The Top 25 Things You Need to Know for Top Scores in Math Level 1

1. Mathematical Expressions

Practice evaluating expressions. Be able to substitute a given value for a variable. Know the order of operations as well as how to perform calculations with fractions, improper fractions, and mixed numbers. Know how to simplify fractions so that you can present answers in the lowest, or simplest, terms.

See Chapter 4, pp. 41–46.

2. Percents

Be able to convert between percents and decimals or fractions within a larger mathematical problem. Know how to find a certain percent of a given number. Be able to determine the relationship between two numbers.

See Chapter 4, pp. 46–48.

3. Exponents

Be familiar with the rules of exponents and avoid common mistakes, such as incorrectly addressing exponents or multiplying exponents when they should be added. Know how to work with rational exponents and negative exponents. Also be familiar with variables in an exponent.

See Chapter 4, pp. 48–51.

4. Real Numbers

Familiarize yourself with:

- the different types of real numbers
- rational numbers
- natural numbers
- integers
- radicals
- the properties of addition and multiplication, especially the distributive property
- the properties of positive and negative numbers
- the concept of absolute value

See Chapter 4, pp. 52–60.

5. Polynomials

Know how to add, subtract, and multiply polynomials. Practice finding factors of polynomials. Be familiar with the difference of perfect squares. Be comfortable factoring quadratic equations, using the quadratic formula, and solving by substitution.

See Chapter 4, pp. 60–68.

6. Inequalities

Know that the rules for solving inequalities are basically the same as those for solving equations. Be able to apply the properties of inequalities, to solve inequalities with absolute values, and to relate solutions of inequalities to graphs.

See Chapter 4, pp. 68–70.

7. Rational Expressions

Know that a rational expression is one that can be expressed as the quotient of polynomials. Be comfortable solving addition, subtraction, multiplication, and division equations with rational expressions.

See Chapter 4, pp. 71–74.

8. Systems

Know how to solve by substitution and linear combination. Be able to differentiate among a single solution, no solution, and infinite solutions. Be comfortable solving word problems by setting up a system and then solving it.

See Chapter 4, pp. 74–79.

9. Geometric Terms

Make sure you understand:

- points
- lines
- planes
- segments
- rays

Recognize the different methods of describing each. Refer to any diagrams provided or consider drawing your own to visualize the given information.

See Chapter 5, pp. 81–85.

10. Angles

Be able to recognize an angle and to classify angles by their measure. Know supplementary, complementary, and vertical angles. Know how to complete several calculations to determine the measure of a specific angle.

See Chapter 5, pp. 85–89.

11. Triangles

Be able to classify a triangle by its angles or by its sides. Know the sum of the interior angles of a triangle as well as the exterior angles. This will enable you to determine the measures of missing angles. For example, a question may provide you with the measure of two interior angles and ask you to classify the triangle by its angles. You will have to use the given angles to determine the measure of the third angle in order to find the answer. Other questions may involve understanding medians, altitudes, and angle bisectors.

You should be able to recognize congruent triangles and to apply the SSS, SAS, and ASA Postulates as well as the AAS Theorem. Familiarize yourself with the Triangle Inequality Theorem because a question may ask you to identify a set of numbers that could be the lengths of the sides of a triangle. Study the properties of right triangles, know how to use the Pythagorean Theorem to solve problems, and review special right triangles.

See Chapter 5, pp. 89–101.

12. Polygons

Memorize the different types of polygons. Be able to name polygons by their number of sides and give the sum of the interior and exterior angles. Know how to draw diagonals in a polygon because a question may ask you to find the number of diagonals that can be drawn from one vertex of a polygon. Review special quadrilaterals and be able to compare them. A question may ask you to name a quadrilateral given its description or it may ask you to name the same quadrilateral in different ways.

Also be sure to understand similarity. Some questions may require you to find the measure of a missing side of a polygon based on the measures of a similar polygon. Others will ask you to calculate perimeter and area.

See Chapter 5, pp. 101–109.

13. Circles

Know the properties of circles. Be able to select chords, tangents, arcs, and central angles from a diagram. Questions may ask you to use a diagram to calculate circumference, area, or arc length.

See Chapter 5, pp. 109–118.

14. Solid Figures

Familiarize yourself with vocabulary for describing polyhedra. For example, questions may ask you to describe figures by the number of faces, edges, or vertices. They might also ask you to recognize the shape of the bases. Know the characteristics of prisms, cylinders, pyramids, cones, and spheres. A question might ask you to calculate volume or lateral surface area given such information as the dimensions of the base and the height.

See Chapter 6, pp. 123–134.

15. Coordinate Geometry

Knowing how to describe a point on a plane rectangular system will enable you to answer several different types of questions. For example, you may be asked to identify the ordered pair that names a point or find solutions of an equation in two variables. Be able to find the midpoint of a line segment and the distance between two points. Other types of questions may ask you to find the area of a figure given its vertices or the slope of a line. Of particular importance is to know the standard form of the equation of a line as well as the point-slope form and the slope-intercept form. A question may ask you to find the equation of a line given the slope and a point or a line parallel to it.

See Chapter 7, pp. 136–145.

16. Graphing Circles and Parabolas

You may encounter the standard form for the equation of a circle or a parabola. A question may ask you to find the x- and y-intercepts of a circle given a specific equation or to find the equation given a description of the figure. The question may provide a description and/or a graph. Other questions may ask you to find the vertex of a parabola given an equation.

See Chapter 7, pp. 145–150.

17. Graphing Inequalities and Absolute Value

Graphing an inequality is similar to graphing a line. The difference is that the set of ordered pairs that make the inequality true is usually infinite and illustrated by a shaded region in the plane. A question may ask you to identify the correct graph to represent an inequality or to describe a characteristic of the graph, such as whether the line is solid or dashed. Know that absolute value graphs are V-shaped and be able to match a graph to an absolute value equation.

See Chapter 7, pp. 151–152.

18. Trigonometry

Study the trigonometric ratios and identities that relate the sides of a right triangle. A question may ask you to find the length of a side given the length of another side and the measure of an angle. The information may be embedded within a word problem and may include a diagram. As always, feel free to draw a diagram to help visualize the problem, but make sure you then use your diagram to choose the correct answer from among the choices.

See Chapter 8, pp. 153–162.

19. Functions

You should be able to recognize a function and determine its domain and range. A question may ask you to identify a function from a mapping diagram or a set notation. It may ask you to identify the domain of a given function from an equation or a graph. Be able to differentiate between functions and relations, and recognize graphs of common functions. Review compositions of functions and be able to select from among identity, zero, and constant functions. Know how to determine the maximum or minimum of a function and find roots of a quadratic function. You may also need to find the inverse of a function or the properties of rational functions, higher-degree polynomial functions, and exponential functions.

See Chapter 9, pp. 164–179.

20. Counting Problems

Some questions may require you to use the Fundamental Counting Principle. For example, you may need to calculate the number of possible combinations given a number of models of sofa and a number of different fabric patterns. Know what it means for events to be mutually exclusive. Be familiar with factorials and the process of finding permutations.

See Chapter 10, pp. 181–183.

21. Probability

Practice determining the probability that an event will occur. Read every question carefully. Identify the desired event and the total number of possible outcomes. Differentiate between dependent and independent events. Some questions may ask you to determine the probability that an event will *not* occur. Pay attention to the wording as you read the answer choices so that you choose the answer that correctly answers the question posed.

See Chapter 10, pp. 183–184.

22. Central Tendency and Data Interpretation

Knowing common measures of central tendency will enable you to answer some questions involving statistics. For example, a question may provide a set of data and ask you to determine the mean, median, or mode. Others may provide you with one of the measures of central tendency and ask you to determine missing data. Some questions may ask you to reach a conclusion based on a histogram or frequency distribution.

See Chapter 10, pp. 184–187.

23. Invented Operations and "In Terms Of" Problems

There is a good possibility that you will see a question that introduces an invented operation. This type of question will show a new symbol that represents a made-up mathematical operation. The symbol will not be familiar to you, but it will be defined for you. You will need to use the definition to solve for a given variable. You may also encounter a question involving more than one unknown variable. In these questions, you must solve for one variable in terms of another.

See Chapter 11, pp. 189–190.

24. Sequences

Sequences are common question topics. Be able to distinguish between finite and infinite sequences as well as between arithmetic and geometric sequences. Questions may ask you to find the sum of the terms for a given sequence or the nth term in a sequence.

See Chapter 11, pp. 190–194.

25. Logic and Number Theory

Questions in this category require you to use reason to identify the correct answer. Review conditional statements, converses, inverses, and contrapositives. A question may provide a statement and ask you to identify a statement that is equivalent. Other questions may provide descriptions of variables and ask you to identify true statements about those variables. Once you determine an answer, try actual values in the problem to check your conclusion.

See Chapter 11, pp. 194–197.

McGRAW-HILL's

SAT

SUBJECT TEST

MATH LEVEL 1

Second Edition

John J. Diehl, Editor

Mathematics Department
Hinsdale Central High School
Hinsdale, IL

Christine E. Joyce

New York / Chicago / San Francisco / Lisbon / London / Madrid / Mexico City
Milan / New Delhi / San Juan / Seoul / Singapore / Sydney / Toronto

McGRAW-HILL's SAT Subject Test: Math Level 1

Copyright © 2009, 2006 by The McGraw-Hill Companies, Inc. All rights reserved. Printed in the United States of America. Except as permitted under the Copyright Act of 1976, no part of this publication may be reproduced or distributed in any forms or by any means, or stored in a database or retrieval system, without the prior written permission of the publisher.

2 3 4 5 6 7 8 9 0   WDQ WDQ   0 1 4 3 2 1 0

ISBN 978-0-07-160922-7
MHID 0-07-160922-9

SAT is a registered trademark of the College Entrance Examination Board, which was not involved in the production of, and does not endorse, this product.

This publication is designed to provide accurate and authoritative information in regard to the subject matter covered. It is sold with the understanding that neither the author nor the publisher is engaged in rendering legal, accounting, futures/securities trading, or other professional service. If legal advice or other expert assistance is required, the services of a competent professional person should be sought.

> *—From a Declaration of Principles jointly adopted by a Committee of the American Bar Association and a Committee of Publishers*

This book is printed on acid-free paper.

CONTENTS

PART I

ABOUT THE SAT MATH LEVEL 1 TEST

CHAPTER 1
TEST BASICS

About the Math Level 1 Test

The SAT Math Level 1 test is one of the Subject Tests offered by the College Board. It tests your knowledge of high school math concepts and differs from the SAT general test, which tests your math *aptitude.* The test consists of 50 multiple-choice questions and is one hour long.

The SAT Subject Tests (formerly known as SAT II Tests or Achievement Tests) are the lesser-known counterpart to the SAT, offered by the same organization—the College Board. But whereas the SAT tests general verbal, writing, and mathematical reasoning skills, the SAT Subject Tests cover specific knowledge in a wide variety of subjects, including English, mathematics, history, science, and foreign language. SAT Subject Tests are only one hour long, significantly shorter than the SAT, and you can take up to three during any one test administration. You can choose which SAT Subject Tests to take and how many to take on one test day, but you cannot register to take both the SAT and Subject Tests on the same test day.

The Math Level 1 test covers the following topics:

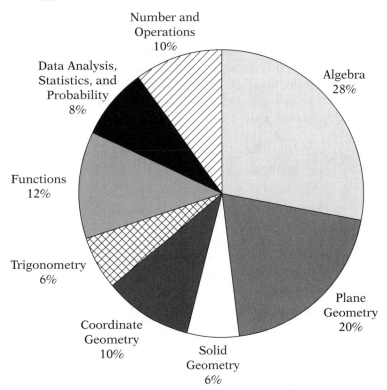

Approximate Breakdown of Topics on the Level 1 Test

The Math Level 1 test is designed to test a student's math knowledge, ability to apply concepts, and higher-order thinking. Students are not expected to know every topic covered on the test.

When determining which SAT Subject Tests to take and when to take them, consult your high school guidance counselor and pick up a copy of the "Taking the SAT Subject Tests" bulletin published by the College Board. Research the admissions policies of colleges to which you are considering applying to determine their SAT Subject Test requirements and the average scores students receive. Also, visit the College Board's Web site at www. collegeboard.com to learn more about what tests are offered.

Use this book to become familiar with the content, organization, and level of difficulty of the Math Level 1 test. Knowing what to expect on the day of the test will allow you to do your best.

When to Take the Test

The Math Level 1 test is recommended for students who have completed three years of college-preparatory mathematics. Most students taking the Level 1 test have studied two years of algebra and one year of geometry. Many students take the math subject tests at the end of their junior year or at the beginning of their senior year.

Colleges look at SAT Subject Test scores to see a student's academic achievement, as the test results are less subjective than other parts of a college application, such as GPA, teacher recommendations, student background information, and the interview. Many colleges require at least one SAT Subject Test score for admission, but even schools that don't require SAT Subject Tests may review your scores to get an overall picture of your qualifications. Colleges may also use SAT Subject Test scores to enroll students in appropriate courses. If math is your strongest subject, then a high SAT Math score, combined with good grades on your transcript, can convey that strength to a college or university.

To register for SAT Subject Tests, pick up a copy of the *Registration Bulletin*, "Registering for the SAT: SAT Reasoning Test, SAT Subject Tests," from your guidance counselor. You can also register at www.collegeboard.com or contact the College Board directly at:

College Board SAT Program
901 South 42nd Street
Mount Vernon, IL 62864
(866) 756-7346

General inquiries can be directed via email through the website's email inquiry form or by telephone at (866) 756-7346.

The SAT Math Level 1 test is administered six Saturdays (or Sunday if you qualify because of religious beliefs) a year in October, November, December, January, May, and June. Students may take up to three SAT Subject Tests per test day.

The Level 1 vs. Level 2 Test

As mentioned, the Math Level 1 test is recommended for students who have completed three years of college-preparatory mathematics. The Math Level 2 test is recommended for students who have completed *more than* three years of college-preparatory mathematics. Most students taking the Level 2 test have studied two years of algebra, one year of geometry, and one year of precalculus (elementary functions) and/or trigonometry.

Typically, students who have received A or B grades in precalculus and trigonometry elect to take the Level 2 test. If you have taken more than three years of high school math and are enrolled in a precalculus or calculus program, don't think that taking the Level 1 test guarantees a higher score. Many of the topics on the Level 1 test will be concepts studied years ago.

Although the topics covered on the two tests overlap somewhat, they differ as shown in the table below. The College Board gives an approximate outline of the mathematics covered on each test as follows:

Topic	Level 1 Test	Level 2 Test
Algebra and Functions	38–42%	48–52%
Plane Euclidean Geometry	18–22%	—
Three-Dimensional Geometry	4–6%	4–6%
Coordinate Geometry	8–12%	10–14%
Trigonometry	6–8%	12–16%
Data Analysis, Statistics, and Probability	6–10%	6–10%
Number and Operations	10–14%	10–14%

Overall, the Level 2 test focuses on more advanced content in each area. As shown in the table, the Level 2 test does not directly cover Plane Euclidean Geometry, although Plane Euclidean Geometry concepts may be applied in other types of questions. Number and Operations was formerly known as Miscellaneous topics.

This book provides a detailed review of all the areas covered on the Math Level 1 test.

Scoring

The scoring of the Math Level 1 test is based on a 200 to 800-point scale, similar to that of the math and verbal sections of the SAT. You receive one point for each correct answer and lose one-quarter of a point for each incorrect answer. You do not lose any points for omitting a question. In addition to your scaled score, your score report shows a percentile ranking indicating the percentage of students scoring below your score. Because there are considerable differences between the Math Level 1 and Level 2 tests, your score on one is not an accurate indicator of your score on the other.

You can view your scores online by logging into your My SAT account approximately three weeks after the test. Refer to the College Board website to see on what date your score will become available. Just like the SAT, you can choose up to four college/scholarship program codes to which to send your scores, for free and the College Board will send a cumulative report of all of your SAT and SAT Subject Test scores to these programs. Additional score reports can be requested, for a fee, online or by phone.

How to Use This Book

- **Become familiar with the SAT: Math Level 1 test.** Review Chapters 1 and 2 to become familiar with the Level 1 test and the guidelines for calculator usage.

- **Identify the subject matter that you need to review.** Complete the diagnostic test in Chapter 3 and evaluate your score. Identify your areas of weakness and focus your test preparation on these areas.

- **Study smart.** Focus your studying on areas that will benefit you. Strengthen your ability to answer the types of questions that appear on the test by reviewing Chapters 4 to 11 as necessary, beginning with your weaker areas. Work through each of the questions in the chapters in which you are weak. Skim the other chapters as needed, and work through problems that are not clear to you.

- **Practice your test-taking skills and pacing.** Complete the practice tests under actual test-like conditions. Evaluate your score and, again, review your areas of weakness.

CHAPTER 2
CALCULATOR TIPS

The SAT: Math Level 1 test requires the use of a scientific or graphing calculator. The Math Level 1 and Level 2 tests are actually the only Subject Tests for which calculators are allowed. It is not necessary to use a calculator to solve every problem on the test. In fact, there is no advantage to using a calculator for 50 to 60 percent of the Level 1 test questions. That means a calculator is helpful for solving approximately 40 to 50 percent of the Level 1 test questions.

It is critical to know how and when to use your calculator effectively . . . and how and when to NOT use your calculator. For some problems, using a calculator may actually take longer than solving the problem by hand. Knowing how to properly operate your calculator will affect your test score, so practice using your calculator when completing the practice tests in this book.

The Level 1 test is created with the understanding that most students know how to use a graphing calculator. Although you have a choice of using either a scientific or a graphing calculator, *choose a graphing calculator.* A graphing calculator provides much more functionality (as long as you know how to use it properly!). A graphing calculator is an advantage when solving many problems related to coordinate geometry and functions.

Remember to make sure your calculator is working properly before your test day. Become comfortable with using it and familiar with the common operations. Since calculator policies are ever-changing, refer to www.college board.com for the latest information. According to the College Board, the following types of calculators are NOT allowed on the SAT Math test:

- Calculators with QWERTY (typewriterlike) keypads
- Calculators that contain electronic dictionaries
- Calculators with paper tape or printers
- Calculators that "talk" or make noise
- Calculators that require an electrical outlet
- Cell-phone calculators
- Pocket organizers or personal digital assistants
- Handheld minicomputers or laptop computers
- Electronic writing pads or pen-input/stylus-driven devices (such as a Palm Pilot).

There are a few rules to calculator usage on the SAT Math test. Of course, you may not share your calculator with another student during the test. Doing so may result in dismissal from the test. If your calculator has a large or raised display that can be seen by other test takers, the test supervisor has the right to assign you to an appropriate seat, presumably not in the line of sight of other students. Calculators may not be on your desk during other SAT Subject Tests, aside from the Math Level 1 and Level 2 tests. If your calculator malfunctions during the test and you don't have a backup or extra batteries, you can either choose to continue the test without a calculator or choose to cancel your test score. You must cancel the score before leaving the test center. If you leave the test center, you must cancel scores for all subject tests taken on that date.

When choosing what calculator to use for the test, make sure your calculator performs the following functions:

- Squaring a number
- Raising a number to a power other than 2 (usually the {^} button)
- Taking the square root of a number
- Taking the cube root of a number (or, in other words, raising a number to the $\frac{1}{3}$ power)
- Sine, cosine, and tangent
- Sin $^{-1}$, cos $^{-1}$, tan $^{-1}$
- Can be set to degree mode

Also know where the π button and the parentheses buttons are, and understand the difference between the subtraction symbol and the negative sign.

Since programmable calculators are allowed on the SAT Math test, some students may frantically program their calculator with commonly used math formulas and facts, such as distance, the quadratic formula, midpoint, slope, circumference, area, volume, surface area, lateral surface area, the trigonometric ratios, trigonometric identities, the Pythagorean Theorem, combinations, permutations, and nth terms of geometric/arithmetic sequences. Of course, if you do not truly understand these math facts and when to use them, you end up wasting significant time scrolling through your calculator searching for them.

On the Day of the Test

- Make sure your calculator works! (Putting new batteries in your calculator will provide you with peace of mind.)
- Bring a backup calculator and extra batteries to the test center.
- Set your calculator to degree mode, since all of the angles on the Level 1 test are given in degrees.

CHAPTER 3

DIAGNOSTIC TEST

To most effectively prepare for the Math Level 1 test, you should identify the areas in which your skills are weak. Then, focus on improving your skills in these areas. (Of course, also becoming stronger in your strong areas will only help your score!) Use the results of the diagnostic test to prioritize areas in which you need further preparation.

The following diagnostic test resembles the format, number of questions, and level of difficulty of the actual Math Level 1 test. It incorporates questions in the following eight areas:

1. Algebra
2. Plane Geometry
3. Solid Geometry
4. Coordinate Geometry
5. Trigonometry
6. Functions
7. Data Analysis, Statistics, and Probability
8. Number and Operations

When you're finished with the test, determine your score and carefully read the answer explanations for the questions you answered incorrectly. Identify your weak areas by determining the areas in which you made the most errors. Review these chapters of the book first. Then, as time permits, go back and review your stronger areas.

Allow one hour to take the diagnostic test. Time yourself and work uninterrupted. If you run out of time, take note of where you ended after one hour, and continue until you have tried all 50 questions. To truly identify your weak areas, you need to complete the test. Remember that you lose $\frac{1}{4}$ of a point for each incorrect answer. Because of this penalty, do not guess on a question unless you can eliminate one or more of the answers. Your score is calculated using the following formula:

$$\text{Number of correct answers} - \frac{1}{4}(\text{Number of incorrect answers})$$

The diagnostic test will be an accurate reflection of how you'll do on the Level 1 test if you treat it as the real examination. Here are some hints on how to take the test under conditions similar to the actual test day:

- Complete the test in one sitting.
- Time yourself.
- Use a scientific or graphing calculator. Remember that a calculator may be useful in solving about 40 to 50 percent of the test questions and is not needed for about 50 to 60 percent of the test.
- Tear out your answer key and fill in the ovals just as you would on the actual test day.
- Become familiar with the directions to the test and the reference information provided. You'll save time on the actual test day by already being familiar with this information.

DIAGNOSTIC TEST
MATH LEVEL 1

ANSWER SHEET

Tear out this answer sheet and use it to complete the diagnostic test. Determine the BEST answer for each question. Then, fill in the appropriate oval using a No. 2 pencil.

1. (A) (B) (C) (D) (E)	21. (A) (B) (C) (D) (E)	41. (A) (B) (C) (D) (E)
2. (A) (B) (C) (D) (E)	22. (A) (B) (C) (D) (E)	42. (A) (B) (C) (D) (E)
3. (A) (B) (C) (D) (E)	23. (A) (B) (C) (D) (E)	43. (A) (B) (C) (D) (E)
4. (A) (B) (C) (D) (E)	24. (A) (B) (C) (D) (E)	44. (A) (B) (C) (D) (E)
5. (A) (B) (C) (D) (E)	25. (A) (B) (C) (D) (E)	45. (A) (B) (C) (D) (E)
6. (A) (B) (C) (D) (E)	26. (A) (B) (C) (D) (E)	46. (A) (B) (C) (D) (E)
7. (A) (B) (C) (D) (E)	27. (A) (B) (C) (D) (E)	47. (A) (B) (C) (D) (E)
8. (A) (B) (C) (D) (E)	28. (A) (B) (C) (D) (E)	48. (A) (B) (C) (D) (E)
9. (A) (B) (C) (D) (E)	29. (A) (B) (C) (D) (E)	49. (A) (B) (C) (D) (E)
10. (A) (B) (C) (D) (E)	30. (A) (B) (C) (D) (E)	50. (A) (B) (C) (D) (E)
11. (A) (B) (C) (D) (E)	31. (A) (B) (C) (D) (E)	
12. (A) (B) (C) (D) (E)	32. (A) (B) (C) (D) (E)	
13. (A) (B) (C) (D) (E)	33. (A) (B) (C) (D) (E)	
14. (A) (B) (C) (D) (E)	34. (A) (B) (C) (D) (E)	
15. (A) (B) (C) (D) (E)	35. (A) (B) (C) (D) (E)	
16. (A) (B) (C) (D) (E)	36. (A) (B) (C) (D) (E)	
17. (A) (B) (C) (D) (E)	37. (A) (B) (C) (D) (E)	
18. (A) (B) (C) (D) (E)	38. (A) (B) (C) (D) (E)	
19. (A) (B) (C) (D) (E)	39. (A) (B) (C) (D) (E)	
20. (A) (B) (C) (D) (E)	40. (A) (B) (C) (D) (E)	

DIAGNOSTIC TEST
Time: 60 Minutes

Directions: Select the BEST answer for each of the 50 multiple-choice questions. If the exact solution is not one of the five choices, select the answer that is the best approximation. Then, fill in the appropriate oval on the answer sheet.

Notes:

1. A calculator will be needed to answer some of the questions on the test. Scientific, programmable, and graphing calculators are permitted. It is up to you to determine when and when not to use your calculator.

2. All angles on the Level 1 test are measured in degrees, not radians. Make sure your calculator is set to degree mode.

3. Figures are drawn as accurately as possible and are intended to help solve some of the test problems. If a figure is not drawn to scale, this will be stated in the problem. All figures lie in a plane unless the problem indicates otherwise.

4. Unless otherwise stated, the domain of a function f is assumed to be the set of real numbers x for which the value of the function, $f(x)$, is a real number.

5. Reference information that may be useful in answering some of the test questions can be found below.

Reference Information	
Right circular cone with radius r and height h:	Volume $= \dfrac{1}{3}\pi r^2 h$
Right circular cone with circumference of base c and slant height ℓ:	Lateral Area $= \dfrac{1}{2}c\ell$
Sphere with radius r:	Volume $= \dfrac{4}{3}\pi r^3$ Surface Area $= 4\pi r^2$
Pyramid with base area B and height h:	Volume $= \dfrac{1}{3}Bh$

GO ON TO THE NEXT PAGE

1. $(x + y + 3)(x + y - 3) =$
    (A) $x^2 + y^2 - 3^2$
    (B) $(x + y)^2 + 6(x + y) + 9$
    (C) $(x + y)^2 + 6(x + y)$
    (D) $(x + y)^2 - 9$
    (E) $x^2 + 2xy + y^2 + 3^2$

2. In square $ABCD$ in Figure 1, what are the coordinates of vertex B?
    (A) $(4, -2)$
    (B) $(5, -2)$
    (C) $(-2, 5)$
    (D) $(-2, 1)$
    (E) $(1, 2)$

3. If $a = -3$, then $(a + 6)(a - 3) =$
    (A) -18
    (B) 18
    (C) 0
    (D) 27
    (E) -54

4. Assuming $x \neq 0$, $\dfrac{1}{(x/3)^2} =$

    (A) $\dfrac{x^2}{3}$

    (B) $\dfrac{1}{3x^2}$

    (C) $\dfrac{x^2}{9}$

    (D) $\dfrac{9}{x}$

    (E) $\dfrac{9}{x^2}$

USE THIS SPACE AS SCRATCH PAPER

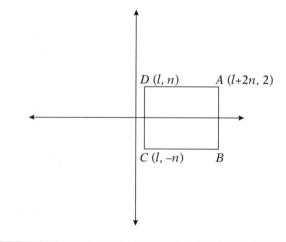

Figure 1

GO ON TO THE NEXT PAGE

5.   If $\frac{1}{2}x - 2x = 3x - 9$, then $x =$

    (A) −6
    (B) 2
    (C) 6
    (D) $\frac{1}{2}$
    (E) 3

6.   If $\sqrt[3]{\sqrt[2]{x}} = 3$, then $x =$

    (A) 9
    (B) 27
    (C) 81
    (D) 243
    (E) 729

7.   If $2n + m = 10$ and $3n - m = -5$, then $m =$

    (A) 6
    (B) 1
    (C) 8
    (D) 4
    (E) 2

8.   In Figure 2, if $\ell_1 \| \ell_2$ and both lines are intersected by line t, then $y =$

    (A) 55°
    (B) 45°
    (C) 135°
    (D) 90°
    (E) 180°

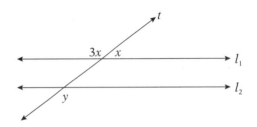

Figure 2

9.   What is the y-intercept of the graph of $3x + 4y = 24$?

    (A) (0, 24)
    (B) (0, 6)
    (C) (0, 8)
    (D) (0, 4)
    (E) (0, 2)

10.   If $2n^2 = 5$, then $5(2n^2) =$

    (A) $\frac{25}{4}$
    (B) $\frac{5}{2}$
    (C) 5
    (D) 25
    (E) $\frac{5\sqrt{5}}{2}$

GO ON TO THE NEXT PAGE

11. A cone and a cylinder both have a height h and a radius r. If the volume of the cone is 12π cm³, what is the volume of the cylinder?

    (A) 4π cm³
    (B) 12π cm³
    (C) 24π cm³
    (D) 36π cm³
    (E) 48π cm³

USE THIS SPACE AS SCRATCH PAPER

12. In Figure 3, $XY = YZ$ in $\triangle XYZ$. If the measure of $\angle Y$ is 50°, what is the measure of $\angle Z$?

    (A) 50°
    (B) 130°
    (C) 65°
    (D) 75°
    (E) 25°

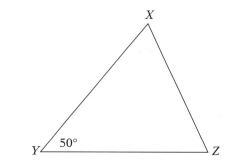

Figure 3

13. In terms of x, what is the average (arithmetic mean) of $2x + 1$, $3x - 4$, $2x + 7$, and $5x$?

    (A) $3x + 1$
    (B) $3x + 4$
    (C) $12x + 1$
    (D) $4x + 4$
    (E) $12x + 4$

14. What is the measure of the angle formed by the hands of a clock at 5 o'clock?

    (A) 120°
    (B) 140°
    (C) 150°
    (D) 160°
    (E) 170°

15. If $f(x) = \dfrac{1}{2x^2 + 1}$, then $f\left(-\dfrac{1}{2}\right) =$

    (A) $\dfrac{1}{3}$
    (B) 2
    (C) $\dfrac{1}{2}$
    (D) $\dfrac{3}{2}$
    (E) $\dfrac{2}{3}$

GO ON TO THE NEXT PAGE

16. If $24^x = 6^3 \times 4^3$, then $x =$

    (A) 2
    (B) 12
    (C) 9
    (D) 6
    (E) 3

17. If three coins are tossed, what is the probability that exactly two are heads?

    (A) $\dfrac{2}{3}$

    (B) $\dfrac{1}{3}$

    (C) $\dfrac{1}{4}$

    (D) $\dfrac{3}{8}$

    (E) $\dfrac{1}{2}$

18. A circle has a circumference of 16π cm. What is its area?

    (A) 8π cm^2
    (B) 16π cm^2
    (C) 332π cm^2
    (D) 64π cm^2
    (E) 256π cm^2

19. If $|x + 4| > 2$, what values of x satisfy the inequality?

    (A) $x < -6$ or $x > -2$
    (B) $-6 < x < -2$
    (C) $x > -2$
    (D) $x < 2$ or $x > 6$
    (E) $-6 < x < 2$

20. In Figure 4, $\overline{PQ}$ and $\overline{PR}$ are tangent segments to circle O. If the $m\angle P = \dfrac{4}{5} m\angle O$, then $m\angle O =$

    (A) 40°
    (B) 50°
    (C) 80°
    (D) 100°
    (E) 120°

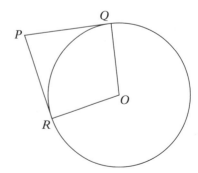

Figure 4

GO ON TO THE NEXT PAGE

21. In Table 1, $f(x)$ is a linear function. What is the value of n?

(A) 9
(B) −7
(C) −11
(D) −15
(E) −5

Table 1

x	f(x)
−2	13
0	5
1	1
2	−3
4	n

22. The slope of $\leftrightarrow AB$ is $\dfrac{1}{4}$. If A has coordinates (10, −8) and B has coordinates (6, y), then $y =$

(A) −24
(B) −9
(C) −7
(D) −2
(E) 7

23. Mark wears a uniform to school. According to the school's dress code, he can wear one of 2 types of pants, one of 4 shirts, and one of 2 pairs of shoes. How many pants-shirt-shoes combinations are possible?

(A) 2
(B) 6
(C) 8
(D) 16
(E) 32

24. A bike has wheels with radii of 8 inches. How far does the bike travel in two complete revolutions of its wheels?

(A) 8π inches
(B) 16π inches
(C) 32π inches
(D) 64π inches
(E) 128π inches

GO ON TO THE NEXT PAGE

25. In Figure 5, a circle is inscribed in a square whose sides have a length of 6 inches. What is the area of the shaded region?

    (A) 36 in^2
    (B) $27\pi \text{ in}^2$
    (C) $36 - 9\pi \text{ in}^2$
    (D) $36 - 36\pi \text{ in}^2$
    (E) $9\pi \text{ in}^2$

26. Two circles have diameters in the ratio of 2:1. If the circumference of the larger circle is 9π centimeters more than the circumference of the smaller circle, what is the radius of the smaller circle?

    (A) 4.5 cm
    (B) 9 cm
    (C) 18 cm
    (D) $\sqrt{3}$ cm
    (E) 12 cm

27. What is the equation of the line containing the point $(1, -2)$ and perpendicular to the line $y = -3x + 7$?

    (A) $y = -3x - 2$
    (B) $y = -3x + 1$
    (C) $y = -\dfrac{1}{3}x$
    (D) $y = \dfrac{1}{3}x + 7$
    (E) $y = \dfrac{1}{3x} - \dfrac{7}{3}$

28. In Figure 6, if $x = 37°$, what is the value of a?

    (A) 6.03
    (B) 6.39
    (C) 10.02
    (D) 10.62
    (E) 13.29

29. The product of the roots of a quadratic equation is -15 and their sum is -2. Which of the following could be the quadratic equation?

    (A) $x^2 - 2x - 15 = 0$
    (B) $x^2 + 2x - 15 = 0$
    (C) $x^2 - 2x + 15 = 0$
    (D) $x^2 + 15x - 2 = 0$
    (E) $x^2 - 15x - 2 = 0$

USE THIS SPACE AS SCRATCH PAPER

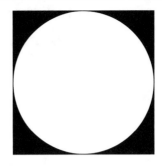

Figure 5

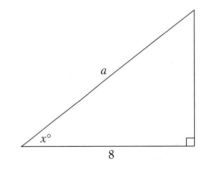

Figure 6

GO ON TO THE NEXT PAGE

30. The line with the equation $x + y = 3$ is graphed on the same xy-plane as the parabola with vertex $(0, 0)$ and focus $(0, -3)$. What is the point of intersection of the two graphs?

    (A) $(0, 3)$
    (B) $(0, -3)$
    (C) $(0.46, 2.54)$
    (D) $(-0.5, 3.5)$
    (E) $(6, -3)$

31. What is the measure of each interior angle of a regular hexagon?

    (A) $180°$
    (B) $720°$
    (C) $60°$
    (D) $120°$
    (E) $90°$

32. In Mr. Taylor's first-period geometry class, the mean score of 30 students on a test is 76 percent. In his second-period class, the mean score of 22 students is 82 percent. What is the mean score of the 52 students?

    (A) 77%
    (B) 78%
    (C) 78.5%
    (D) 79%
    (E) 79.5%

33. The sum of two numbers is 27, and the difference of their squares is also 27. What are the two numbers?

    (A) $\{13, 14\}$
    (B) $\{12, 15\}$
    (C) $\{16, 11\}$
    (D) $\{10, 17\}$
    (E) $\{9, 18\}$

34. If 8 percent of an 18-gallon solution is chlorine, how many gallons of water must be added to make a new solution that is 6 percent chlorine?

    (A) 6 gallons
    (B) 8 gallons
    (C) 10 gallons
    (D) 12 gallons
    (E) 18 gallons

USE THIS SPACE AS SCRATCH PAPER

GO ON TO THE NEXT PAGE

35. Which of the following equations does NOT represent the line containing the points (15, 14) and (10, 10)?

    (A) $y = \dfrac{4}{5}x + 2$

    (B) $y - 10 = \dfrac{4}{5}(x - 10)$

    (C) $y - 14 = \dfrac{4}{5}(x - 15)$

    (D) $4x - 5y + 10 = 0$

    (E) $4x + 5y = -10$

36. What is the maximum value of the function $f(x) = -x^2 + 8x - 20$?

    (A) 4
    (B) 28
    (C) 3
    (D) −4
    (E) −36

37. What is the nth term of the geometric sequence 3, $3\sqrt{3}$, 9, $9\sqrt{3}$, 27, . . . ?

    (A) $2n\sqrt{3}$

    (B) $n\sqrt{3}$

    (C) $\left(\sqrt{3}\right)^n$

    (D) $\left(\sqrt{3}\right)^{n-1}$

    (E) $\left(\sqrt{3}\right)^{n+1}$

38. If $4^{-1} - 8^{-1} = x^{-1}$, then $x =$

    (A) −4
    (B) −8
    (C) $\dfrac{1}{2}$
    (D) 8
    (E) 4

GO ON TO THE NEXT PAGE

39. The cube in Figure 7 has edges of length 5. What is the distance from vertex H to vertex K?

    (A) $5\sqrt{2}$
    (B) $5\sqrt{3}$
    (C) 5
    (D) $10\sqrt{2}$
    (E) $5\sqrt{5}$

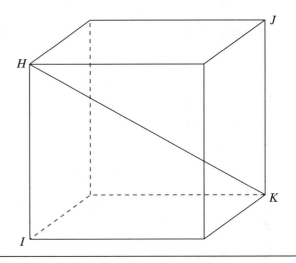

Figure 7

40. At the end of 2000, the number of students attending a certain high school was 850. If the number of students increases at a constant rate of 2.25 percent each year, how many students will attend the high school at the end of 2012?

    (A) 1062
    (B) 1086
    (C) 1110
    (D) 1135
    (E) 1161

41. If $f(x) = \dfrac{x+3}{2}$ and f^{-1} is the inverse function of f, what is $f^{-1}(-5)$?

    (A) 1
    (B) 4
    (C) −13
    (D) 7
    (E) −7

42. The area of the rhombus $TUVW$ in Figure 8 is

    (A) 64
    (B) 32
    (C) 5.7
    (D) 45.3
    (E) $64\sqrt{2}$

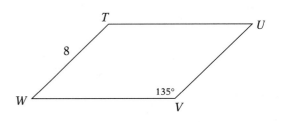

Figure 8

GO ON TO THE NEXT PAGE

43. Which of the following is equal to $(\sec \theta)(\cot \theta)$?

    (A) $\sin \theta$
    (B) $\cos \theta$
    (C) $\sec \theta$
    (D) $\csc \theta$
    (E) $\cot \theta$

44. If $i^2 = -1$, then $i^8 =$

    (A) i
    (B) $-i$
    (C) 1
    (D) -1
    (E) -4

45. The statement, "If a triangle is equilateral, then it is *not* scalene," is logically equivalent to which of the following?

    I.   If a triangle is not scalene, then it is equilateral.
    II. If a triangle is not equilateral, then it is scalene.
    III. If a triangle is scalene, then it is not equilateral.

    (A) I only
    (B) II only
    (C) III only
    (D) I and II only
    (E) I and III only

46. $(2\sin x)(9\sin x) - (6\cos x)(-3\cos x) =$

    (A) 18
    (B) $18\sin^2 x - 18\cos^2 x$
    (C) $18\sin x + 18\cos x$
    (D) 36
    (E) 1

47. If the sides of a right triangle have lengths $x - 3$, $x + 1$, and $x + 5$, then $x =$

    (A) -1
    (B) 15
    (C) 4
    (D) 5
    (E) 12

48. If $x^2 - y^2 = x + y$ and $x \neq -y$, then $x - y =$

    (A) -1
    (B) 1
    (C) 0
    (D) -2
    (E) Cannot be determined

USE THIS SPACE AS SCRATCH PAPER

GO ON TO THE NEXT PAGE

49. $\dfrac{\sqrt{6}}{\sqrt{3}+\sqrt{2}} =$

    (A) $\dfrac{\sqrt{6}}{\sqrt{5}}$

    (B) $\sqrt{2}+\sqrt{3}$

    (C) $\dfrac{3\sqrt{2}-2\sqrt{3}}{5}$

    (D) $2\sqrt{3}-3\sqrt{2}$

    (E) $3\sqrt{2}-2\sqrt{3}$

50. A rectangular swimming pool has dimensions 15 feet, 12 feet, and 5 feet. The pool is to be filled using a right cylindrical bucket with a base radius of 6 inches and a height of 2 feet. Approximately, how many buckets of water will it take to fill the swimming pool?

    (A) 75
    (B) 3,438
    (C) 24
    (D) 143
    (E) 573

STOP

IF YOU FINISH BEFORE TIME IS CALLED, GO BACK AND CHECK YOUR WORK.

ANSWER KEY

1. D	11. D	21. C	31. D	41. C
2. B	12. C	22. B	32. C	42. D
3. A	13. A	23. D	33. A	43. D
4. E	14. C	24. C	34. A	44. C
5. B	15. E	25. C	35. E	45. C
6. E	16. E	26. A	36. D	46. A
7. C	17. D	27. E	37. E	47. B
8. C	18. D	28. C	38. D	48. B
9. B	19. A	29. B	39. B	49. E
10. D	20. D	30. E	40. C	50. E

ANSWERS AND SOLUTIONS

1. **D** You don't need to start multiplying the second trinomial by the first. Instead, group x and y as a single expression.

$$(x + y + 3)(x + y - 3)$$
$$= [(x + y) + 3][(x + y) - 3]$$
$$= (x + y)^2 - 3(x + y) + 3(x + y) - 9$$
$$= (x + y)^2 - 9$$

2. **B** Recognize that $ABCD$ is a square, so all four sides have equal measure. You know $n = 2$ because there is no change in the $y =$ coordinate on side AD. B has an x-coordinate of $1 + 2n$, which equals $1 + 2(2) = 5$ and a y-coordinate of -2. B has coordinates $(5, -2)$.

3. **A** Substitute $a = -3$ into the expression to get

$$(-3 + 6)(-3 - 3)$$
$$= 3(-6)$$
$$= -18$$

4. **E** To simplify the complex fraction, multiply the numerator and denominator by an expression equivalent to 1 that will eliminate the fraction in the denominator.

$$\frac{1}{(x/3)^2} \times \frac{3^2}{3^2}$$
$$= \frac{3^2}{x^2}$$
$$= \frac{9}{x^2}$$

5. **B** Solve for x by isolating the variable on one side of the equation.

Multiply both sides by 2. $\frac{1}{2}x - 2x = 3x - 9$

$$x - 4x = 6x - 18$$
$$-3x = 6x - 18$$
$$-9x = -18$$
$$x = 2$$

6. **E** Cubing is the inverse of cube rooting, so cube both sides first.

$$\left(\sqrt[3]{\sqrt[2]{x}}\right)^3 = 3^3$$
$$\sqrt[3]{\sqrt[2]{x}} = 27$$

Now square both sides to solve x.

$$\left(\sqrt[2]{x}\right)^2 = 27^2$$
$$x = 729$$

An alternate way of solving the problem is to rewrite the given equation using rational exponents: $\sqrt[3]{\sqrt[2]{x}} = \left(x^{\frac{1}{2}}\right)^{\frac{1}{3}} = x^{\frac{1}{6}}$. Raise each side to the sixth power to solve for x.

$$\left(x^{\frac{1}{6}}\right)^6 = 3^6 = 729$$

7. **C** Since you have two variables and two unknowns, set up a system to solve for n and m.

$$2n + m = 10$$
$$\underline{+\ 3n - m = -5}$$
$$5n \qquad = -5$$
$$n \qquad = 1$$

Since $2n + m = 10$, you can substitute $n = 1$ to get $2(1) + m = 10$. $m = 10 - 2 = 8$.

8. **C** Since the angles measuring $3x$ and x are a linear pair:

$$3x + x = 180°$$
$$4x = 180°$$
$$x = \frac{180}{4} = 45°$$

The angle measuring y and the angle measuring $3x$ are alternate exterior angles and are, therefore, congruent.

$$y = 3x = 3(45) = 135°$$

9. **B** Recognize that the line crosses the y-axis when x equals zero. Substitute $x = 0$ into the equation to get

$$3x + 4y = 24$$
$$3(0) + 4y = 24$$
$$4y = 24$$
$$y = \frac{24}{4} = 6$$

The y-intercept is the point $(0, 6)$.

10. **D** This is a straightforward substitution problem, so don't waste time solving for n. Simply substitute 5 for $2n^2$ to get

$$5(2n^2) = 5(5) = 25$$

11. **D** The formula for the volume of a cone is $V = \frac{1}{3}\pi r^2 h$ (as given in the Reference Information), while the formula for the volume of a cylinder is $V = \pi r^2 h$. Since the cone and cylinder have the same radius and height, you know that the cylinder's volume is three times that of the cone.

$$V_{\text{cone}} = \frac{1}{3}\pi r^2 h = 12\pi$$

$$V_{\text{cylinder}} = \pi r^2 h = 3(12\pi) = 36\pi$$

$$V_{\text{cylinder}} = 36\pi \text{ cm}^3$$

12. **C** Since ΔXYZ is an isosceles triangle, its two base angles, $\angle X$ and $\angle Z$, are congruent. The vertex angle, $\angle Y$, equals $50°$, and the measures of all three angles of the triangle must add up to $180°$.

$$180 - 50 = 130°$$
$$\frac{130}{2} = 65°$$

Each base angle measures $65°$, so $m\angle Z = 65$.

13. **A** The average is found by dividing the sum of the terms by the number of terms. In this case, there are 4 given terms. The average is

$$\frac{2x + 1 + 3x - 4 + 2x + 7 + 5x}{4}$$
$$= \frac{12x + 4}{4} = \frac{4(3x + 1)}{4} = 3x + 1$$

14. **C** Since a clock is circular, the hands travel $360°$ in one full rotation. There are 12 numbers on the clock, so there are $\frac{360}{12}$ or $30°$ between each number and the next. At 5 o'clock, the hands form an angle of

$$30°(5) = 150°$$

15. **E** Since $f(x) = \frac{1}{2x^2 + 1}, f\left(\frac{-1}{2}\right)$

$$= \frac{1}{\left[2(-1/2)^2 + 1\right]}$$
$$= \frac{1}{\left[2(1/4) + 1\right]}$$
$$= \frac{1}{(1/2 + 1)}$$
$$= \frac{1}{(3/2)}$$
$$= \frac{2}{3}$$

16. **E** One property of exponents states that $(ab)^n = a^n \times b^n$. The expression 24^x can be written as follows:

$$24^x = (6 \times 4)^x = 6^x \times 4^x$$
$$6^x \times 4^x = 6^3 \times 4^3$$
$$x = 3$$

17. **D** The probability that an event, E, occurs is

$$P(E) = \frac{\text{the number of possible outcomes of } E}{\text{the total number of possible outcomes}}$$

In this example, there are 2^3 or 8 possible outcomes for the coin toss. If exactly 2 coins must be heads, the following outcomes are possible:

> *HHT*
>
> *HTH*
>
> *THH*

3 out of the 8 possible outcomes result in exactly 2 heads, so the probability is 3/8.

18. **D** The formula for the circumference of a circle is $C = 2\pi r$. The circumference is 16π, so:

$$2\pi r = 16\pi$$

$$r = \frac{16\pi}{2\pi} = 8$$

Area is given by the formula $A = \pi r^2$.

$$A = \pi(8)^2 = 64\pi \text{ cm}^3$$

19. **A** If $|x + 4| > 2$, then

$x + 4 > 2$	or	$-(x + 4) > 2$
$x > -2$		$-x - 4 > 2$
		$-x > 6$
		$x < -6$

Since a value cannot be greater than -2 and less than -6, the solution is a disjunction, meaning that the two inequalities are joined by "or." The solution is

> $x < -6$ or $x > -2$

20. **D** $\overline{PQ}$ and $\overline{PR}$ are tangent segments and are, therefore, congruent to each other and perpendicular to the radius of circle O. $\angle PQO$ and $\angle PRO$ are right angles. Draw segment $\overline{OP}$ in Figure 9 to create two congruent, right triangles. Then, let $m\angle POR$ and the $m\angle POQ$ equal x. The angles in a triangle must sum to 180°, so $m\angle QPO$ and $m\angle RPO$ must equal $90 - x$. See Figure 9.

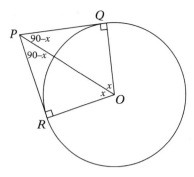

Figure 9

$$m\angle P = \frac{4}{5}m\angle O$$

$$2(90 - x) = \frac{4}{5}(2x)$$

$$10(90 - x) = 8x$$

$$900 - 10x = 8x$$

$$900 = 18x$$

$$x = \frac{900}{18} = 50$$

The $m\angle O = 2x = 2(50) = 100°$.

21. **C** Since this is a linear function, it has a constant rate of change. Recognize that for each increase of 1 in x, $f(x)$ decreases by 4. For example, as x increases from 0 to 1, $f(x)$ decreases from 5 to 1. Also, $-3 - 1 = -4$. If a row in the table represented $x = 3$, $f(3)$ would equal

> $-3 - 4 = -7$

When $x = 4$, $f(x)$ would again decrease by 4:

> $f(4) = -7 - 4 = -11$

As an alternate solution, observe that an increase of 2 in x corresponds to a decrease of 8 in y; therefore, $n = -3 - 8 = -11$.

22. **B** Slope is determined using the formula

$$m = \frac{y_2 - y_1}{x_2 - x_1}$$

Set m equal to $\frac{1}{4}$ to get

$$\frac{y - -8}{6 - 10} = \frac{1}{4}$$

$$\frac{y + 8}{-4} = \frac{1}{4}$$

Then, cross multiply to solve for y.

$$4(y + 8) = -4(1)$$

$$4y + 32 = -4$$

$$4y = -36$$

$$y = -9$$

23. **D** Use the Fundamental Counting Principle to solve for the number of outfit combinations. It states that if one action can be done in a ways, and for each of these a second action can be done in b ways, the number of ways the two actions can be done in order is $a \times b$. Since Mark has 2 pants, 4 shirts, and 2 pairs of shoes, he can create

$$2 \times 4 \times 2 = 16 \text{ outfits}$$

24. **C** In one complete revolution of its wheels, the bike travels a distance equal to the wheels' circumference. Circumference is given by the formula

$$C = 2\pi r$$

Since each wheel has a radius of 8 inches and the bike travels 2 revolutions, the distance is determined by

$$C = 2[2\pi(8)]$$

$$= 2(16\pi)$$

$$= 32\pi \text{ inches}$$

25. **C** The area of the shaded region equals the area of the square minus the area of the inscribed circle. The square has sides of length s, so its area is 6(6), or 36 in².

The diameter of the circle is also 6 inches, so its radius is half the diameter, 3 inches. Its area is $\pi r^2 = \pi(3)^2 = 9\pi$ in².

The shaded region, therefore, has an area of

$$36 - 9\pi \text{ in}^2$$

26. **A** Let the diameter of the larger circle equal $2x$ and the diameter of the smaller circle equal x. Circumference is determined using the equation $C = \pi d$, so the circumference of the larger circle is $C = 2x\pi$, and

the circumference of the smaller circle is $C = x\pi$. Knowing that the larger circle's diameter is 9π cm greater than the smaller, set up the following equation and solve for x.

$$2x\pi = x\pi + 9\pi$$

$$x\pi = 9\pi$$

$$x = 9 \text{ cm}$$

Remember to answer the question asked. x = the diameter of the smaller circle. The radius of the smaller circle must be half of x, or 4.5 cm.

27. **E** The slopes of perpendicular lines are negative reciprocals. The given line, $y = -3x + 7$, is in slope-intercept form, so you can determine that its slope is simply the coefficient of x, -3. Any lines perpendicular to it must have a slope of

$$m = -\left(-\frac{1}{3}\right) = \frac{1}{3}$$

Notice that all of the answers are also in slope intercept form. So far, you know m, so the equation of the line perpendicular to the given line is

$$y = \frac{1}{3}x + b$$

Use the point $(1, -2)$ to substitute values for x and y, and then solve for b.

$$-2 = \frac{1}{3}(1) + b$$

$$-2 - \frac{1}{3} = b$$

$$-\frac{7}{3} = b$$

The equation of the line is $y = \frac{1}{3}x - \frac{7}{3}$.

28. **C** Use trigonometry to solve for a. First, determine which trigonometric ratio is appropriate to use: sine, cosine, or tangent. Recall SOH CAH TOA. Since you know the side adjacent to the angle measures 8 and you're solving for the hypotenuse of the triangle, it makes sense to use cosine.

$$\text{cosine} = \frac{\text{adjacent}}{\text{hypotenuse}}$$

$$\cos 37° = \frac{8}{a}$$

$$a(\cos 37°) = 8$$

$$a = \frac{8}{\cos 37°} \approx 10.02$$

29. **B** A quadratic equation can be thought of as

$$a[x^2 - (\text{sum of the roots})x + (\text{product of the roots})] = 0$$

Since the sum of the two roots is -2 and the product is -15, substitute these values into the equation. Let's assume $a = 1$ and see if the answer matches one of the given answers.

$$1[x^2 - (-2)x + (-15)] = 0$$

$$x^2 + 2x - 15 = 0$$

If you didn't remember the theorem about the sum and product of the roots of a quadratic equation, try factoring the answers and examining the roots. Factoring answer B results in

$$x^2 + 2x - 15 = 0$$

$$(x + 5)(x - 3) = 0$$

$$x = -5 \text{ and } x = 3$$

You can see that $-5 + 3 = -2$ and $-5(3) = -15$.

30. **E** First, determine the equation of the parabola. Since the vertex is at the origin and the focus is $(0, -3)$, the parabola is concave down and the distance between the vertex and focus, c, is 3 units. In standard form, the equation of the parabola is

$$y = -ax^2$$

Recall that $a = \dfrac{1}{4c}$. Since $c = 3$, $a = \dfrac{1}{12}$ and the parabola's equation becomes

$$y = \frac{-1}{12}x^2$$

Solve for y in the equation of the line: $y = -x + 3$. Then, substitute this value of y into the equation of the parabola and solve for x.

$$-x + 3 = \frac{-1}{12}x^2$$

$$-12x + 36 = -x^2$$

$$x^2 - 12x + 36 = 0$$

$$(x - 6)(x - 6) = 0$$

$$x = 6$$

The y-coordinate of the point is $y = -x + 3 = -6 + 3 = -3$.

31. **D** Recall that the sum of the interior angles of any polygon is given by the formula

$$S = 180(n - 2)$$

where $n =$ the number of sides of the polygon.

The sum of the 6 angles in a hexagon is therefore

$$S = 180(6 - 2) = 180(4) = 720°$$

Since the hexagon is *regular*, all 6 angles are congruent. Each one measures 720/6 or 120°.

32. **C** The total number of students in both classes is 52. Set up an equation so that the mean is the sum of all 52 test scores divided by 52.

$$\frac{76(30) + 82(22)}{52}$$

$$= \frac{4084}{52} \approx 78.5\%$$

33. **A** Let x and y be the two numbers. You know that

$$x + y = 27 \text{ and}$$

$$x^2 - y^2 = 27$$

Solve for x in the first equation and substitute this value for x in the second equation.

$$x = 27 - y$$

$$(27 - y)^2 - y^2 = 27$$

$$27^2 - 54y + y^2 - y^2 = 27$$

$$27^2 - 54y = 27$$

$$27^2 - 27 = 54y$$

$$\frac{702}{54} = 13 = y$$

Since $y = 13$, $x = 27 - y = 27 - 13 = 14$.

As an alternate solution, you know $x^2 - y^2 = 27$, so

$$(x + y)(x - y) = 27$$

$27(x - y) = 27$, because $x + y = 27$.

$$x - y = 1$$

Therefore, the correct answer choice is A.

34. **A** This is a typical mixture problem. Set up an equation to represent the percent of chlorine in the solution. Remember that you are diluting the mixture by adding pure water to the existing chlorine solution, so the water added is 0 percent chlorine. Let $x =$ the number of gallons of water added.

$$8\%(18) + 0\%(x) = 6\%(18 + x)$$

Now multiply by 100 to simplify the percents and solve for x.

$$8(18) + 0 = 6(18 + x)$$

$$144 = 108 + 6x$$

$$36 = 6x$$

$$x = 6 \text{ gallons}$$

35. **E** Answer A is in slope-intercept form. Answers B and C are in point-slope form, and answers D and E are in a variation on the standard form of the equation of a line. One way to solve the problem is to find the slope of the line and then write the equation of the line in the various forms.

An alternate way to solve the problem is to substitute the x- and y-coordinates of the two points into the given equations and determine if the points are, in fact, on the lines.

Try substituting (10, 10) into answer E.

$$4(10) + 5(10) = -10$$

$$40 + 50 = -10$$

$$90 = -10 \quad \text{Not true}$$

The line given by the equation $4x + 5y = -10$ does not contain the point (10, 10).

36. **D** The maximum or minimum value of a quadratic function, $f(x) = Ax^2 + Bx + C$, is the y-coordinate of the parabola's vertex. You can determine this value by graphing the parabola and finding its vertex or by using

$$x = \frac{-B}{2A}$$

For this equation $A = -1$ and $B = 8$, so

$$x = \frac{-8}{2(-1)} = 4$$

This answer is the value for x that results in the maximum value of the function, so find $f(4)$:

$$f(4) = -(4)^2 + 8(4) - 20$$

$$= -16 + 32 - 20 = -4$$

37. **E** Geometric sequences have a common ratio between consecutive terms. The common ratio in this sequence is

$$\frac{3\sqrt{3}}{3} = \sqrt{3}$$

n = the number of the term. When $n = 1$, $3 = \left(\sqrt{3}\right)^2$ and when $n = 2$, $3\sqrt{3} = \left(\sqrt{3}\right)^3$. In generalizing the nth term, evaluate the power to which the common ratio, $\sqrt{3}$, is raised. The nth term is therefore $\left(\sqrt{3}\right)^{n+1}$.

38. **D** Knowing that $a^{-1} = \dfrac{1}{a}$, simplify the equation by writing it without negative exponents.

$$\frac{1}{4} - \frac{1}{8} = \frac{1}{x}$$

Multiply both sides of the equation by the LCD, $8x$:

$$8x\left(\frac{1}{4} - \frac{1}{8}\right) = 8x\left(\frac{1}{x}\right)$$

$$2x - x = 8$$

$$x = 8$$

39. **B** This is a distance problem where you use the Pythagorean Theorem *twice*. Sketch a right triangle whose hypotenuse is the segment $\overline{HK}$. One possible triangle has a leg $\overline{HI}$, a right angle at $\angle HIK$, and a leg $\overline{IK}$. You know $\overline{HI} = 5$, so find the $\overline{IK}$ by using the Pythagorean Theorem.

$$5^2 + 5^2 = \overline{IK}^2$$

$$50 = \overline{IK}^2$$

$$5\sqrt{2} = \overline{IK}$$

(Since $\overline{IK}$ is the hypotenuse of an isosceles right triangle, you could have used the ratios of the sides of a 45°-45°-90° triangle to find $\overline{IK}$.)

Now use the Pythagorean Theorem again to solve for HK.

$$\overline{HI}^2 + \overline{IK}^2 = \overline{HK}^2$$

$$5^2 + \left(5\sqrt{2}\right)^2 = \overline{HK}^2$$

$$25 + 50 = \overline{HK}^2$$

$$75 = \overline{HK}^2$$

$$\overline{HK} = \sqrt{75} = 5\sqrt{3}$$

40. **C** Each year, the number of students increases by 2.25 percent of the previous year's number of students. So, although the increase is the same percentage each year, it is a different number of students each year.

The rate of change can be represented by 1.0225. To determine the number of students for a given year, multiply the previous year's number of students by 1.0225. To find the number of students in the year 2012, you would raise the rate of change to a power of 12 (for the years from 2000 to 2012) and multiply that result by 850.

$850(1.0225) = 1110.142$. Round the answer to the nearest whole number. The answer is 1110 students.

41. **C** The inverse of a function is found by interchanging y and x and solving for the new y value.

$$f(x) = \frac{x + 3}{2}$$

$$y = \frac{x + 3}{2}$$

$$x = \frac{y + 3}{2}$$

$$2x = y + 3$$

$$2x - 3 = y$$

$$f^{-1} = 2x - 3$$

(Check your solution by graphing the original function and the inverse function on your calculator. The inverse function is obtained by reflecting the original function over the line $y = x$.)

$$f^{-1}(-5) = 2(-5) - 3 = -13$$

42. **D** Knowing one of the angle measures of the rhombus should provide a hint that either trigonometry or a special right triangle needs be used to solve the problem. Since $m\angle WVU = 135°$, then the angle opposite it, $\angle WTU$, also measures 135°. Draw the altitude from vertex T to the opposite side, and name the point where the altitude intersects the opposite side X. You now have a 45°-45°-90° right triangle in $\triangle TXW$.

The side opposite the 90° in $\triangle TXW$ measures 8. Using the ratio of the sides of a 45°-45°-90°, you know the two, congruent legs must measure $\frac{8\sqrt{2}}{\sqrt{2}}$, or $4\sqrt{2}$.

$4\sqrt{2} \approx 5.657$.

Figure 10 helps to visualize the problem.

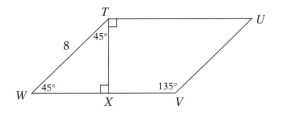

Figure 10

An alternate way to solve for the height of the rhombus is to use trigonometry.

$$\sin 45° = \frac{TX}{8}$$
$$8(\sin 45°) = 5.657 = TX$$

The area of the rhombus is found by

$$A = BH = 8(5.657) = 45.3$$

43. **D** Secant is the cofunction of the cosine function, and cotangent is the cofunction of the tangent function.

$$(\sec \theta)(\cot \theta)$$

$$= \left(\frac{1}{\cos \theta}\right)\left(\frac{\cos \theta}{\sin \theta}\right)$$

$$= \frac{1}{\sin \theta} = \csc \theta$$

44. **C** Imaginary numbers are more of a focus of the SAT II Math Level 2 test. Although you may be unfamiliar with the imaginary number i, you know enough information to solve this problem. It is given that $i^2 = -1$, so the problem is simply an application of properties of exponents.

Write i^8 in terms of factors of i^2.

$$i^8 = (i^2)^4 = i^2 \times i^2 \times i^2 \times i^2$$

$$i^8 = -1 \times -1 \times -1 \times -1 = 1$$

45. **C** A conditional (if-then) statement is equivalent to its contrapositive. Think of the given statement, "If a triangle is equilateral, then it is *not* scalene," as "If p, then q" where p = "If a triangle is equilateral" and q = "it is not scalene."

The contrapositive of the statement must be in the form "if not q, then not p." Manipulating the original statement to create the contrapositive results in:

"If a triangle is NOT not scalene, then it is NOT equilateral." This is equivalent to statement III, "If a triangle is scalene, then it is not equilateral."

Note: A conditional statement is NOT equivalent to its converse, nor to its inverse, eliminating I and II.

46. **A** Use the trigonometric identity $\sin^2 x + \cos^2 x = 1$ to simplify the expression.

$$(2\sin x)(9\sin x) - (6\cos x)(-3\cos x)$$

$$= 18\sin^2 x - -18\cos^2 x$$

$$= 18(\sin^2 x + \cos^2 x)$$

$$= 18(1) = 18$$

47. **B** Use the Pythagorean Theorem to solve for x. The hypotenuse, c, must be the largest value.

$$(x - 3)^2 + (x + 1)^2 = (x + 5)^2$$

$$x^2 - 6x + 9 + x^2 + 2x + 1 = x^2 + 10x + 25$$

$$2x^2 - 4x + 10 = x^2 + 10x + 25$$

$$x^2 - 14x - 15 = 0$$

$$(x - 15)(x + 1) = 0$$

$$x = 15$$

($x = -1$ would not result in the measures of sides of a triangle, since one side would equal zero and one side would be negative.)

48. **B** Recognize that $x^2 - y^2$ is the difference of perfect square binomials. Then, factor $x^2 - y^2$ and solve for $x - y$.

$$x^2 - y^2 = x + y$$

$$(x + y)(x - y) = x + y$$

$$(x + y)(x - y) - (x + y) = 0$$

$$(x + y)[(x - y) - 1] = 0$$

$$(x + y) = 0 \text{ or } (x - y) = 1$$

$$x = -y$$

The problem states that $x \neq -y$, so the only solution to the problem is $(x - y) = 1$.

49. **E** Rationalize the denominator by multiplying the numerator and denominator by the conjugate of $\sqrt{3} + \sqrt{2} : \sqrt{3} - \sqrt{2}$.

$$\frac{\sqrt{6}}{\sqrt{3} + \sqrt{2}} \times \frac{\sqrt{3} - \sqrt{2}}{\sqrt{3} - \sqrt{2}}$$

$$= \frac{\sqrt{6}\left(\sqrt{3} - \sqrt{2}\right)}{\left(\sqrt{3} + \sqrt{2}\right)\left(\sqrt{3} - \sqrt{2}\right)}$$

$$= \frac{\sqrt{18} - \sqrt{12}}{3 - 2}$$

$$= \frac{3\sqrt{2} - 2\sqrt{3}}{1}$$

$$= 3\sqrt{2} - 2\sqrt{3}$$

50. **E** The volume of the pool is given by

$$V = \ell \times w \times h$$

$$V = 15 \times 12 \times 5 = 900 \text{ ft}^3$$

Remember to convert the radius of the base of the bucket to feet: 6 inches = $\frac{1}{2}$ foot. The volume of the right cylindrical bucket is then given by

$$V = \pi r^2 h$$

$$V = \pi \left(\frac{1}{2}\right)^2 2$$

$$V \approx 1.57 \text{ ft}^3$$

Divide the volume of the pool by the volume of the bucket to get

$$\frac{900}{1.57} \approx 573 \text{ buckets}$$

Diagnose Your Strengths and Weaknesses

Check the number of each question answered correctly and "X" the number of each question answered incorrectly.

Algebra	1	3	4	5	6	7	10	13	16	19	33	34	38	48	49	Total Number Correct
15 questions																

Plane Geometry	8	12	14	18	20	24	25	26	31	47	Total Number Correct
10 questions											

Solid Geometry	11	39	50	Total Number Correct
3 questions				

Coordinate Geometry	2	9	22	27	35	40	Total Number Correct
6 questions							

Trigonometry	28	42	43	46	Total Number Correct
4 questions					

Functions	15	21	29	30	36	41	Total Number Correct
6 questions							

Data Analysis, Statistics, and Probability	17	23	32	Total Number Correct
3 questions				

Number and Operations	37	44	45	Total Number Correct
3 questions				

Number of correct answers $- \frac{1}{4}$ **(Number of incorrect answers) = Your raw score**

_____ $- \frac{1}{4} ($_____$) = $_____

Compare your raw score with the approximate SAT subject test score below:

	Raw Score	**SAT Subject Test Approximate Score**
Excellent	46–50	750–800
Very Good	41–45	700–750
Good	36–40	640–700
Above Average	29–35	590–640
Average	22–28	510–590
Below Average	<22	<510

PART II
MATH REVIEW

CHAPTER 4

ALGEBRA

This chapter provides a review of basic algebraic principles. Thirty-eight to forty-two percent of the Level 1 test questions relate to algebra and functions. That translates to about 28 percent of the test questions relating specifically to algebra. In reality, however, algebra is needed to answer nearly all of the questions on the test, including coordinate geometry, plane geometry, and, especially, functions. The pie chart shows approximately how much of the Level 1 test is related to algebra:

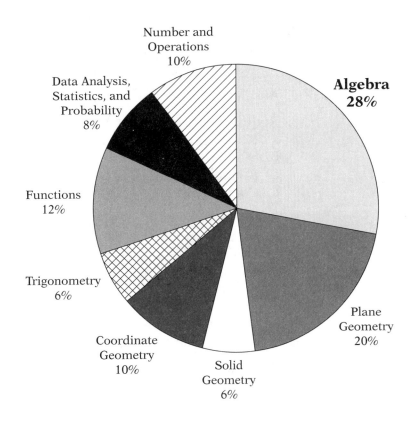

A wide variety of algebra topics are covered in this chapter to help best prepare you for the Math Level 1 test. The topics are

1. Evaluating Expressions

2. Order of Operations

3. Fractions
   a. Simplifying Fractions
   b. Least Common Denominator
   c. Multiplying Fractions
   d. Using Mixed Numbers and Improper Fractions
   e. Variables in the Denominator

4. Percents
   a. Converting Percents to Decimals
   b. Converting Fractions to Percents
   c. Percent Problems

5. Exponents
   a. Properties of Exponents
   b. Common Mistakes with Exponents
   c. Rational Exponents
   d. Negative Exponents
   e. Variables in an Exponent

6. Real Numbers
   a. Vocabulary
   b. Properties of Real Numbers
      i. Properties of Addition
      ii. Properties of Multiplication
      iii. Distributive Property
      iv. Properties of Positive and Negative Numbers

7. Absolute Value

8. Radical Expressions
   a. Roots of Real Numbers
   b. Simplest Radical Form
   c. Rationalizing the Denominator
   d. Conjugates

9. Polynomials
   a. Vocabulary
   b. Adding and Subtracting Polynomials
   c. Multiplying Polynomials
   d. Factoring
      i. Trinomials
      ii. Difference of Perfect Squares
      iii. Sum and Difference of Cubes

10. Quadratic Equations
    a. Factoring
    b. Quadratic Formula
    c. Solving by Substitution
    d. The Discriminant
    e. Equations with Radicals

11. Inequalities
    a. Transitive Property of Inequality
    b. Addition and Multiplication Properties
    c. "And" vs. "Or"
    d. Inequalities with Absolute Value

12. Rational Expressions
    a. Simplifying Rational Expressions
    b. Multiplying and Dividing Rational Expressions
    c. Adding and Subtracting Rational Expressions
    d. Solving Equations with Rational Expressions

Evaluating Expressions

Problems asking you to evaluate an expression represent the easiest of the algebra questions on the Math Level 1 test. To answer this type of question, simply substitute the value given for the variable.

EXAMPLE:

If $x = n^3$ and $n = \dfrac{1}{2}y$, then find the value of x when $y = 4$.

Substitute $y = 4$ into the second equation to get $n = \dfrac{1}{2}(4) = 2$.

Now substitute $n = 2$ into the first equation to get $x = 2^3 = 8$.

The correct answer is 8.

Order of Operations

The order of operations specifies which step to do first when solving an equation. Students usually remember the order by "PEMDAS" or "Please Excuse My Dear Aunt Sally." Both expressions stand for **P**arentheses (or other grouping symbols like brackets, radicals, or fraction bars), **E**xponents, **M**ultiplication/**D**ivision, and **A**ddition/**S**ubtraction.

Within a grouping symbol, work from the innermost to the outermost expression. Evaluate exponents and roots from left to right. Then, perform multiplication and division in order from left to right. Finally, perform addition and subtraction in order from left to right.

EXAMPLE:

Simplify $16 - 2 + [52 \div (7 - 3)]$.

$= 16 - 2 + [52 \div 4]$

$= 16 - 2 + 13$

$= 14 + 13$

$= 27 \quad$ Answer

Fractions

SIMPLIFYING FRACTIONS

Fractions are in simplest form when the numerator and denominator have no common factor other than 1. To simplify a fraction, factor both the numerator and denominator.

EXAMPLE:

Simplify $\dfrac{4}{12}$.

4 and 12 have a common factor of 4. Divide both the numerator and denominator by 4 to get $\dfrac{1}{3}$.

Don't cancel terms that are not common factors.

   Following is a common mistake:

$$\dfrac{(x^2 - 4)}{8} \neq \dfrac{x^2}{2}$$

   $x^2 - 4$ and 8 do not have a common factor, so this expression is already in simplest form.

EXAMPLE:

Simplify $\dfrac{(3x + 12)}{(3x + 3y)}$

$= \dfrac{3(x + 4)}{3(x + y)}$ Factor the numerator and denominator. 3 is a common factor.

$= \dfrac{(x + 4)}{(x + y)}$ $(x \neq -y)$ (This restriction is important because you cannot divide by zero!)   Answer

LEAST COMMON DENOMINATOR

The least common denominator (LCD) of two or more fractions is the least common multiple (LCM) of their denominators. To find the LCD:

1. Factor each denominator completely, and write as the product of prime factors. (Factor trees are usually used for this.)
2. Take the greatest power of each prime factor.
3. Find the product of these factors.

EXAMPLE:

Find the LCD of $\dfrac{1}{4}$ and $\dfrac{7}{30}$.

$4 = 2 \times 2 = 2^2$ $30 = 2 \times 3 \times 5$

The greatest power of 2 is 2^2. The greatest power of 3 is 3. The greatest power of 5 is 5.

$2^2 \times 3 \times 5 = 60$

60 is the LCD.   Answer

The least common denominator is helpful when adding and subtracting fractions.

EXAMPLE:

Simplify $\dfrac{1}{4} + \dfrac{7}{30}$.

You already know that the LCD of 4 and 30 is 60. Rewrite each fraction using 60 as the denominator.

$$\dfrac{1 \times 15}{4 \times 15} = \dfrac{7 \times 2}{30 \times 2}$$

$$= \dfrac{15}{60} + \dfrac{14}{60}$$

$$= \dfrac{29}{60} \quad \text{Answer}$$

The least common denominator is also used when simplifying complex fractions. A *complex fraction* is a fraction whose numerator or denominator contains one or more fractions. Find the LCD of the simple fractions and multiply the numerator and denominator of the complex fraction by it.

EXAMPLE:

Simplify $\dfrac{\dfrac{5}{x}}{\left(\dfrac{1}{x} - \dfrac{1}{5x}\right)}$.

Multiply the numerator and the denominator by the LCD of the simple fractions, *5x*.

$$= \dfrac{\dfrac{5}{x}}{\left(\dfrac{1}{x} - \dfrac{1}{5x}\right)} \times \dfrac{5x}{5x}$$

$$= \dfrac{5 \times 5}{(5 - 1)}$$

$$= \dfrac{25}{4} \quad \text{Answer}$$

MULTIPLYING FRACTIONS

To multiply fractions, simply multiply straight across. $\frac{a}{b} \times \frac{c}{d} = \frac{ac}{bd}$.

EXAMPLE:

Simplify $\frac{2}{5} \times \frac{3}{6} \times \frac{4}{7}$.

$= \frac{2 \times 3 \times 4}{5 \times 6 \times 7}$

$= \frac{24}{210}$ Divide by a common factor to simplify.

$= \frac{4}{35}$ Answer

You can also simplify the fractions before multiplying to save time.

EXAMPLE:

$\frac{2}{5} \times \frac{3}{6} \times \frac{4}{7} = \frac{1}{5} \times \frac{1}{1} \times \frac{4}{7}$ Remove the common factors of 2 and 3.

$= \frac{1 \times 1 \times 4}{5 \times 1 \times 7}$

$= \frac{4}{35}$

To divide by a fraction, multiply by its reciprocal. $\frac{a}{b} \div \frac{c}{d} = \frac{a}{b} \times \frac{d}{c}$. This is known as the Division Rule for Fractions. Of course, b, c, and d cannot equal zero, since you cannot divide by zero.

EXAMPLE:

Simplify $18 \div \frac{6}{11}$.

$= 18 \times \frac{11}{6}$

$= 3 \times \frac{11}{1}$ Divide through by a common factor of 6.

$= \frac{3 \times 11}{1} = 33$ Answer

USING MIXED NUMBERS AND IMPROPER FRACTIONS

A mixed number represents the sum of an integer and a fraction. For instance:

$3\frac{1}{4} = 3 + \frac{1}{4}$

In fractional form:

$$3\frac{1}{4} = \frac{4 \times 3 + 1}{4} = \frac{13}{4}$$

When $3\frac{1}{4}$ is written as the fraction $\frac{13}{4}$, it is called an *improper fraction*.

Improper fractions are fractions whose numerator is greater than the denominator. It is often easier to change mixed numerals to improper fractions when simplifying an expression.

EXAMPLE:

Simplify $8\frac{2}{3} \div \frac{1}{6}$.

$$8\frac{2}{3} = \frac{3 \times 8 + 2}{3} = \frac{24 + 2}{3} = \frac{26}{3} \qquad \text{Change to an improper fraction first.}$$

Then $8\frac{2}{3} \div \frac{1}{6} = \frac{26}{3} \times \frac{6}{1}$ Multiply by the reciprocal of $\frac{1}{6}$.

$$\frac{26 \times 6}{3} = \frac{26 \times 2}{1} = 52 \qquad \text{Answer}$$

VARIABLES IN THE DENOMINATOR

Fraction problems get more difficult to solve when there is a variable in the denominator. To solve, find the least common denominator (LCD) of the fractions and multiply both sides of the equation by it.

EXAMPLE:

Solve $4 - \frac{1}{x} = \frac{6}{2x}$

The LCD of $\frac{1}{x}$ and $\frac{6}{2x}$ is $2x$.

$$2x\left(4 - \frac{1}{x}\right) = 2x\left(\frac{6}{2x}\right)$$

$$8x - 2 = 6$$

$$8x = 8$$

$$x = 1 \qquad \text{Answer}$$

Sometimes multiplying both sides of an equation by the LCD transforms the equation into an equation that is NOT equivalent to the original one. Multiplying both sides of an equation by a polynomial may introduce *extraneous roots* that do not satisfy the original equation. It is crucial to go back and check your answer in the original fractional equation.

EXAMPLE:

Solve $\dfrac{2}{\left(x^2 - 7x + 10\right)} = \dfrac{x - 1}{x - 5}$.

Factor $x^2 - 7x + 10$ into $(x - 2)(x - 5)$. Now multiply both sides of the equation by the LCD of the fractions, $(x - 2)(x - 5)$.

$$\frac{2}{\left(x^2 - 7x + 10\right)} \times (x - 2)(x - 5) = \frac{x - 1}{x - 5} \times (x - 2)(x - 5)$$

$$2 = (x - 1)(x - 2)$$

$$2 = x^2 - 3x + 2$$

$$0 = x^2 - 3x$$

$$0 = x(x - 3)$$

$$x = 0 \text{ or } x = 3 \quad \text{Answer}$$

Since you multiplied both sides of the equation by a polynomial, $(x - 2)(x - 5)$, check to ensure the equation does not have extraneous roots. Substituting $x = 0$ into the original equation results in $\dfrac{2}{10} = \dfrac{-1}{-5}$ or $1/5 = 1/5$. Substituting $x = 3$ into the original equation results in $2/-2 = 2/-2$ or $-1 = -1$. Both answers check, so they are not extraneous.

Proportions are another type of problem that may have variables in the denominator. A *proportion* is an equation that sets two ratios (fractions) equal to each other. Don't worry about finding least common denominators when solving a proportion, simply *cross multiply*.

EXAMPLE:

$$\frac{10}{x + 4} = \frac{6}{x}$$

$$10x = 6(x + 4)$$

$$10x = 6x + 24$$

$$4x = 24$$

$$x = 6 \quad \text{Answer}$$

Percents

CONVERTING PERCENTS TO DECIMALS

Percent problems can often be easily translated into simpler equations. Percent means "per one hundred" or "divided by one hundred." To convert a percent to a decimal, move the decimal point two places to the left.

$$5\% = 5 \text{ out of } 100 = \frac{5}{100} = 5 \div 100 = 0.05$$

$$\frac{3}{4}\% = \frac{3}{4} \text{ out of } 100 = \frac{\frac{3}{4}}{100} = \frac{3}{4} \div 100 = 0.75 \div 100 = 0.0075$$

The simplest way to change a fractional percent to a decimal is to change the fraction to a decimal first, and then move the decimal point two places to the *left*.

E X A M P L E :

Simplify $\frac{2}{5}\%$.

$$\frac{2}{5} = 0.4$$

$0.4\% = 0.004$ Answer

CONVERTING FRACTIONS TO PERCENTS

The simplest way to change a fraction to a percent is to change the fraction to a decimal first, and then move the decimal point two places to the *right*.

$$\frac{2}{5} = 0.4$$

$0.4 = 40\%$

E X A M P L E :

When written as a percent, $7\frac{1}{4}$ is what value?

$$7\frac{1}{4} = 7.25$$

725% Answer

PERCENT PROBLEMS

In percent problems, the word "of" means "multiply" and the word "is" means "equals." It is often useful to set up problems in the format *a* **is** *b*% **of** *c* and solve for the unknown variable.

E X A M P L E :

26 is 25% of what number?

$26 = 25\% \times c$ Think *a* **is** *b*% **of** *c*. $26 = a$ and $25 = b$.

$26 = \frac{25}{100}(c)$ so $26 = 0.25c$

$\frac{26}{0.25} = c$

$c = 104$ Answer

EXAMPLE:

What percent of 12 is 4? Round answer to the nearest tenth.

$4 = b\% \times 12$ Think **a is b% of c.** 4 = a and 12 = c.

$\dfrac{4}{12} = b\%$

$\dfrac{4}{12} = \dfrac{b}{100}$

$\dfrac{4 \times 100}{12} = b$

$b = \dfrac{400}{12} = 33.\overline{3}\%$ Answer

EXAMPLE:

Find 85% of 324.

$a = 85\% \times 324$ Think **a is b% of c.** 85 = b and 324 = c.

$a = 0.85 \times 324$

$a = 275.4$ Answer

Exponents

PROPERTIES OF EXPONENTS

Given the expression 2^4, the exponent 4 tells you the number of times the base, 2, is to be used as a factor.

$2^4 = 2 \times 2 \times 2 \times 2 = 16$

Remember that a number raised to the zero power equals 1.

$a^0 = 1 \ (a \neq 0)$ $5^0 = 1$

Rules of Exponents

1. To multiply two powers with the same base, you *add* the exponents:

   $a^m \times a^n = a^{m+n}$ $2^2 \times 2^3 = 2^{2+3} = 2^5$

2. To divide two powers with the same base, you *subtract* the exponents:

   $\dfrac{a^m}{a^n} = a^{m-n}$ $\dfrac{2^5}{2^3} = 2^{5-3} = 2^2$

3. To raise a power to a power, you *multiply* the exponents:

   $(a^m)^n = a^{mn}$ $(2^2)^3 = 2^{2 \times 3} = 2^6$

4. To raise a product to a power, you *raise each factor to the power* and *multiply:*

   $(ab)^m = a^m \times b^m$ $(2 \times 5)^3 = 2^3 \times 5^3$

5. To raise a quotient to a power, you *raise each factor to the power* and *divide:*

$$\left(\frac{a}{b}\right)^m = \frac{a^m}{b^m} \qquad\qquad \left(\frac{8}{4}\right)^2 = \frac{8^2}{4^2}$$

When simplifying expressions involving the rules of exponents, it is easiest to simplify each variable separately as shown in the next example.

EXAMPLE:

Simplify $\dfrac{30x^3y^5}{-5x^2y^3}$.   (Assume x and y do not equal 0.)

$$\frac{30x^3y^5}{-5x^2y^3} = \frac{30}{-5} \times \frac{x^3}{x^2} \times \frac{y^5}{y^3} \qquad \text{Isolate each variable.}$$

$$= -6 \times x^{3-2} \times y^{5-3} \qquad \text{Use rule \#2. Subtract the exponents for each base.}$$

$$= -6 \times x^1 \times y^2$$

$$= -6xy^2 \qquad \text{Answer}$$

EXAMPLE:

Simplify $\dfrac{\left(a^3bc^3\right)^2}{\left(a^2bc\right)^2}$.   (Assume a, b and c do not equal 0.)

$$\frac{\left(a^3bc^3\right)^2}{\left(a^2bc\right)^2} = \frac{a^{3\times2}b^2c^{3\times2}}{a^{2\times2}b^2c^2} \qquad \text{Use rules \#3 and \#5. Multiply the exponents.}$$

$$= \frac{a^6}{a^4} \times \frac{b^2}{b^2} \times \frac{c^6}{c^2} \qquad \text{Isolate each variable.}$$

$$= a^2 \times b^0 \times c^4 \qquad \text{Use rule \#2. Subtract the exponents for each base.}$$

$$= a^2 \times 1 \times c^4$$

$$= a^2c^4 \qquad \text{Answer}$$

COMMON MISTAKES WITH EXPONENTS

When studying for the SAT Subject test, make sure you don't make these common mistakes:

1. $\left(-\dfrac{1}{2}\right)^{-3} \neq \dfrac{1}{8}$

Watch your negative exponents. The quantity $\dfrac{1}{2}$ should be put in the denominator and raised to the third power:

$$\left(-\frac{1}{2}\right)^{-3} = \frac{1}{\left(-\frac{1}{2}\right)^3} = \frac{1}{\left(\frac{(-1)^3}{2^3}\right)} = \frac{8}{-1} = -8$$

2. $3x^3 \neq 27x^3$

$3x^3 \neq (3x)^3$

Only x is raised to the third power here. $3x^3$ is in simplest form.

3. $2^2 + 2^3 \neq 2^5$

   You only add the exponents when finding the *product* of two terms in the same base. $2^2 \times 2^3$ would in fact equal 2^5. There's no rule of exponents that applies to finding the *sum* of two terms, so just simplify each term.

   $2^2 + 2^3 = 4 + 8 = 12$

4. $4^3 \times 4^4 \neq 4^{12}$

   Remember to add the exponents when the bases are the same.

   $4^3 \times 4^4 = 4^7$

5. $2^2 \times 2^3 \neq 4^5$

   It's correct to add the exponents here, but the base should remain unchanged.

6. $(a + b)^2 \neq a^2 + b^2$

   This is a very common error. It is important to understand that raising the quantity $a + b$ to the second power means that the base, $a + b$, is to be used as a factor two times. In other words, $(a + b)^2 = (a + b)(a + b)$. You then need to multiply using the FOIL method:

   $(a + b)(a + b) = a^2 + 2ab + b^2$

RATIONAL EXPONENTS

The previous examples focus on integral exponents. It is possible, however, to define a^x when x is any *rational number*. Remember that a rational number can be expressed as $\dfrac{p}{q}$ and results from dividing an integer by another (nonzero) integer.

$4^{\frac{1}{2}}$ reads as "4 to the one-half power" and equals $\sqrt{4}$.

$5^{\frac{2}{3}}$ reads as "5 to the two-thirds power" and equals $\sqrt[3]{5^2}$ or $\sqrt[3]{25}$. $5^{\frac{2}{3}}$ can also be represented as $\left(\sqrt[3]{5}\right)^2$.

$x^{\frac{a}{b}}$ equals $\sqrt[b]{x^a}$ or $\left(\sqrt[b]{x}\right)^a$ as long as $b \neq 0$. All of the rules of exponents previously discussed also apply to rational exponents.

EXAMPLE:

Simplify $81^{\frac{3}{4}}$.

$81^{\frac{3}{4}} = \left(\sqrt[4]{81}\right)^3$

$\quad = 3^3 = 27 \qquad$ Answer

This problem can also be solved by raising 81 to the third power first.

$\sqrt[4]{81^3} = \sqrt[4]{531,441}$

Finding the fourth root of 531,441 is less obvious than finding the fourth root of 81 as in the solution above.

EXAMPLE:

Simplify $\left(8^4\right)^{\frac{1}{12}}$.

$$\left(8^4\right)^{\frac{1}{12}} = 8^{\frac{4}{12}} = 8^{\frac{1}{3}}$$

$$= \left(2^3\right)^{\frac{1}{3}} = 2^1 = 2 \quad \text{Answer}$$

NEGATIVE EXPONENTS

Given the expression 2^{-4}, rewrite it without the negative exponent by moving 2^4 to the denominator. In other words, 2^{-4} is the reciprocal of 2^4.

$$2^{-4} = \frac{1}{2^4} = \frac{1}{(2 \times 2 \times 2 \times 2)} = \frac{1}{16}$$

Remember that expressions in simplest form typically do not contain negative exponents.

EXAMPLE:

Simplify $\dfrac{x^{-3}}{2y^3}\left(\dfrac{1}{xy}\right)^{-3}$. (Assume x and y do not equal 0.)

$$\frac{x^{-3}}{2y^3}\left(\frac{1}{xy}\right)^{-3} = \frac{x^{-3}}{2y^3}\left(\frac{1^{-3}}{x^{-3}y^{-3}}\right) \quad \text{Use rule \#5.}$$

$$= \left(\frac{1}{2x^3y^3}\right)\left(\frac{x^3y^3}{1}\right) \quad \text{Simplify the negative exponents.}$$

$$= \frac{x^3y^3}{2x^3y^3}$$

$$= \frac{1}{2} \quad \text{Answer}$$

VARIABLES IN AN EXPONENT

Solving an equation with a variable in the exponent can be easily done if both sides can be rewritten in the same base.

EXAMPLE:

Solve $4^x = 32^{x+1}$. Recognize that 4 and 32 can be written in base 2.

$$(2^2)^x = (2^5)^{x+1}$$

$2^{2x} = 2^{5(x+1)}$ Since both sides are in base 2, set the exponents equal and solve.

$$2x = 5(x + 1)$$

$$2x = 5x + 5$$

$$-3x = 5$$

$$x = -\frac{5}{3} \quad \text{Answer}$$

Real Numbers

VOCABULARY

Natural Numbers   {1, 2, 3, . . .}

Whole Numbers   {0, 1, 2, 3, . . .}

Integers   {. . .–2, –1, 0, 1, 2, 3, . . .}

Rational Numbers   Numbers that can be expressed as $\frac{p}{q}$ and result from dividing an integer by another (nonzero) integer. $-\frac{2}{3}$, $\frac{3}{4}$, 0.7, 1.333, . . . and 8 are examples of rational numbers.

Irrational Numbers Numbers that cannot be expressed as $\frac{p}{q}$. In decimal form, they are nonterminating and non-repeating. π and $\sqrt{2}$ are examples of irrational numbers.

Real Numbers   The set of all rational and irrational numbers.

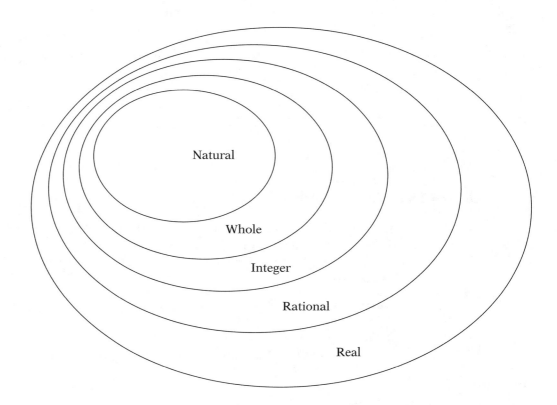

EXAMPLE:

Which of the following is NOT an irrational number?

(A) $\sqrt{2}$ (B) π (C) $\sqrt{50}$ (D) 1.33333. . .   (E) 5.020020002. . .

1.33333 is a repeating decimal so it is rational. Irrational numbers are infinite and nonrepeating, such as answer E. 5.02020202 . . . is a repeating decimal, but 5.020020002 . . . is nonrepeating, since the number of zeros continues to increase.

(D) 1.333333   Answer

PROPERTIES OF REAL NUMBERS

It is important to understand the properties of real numbers in order to move on in algebra. Before getting into the operations of addition and multiplication, let's review examples of the basic properties of equality. These hold true for all real numbers.

- **Reflexive Property** $x = x$ $2 = 2$

- **Symmetric Property**   If $a = b$, then $b = a$.   If $x = 1$, then $1 = x$.

- **Transitive Property**   If $a = b$ and $b = c$, then   If $x = 1$ and $1 = y$,
                              $a = c$.   then $x = y$.

- **Addition Property**   If $a = b$, then $a + c =$ If $x = 4$, then $x + 2 =$
                              $b + c$. $4 + 2$.

- **Multiplication Property** If $a = b$, then $ac = bc$.   If $x = 9$, then $3x =$
                                                                3×9.

The last two properties show the fundamental principle of algebra:

What you do to one side of an equation, you MUST do to the other side.

In other words, if you add 2 to one side of an equation, you must add 2 to the other side to maintain the equality. You can perform nearly any operation on one side as long as you also perform it on the other. Most of this algebra chapter comes back to this fundamental idea. If you take the square root of one side of an equation, you must take the square root of the other side. If you cube one side of an equation, you must cube the other. You get the idea.

As you review the following properties of addition and multiplication, remember these are the properties that allow you to perform operations needed to simplify expressions and solve equations. It is important to be able to perform these operations *and* identify what property is being used. Assume a, b, and c are real numbers.

Properties of Addition

1. **Closure Property of Addition**

   The sum $a + b$ results in a unique real number.

   $3 + 11$ equals the real number 14.

2. **Commutative Property of Addition**

   $a + b = b + a$

   $20 + 5 = 5 + 20$

3. **Associative Property of Addition**

   $(a + b) + c = a + (b + c)$

   $(8 + 9) + 10 = 8 + (9 + 10)$

4. **Identity Property of Addition** (Additive Identity)

   There is a unique real number *zero* such that:

   $a + 0 = a$

   $77 + 0 = 77$

5. **Property of Opposites** (Additive Inverse)

   For each real number *a*, there is a real unique number $-a$ such that:

   $a + -a = 0$

   $-a$ is the *opposite* of *a*. It is also called the *additive inverse* of *a*.

   $6 + -6 = 0$

Properties of Multiplication

1. **Closure Property of Multiplication**

   The product $a \times b$ results in a unique real number.

   3×11 equals the real number 33.

2. **Commutative Property of Multiplication**

   $ab = ba$

   $20 \times 5 = 5 \times 20$

3. **Associative Property of Multiplication**

   $(a \times b) \times c = a \times (b \times c)$

   $(8 \times 9) \times 10 = 8 \times (9 \times 10)$

4. **Identity Property of Multiplication** (Multiplicative Identity)

   There is a unique real number *one* such that:

   $a \times 1 = a$

   $77 \times 1 = 77$

5. **Property of Reciprocals** (Multiplicative Inverse)

   For each real number *a* (except 0), there is a unique real number $\dfrac{1}{a}$ such that:

   $a \times \dfrac{1}{a} = 1$

   $\dfrac{1}{a}$ is the *reciprocal* of *a*. It is also called the *multiplicative inverse* of *a*.

   Zero has no reciprocal, since $\dfrac{1}{0}$ is undefined.

   $6 \times \dfrac{1}{6} = 1$

Distributive Property

The distributive property of multiplication over addition states that:

$$a(b + c) = ab + ac \quad \text{and} \quad (b + c)a = ba + ca$$

$$3(5 + 6) = (3 \times 5) + (6 \times 5) = 15 + 30 = 45$$

EXAMPLE:

Simplify $2(6 - x + 2y)$.

$$2(6 - x + 2y) = (2 \times 6) - (2 \times x) + (2 \times 2y) \quad \text{Distribute the 2.}$$

$$= 12 - 2x + 4y \quad \text{Answer}$$

The example shows that the distributive property also works for trinomials (expressions containing three terms). Does it apply to multiplication over subtraction? Try the next example to see that it does hold true.

EXAMPLE:

Simplify $5(4x^2 - 10)$.

$$5(4x^2 - 10) = (5 \times 4x^2) - (5 \times 10) \quad \text{Distribute the 5.}$$

$$= 20x^2 - 50 \quad \text{Answer}$$

Properties of Positive and Negative Numbers

You should be familiar with working with signed numbers by this point in your math career. Here is a review of the basic properties of positive and negative numbers.

- A positive number times a positive number equals a positive number.

  $3 \times 4 = 12$

- A positive number times a negative number equals a negative number.

  $3 \times -4 = -12$

- A negative number times a negative number equals a positive number.

  $-3 \times -4 = 12$

- To subtract a number, add its opposite.

  $3 - 4 = 3 + (-4) = -1$

  $3 - (-4) = 3 + (+4) = 7$

- The sum of the opposites of two numbers is the opposite of their sum.

  $(-3) + (-4) = -(3 + 4) = -7$

- $x(-1) = -x$ for all real values of x.

  $3(-1) = -3 \quad \text{and} \quad -3(-1) = -(-3) = 3$

- $x(-y) = -(xy)$ for all real values of x and y.

  $3 \times (-4) = -(3 \times 4) = -12$

- $x - y = -(y - x)$.

This is a variation of the property of opposites that usually tricks students. It is often used when simplifying rational expressions and factoring, so it is important to recognize.

$$\frac{(x - y)}{(y - x)} = -1 \qquad \frac{(x - 4)}{(4 - x)} = -1 \qquad (x - 2)(2 - x) = -(x - 2)^2$$

Absolute Value

The absolute value of a number is the distance from the graph of the number on a number line to the origin. For a real number x, the absolute value of x is defined as:

$|x| = x$ if $x > 0$

$|x| = 0$ if $x = 0$

$|x| = -x$ if $x < 0$

EXAMPLE:

Evaluate the expression $|x| - 2|y|$ if $x = 6$ and $y = -3$.

$|x| - 2|y| = |6| - 2|-3|$ Substitute the given values.

$\qquad = 6 - 2 \times 3$

$\qquad = 6 - 6 = 0$ Answer

To solve an equation involving absolute value, think in terms of two separate equations: one where the expression inside the absolute value signs is *positive* and one where the expression inside the absolute value is *negative*.

EXAMPLE:

Solve $|x - 3| = 1$.

$x - 3 = 1 \quad$ or $\quad -(x - 3) = 1$ Recognize when the expression $x - 3$ is positive and negative.

$x = 4 \quad$ or $\quad -x = -2$

The solution set is $\{2, 4\}$ Answer

EXAMPLE:

Graph $y = |x - 1|$.

It is important to recognize immediately that y will never be negative, since it equals the absolute value of an expression. Absolute value, by definition, is a positive distance. If you're unsure what happens to an absolute value graph, try plotting a few points to see what results.

When $x = 1$, $y = |1 - 1| = 0$, so the coordinate $(1,0)$ must be part of the solution. When $x = 2$, $y = |2 - 1| = |1| = 1$, so the coordinate $(2,1)$ must be part of the solution. When $x = 0$, $y = |0 - 1| = |-1| = 1$, so the coordinate $(0,1)$ must be part of the solution. These three points are enough to sketch the graph, which resembles a letter "V" and has a vertex of $(1,0)$.

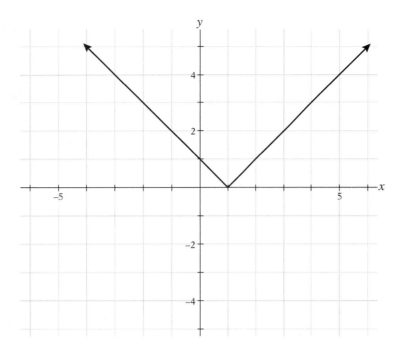

Radical Expressions

ROOTS OF REAL NUMBERS

A radical is a symbol such as $\sqrt[n]{x}$ where n is the *index* and b is the *radicand*. If n is not written, it is assumed to equal 2, for example, $\sqrt[n]{x}$ (read the *square root* of 4). Every positive number x has two square roots: $\sqrt{x}$ and $-\sqrt{x}$. The square roots of 16 are 4 and −4 because both 4^2 and $(-4)^2$ equal 16. The positive square root, 4 in this case, is called the *principal square root*.

Example 1:   Example 2:

Solve $x^2 = 49$.   Solve $\sqrt{x} = 6$.

$x = 7$ or -7 Square both sides to get $x = 6^2$.

The roots are 7 and −7. $x = 36$

Two solutions   **One solution**

It is important to note the distinction in the examples above. When finding the roots of an equation where the variable is raised to an *even* power, remember there's a positive and negative solution. In example 1, it is true that 49 has two real roots, but $\sqrt{49}$ has only one solution. $\sqrt{49} \neq -7$. If the variable is raised to an odd power, however, there's only *one real root*. For instance, there is only one solution for x in the following example:

EXAMPLE 3:

Solve $x^3 = -125$.

Take the cube root of both sides to get $x = \sqrt[3]{-125}$.

$x = -5$ Answer

Check your answer by substituting it back into the original equation. (This is always a good idea!)

$(-5)^3 = (-5)(-5)(-5) = -125$

When working with radicals, remember the product and quotient properties:

- **The Product Property of Radicals** $\sqrt[n]{ab} = \sqrt[n]{a} \times \sqrt[n]{b}$

  $$\sqrt{4 \times 9} = \sqrt{4} \times \sqrt{9} = 2 \times 3 = 6$$

- **The Quotient Property of Radicals** $\sqrt[n]{\dfrac{a}{b}} = \dfrac{\sqrt[n]{a}}{\sqrt[n]{b}}$

  $$\sqrt[3]{\dfrac{64}{8}} = \dfrac{\sqrt[3]{64}}{\sqrt[3]{8}} = \dfrac{4}{2} = 2$$

Be careful not to apply the product and quotient properties to finding the sum of radicals.

$$\sqrt{3^2 + 4^2} = \sqrt{5^2} \text{ but } \sqrt{3^2} + \sqrt{4^2} \neq \sqrt{5^2}$$

SIMPLEST RADICAL FORM

Make sure two things are true when writing an expression, such as $\sqrt[n]{x}$, in *simplest radical form:*

1. Factor all perfect nth powers from the radicand.

2. Rationalize the denominators so that no radicals remain in the denominator and no radicands are fractions.

Write the following examples in simplest radical form.

Example 1:

$\sqrt{75}$

$= \sqrt{25 \times 3}$

Example 2:

$\sqrt[3]{54}$

$= \sqrt[3]{27 \times 2}$

25 is the largest perfect square factor of 75. 27 is the largest perfect cube factor of 54.

$= \sqrt{25} \times \sqrt{3}$

$= 5\sqrt{3}$

$= \sqrt[3]{27} \times \sqrt[3]{2}$

$= 3\sqrt[3]{2}$

RATIONALIZING THE DENOMINATOR

To rationalize a denominator containing a radical, try to create a perfect square, cube, or other nth power. Let's look at a square root with a fractional radicand first.

EXAMPLE:

Simplify $\sqrt{\dfrac{7}{3}}$.

$= \sqrt{\dfrac{7}{3} \times \dfrac{3}{3}}$ Multiplying the denominator by 3 will create a perfect square, 3^2, in the denominator.

$\dfrac{3}{3}$ is another way of writing **1,** the identity element for multiplication.

$= \sqrt{\dfrac{21}{9}}$

$= \dfrac{\sqrt{21}}{3}$ Answer

Solving a cube root with a fractional radicand is nearly identical. You must multiply by a perfect square this time in order to create a perfect cube in the denominator.

EXAMPLE:

Simplify $\sqrt[3]{\dfrac{15}{2}}$.

$= \sqrt[3]{\dfrac{15}{2} \times \dfrac{2^2}{2^2}}$ Multiplying the denominator by 2^2 will create a perfect cube, 2^3, in the denominator.

$\dfrac{2^2}{2^2}$ is another way of writing **1,** the identity element for multiplication.

$= \sqrt[3]{\dfrac{60}{8}}$

$= \dfrac{\sqrt[3]{60}}{2}$ Answer

Now let's look at rationalizing a denominator that contains a radical.

EXAMPLE:

Simplify $\dfrac{\left(\sqrt{20} - \sqrt{6}\right)}{\sqrt{3}}$.

$= \left(\dfrac{\sqrt{20} - \sqrt{6}}{\sqrt{3}} \times \dfrac{\sqrt{3}}{\sqrt{3}}\right)$ Multiplying the denominator by $\sqrt{3}$ will create a perfect square in the denominator's radicand.

$\dfrac{\sqrt{3}}{\sqrt{3}}$ is another way of writing **1.**

$$= \frac{\left[\sqrt{3}\left(\sqrt{20} - \sqrt{6}\right)\right]}{\sqrt{9}} \qquad \text{Distribute } \sqrt{3}.$$

$$= \frac{\left(\sqrt{60} - \sqrt{18}\right)}{3} \qquad \text{The denominator is rationalized here, but the numerator is not in simplest radical form.}$$

$$= \frac{\left(2\sqrt{15} - 3\sqrt{2}\right)}{3} \qquad \text{Answer}$$

CONJUGATES

Conjugates are expressions in the form $\sqrt{a} + \sqrt{b}$ and $\sqrt{a} - \sqrt{b}$. Assuming a and b are integers even if a or b is a perfect square, the product of conjugates will always equal an integer.

$$\left(\sqrt{a} + \sqrt{b}\right) \times \left(\sqrt{a} - \sqrt{b}\right) = \sqrt{a}\sqrt{a} - \sqrt{a}\sqrt{b} + \sqrt{b}\sqrt{a} - \sqrt{b}\sqrt{b} = a - b$$

$$\left(\sqrt{19} + \sqrt{3}\right) \times \left(\sqrt{19} - \sqrt{3}\right) = \sqrt{19}\sqrt{19} - \sqrt{19}\sqrt{3} + \sqrt{3}\sqrt{19} - \sqrt{3}\sqrt{3} = 19 - 3 = 16$$

Conjugates are useful when rationalizing a denominator containing a *binomial radical expression*.

EXAMPLE:

Simplify $\dfrac{\left(1 + \sqrt{2}\right)}{\left(1 - \sqrt{2}\right)}$.

$$\frac{\left(1 + \sqrt{2}\right)}{\left(1 - \sqrt{2}\right)} \times \frac{\left(1 + \sqrt{2}\right)}{\left(1 + \sqrt{2}\right)} \qquad \text{Multiply both numerator and denominator by the conjugate of the denominator } 1 + \sqrt{2}.$$

$$\frac{\left(1 + \sqrt{2}\right)}{\left(1 + \sqrt{2}\right)} \text{ is another way of writing } \textbf{1.}$$

$$= \frac{\left(1 + 2\sqrt{2} + 2\right)}{1 - 2}$$

$$= \frac{\left(3 + 2\sqrt{2}\right)}{-1} \qquad \text{The denominator becomes an integer, } -1. \text{ Now simplify.}$$

$$-3 - 2\sqrt{2} \qquad \text{Answer}$$

Polynomials

VOCABULARY

A *monomial* is a single term, such as a constant, a variable, or the product of constants and variables. 7, x, $5x^2$, and $-3xy^2$ are examples of monomials. A *polynomial* contains many terms. By definition, a polynomial is the sum of monomials. $x^2 - 3x + 2$ is an example of a polynomial containing the *terms* x^2, $3x$, and 2.

　　Polynomials can be added, subtracted, multiplied, and divided following the properties of real numbers.

▨▨ ADDING AND SUBTRACTING POLYNOMIALS

Polynomials can be added and subtracted by *combining like terms*. Like terms have the same variables raised to the same power. In other words, they're terms that differ only by their coefficients.

　　a^2b^3 and $-4a^2b^3$ are like terms that can be combined. $a^2b^3 + (-4a^2b^3) = -3a^2b^3$. x^2y and $2xy$ are not like terms.

E X A M P L E :

Subtract $x^2 - 2x + 5$ from $3x - 4$.

$3x - 4 - (x^2 - 2x + 5)$	Set up your expression. Subtract the first term from the second.
$= 3x - 4 - x^2 + 2x - 5$	Change the subtraction to *adding the opposites*.
$= -x^2 + (3 + 2)x + (-4 + -5)$	Combine like terms.
$= -x^2 + 5x - 9$　　Answer	

▨▨ MULTIPLYING POLYNOMIALS

Multiplying polynomials involves using the distributive property. You are probably most familiar with multiplying a binomial (a polynomial with two terms) by another binomial. For example:

$(x + 4)(x - 6)$

　　The *FOIL method* helps to remember how to multiply terms: **F**irst, **O**uter, **I**nner, **L**ast.

$(x + 4)(x - 6) = x^2 - 6x + 4x - 24$

　　Now, add the outer and inner products to simplify the expression.

$= x^2 - 2x - 24$

E X A M P L E :

Multiply $(2x + 7)(2x - 7)$.

$(2x + 7)(2x - 7) = 4x^2 - 14x + 14x - 49$	FOIL
$= 4x^2 + (-14x + 14x) - 49$	Notice that the inner and outer terms are opposites.
$= 4x^2 - 49$　　Answer	

EXAMPLE:

Multiply $(5a + 1)(1 - 5a)$.

$(5a + 1)(1 - 5a) = (5a + 1)(-(5a - 1))$ Rewrite $(1 - 5a)$ as the opposite of $(5a - 1)$.

$= -(25a^2 - 5a + 5a - 1)$ FOIL

$= -(25a^2 + 5a - 5a + 1)$ Distribute the -1.

$= -25a^2 + 1$ Answer

Remembering these special products of polynomials will help when factoring.

Special Products	Examples
$(a + b)^2 = a^2 + 2ab + b^2$	$(2x + 9)^2 = 4x^2 + 36x + 81$
$(a - b)^2 = a^2 - 2ab + b^2$	$(x - 12)^2 = x^2 - 24x + 144$
$(a + b)(a - b) = a^2 - b^2$	$(x + 3y)(x - 3y) = x^2 - 9y^2$

FACTORING

Now that you've reviewed multiplying polynomials, let's look at its reverse: finding factors. Factoring means expressing a polynomial as a product of other polynomials. The most basic way to factor a polynomial is to distribute out its *greatest monomial factor*. (Remember a monomial is a single term, such as a constant, a variable, or the product of constants and variables.)

Just as 12 can be factored as $2^2 \times 3$, the polynomial $12xy^3 - 2x^2y^2$ can be factored as $2xy^2(6y - x)$. $2xy^2$ is the *greatest monomial factor*, otherwise known as their *GCF*, of the terms $12xy^3$ and $2x^2y^2$.

EXAMPLE:

Factor $xy^3 - xy^2 + x^2y$.

$xy^3 - xy^2 + x^2y = xy(y^2 - y + x)$ The GCF of the terms is xy.

Trinomials

Some trinomials can be factored by recognizing that they're a special product. These are called *perfect square trinomials*:

$a^2 + 2ab + b^2 = (a + b)^2$

$a^2 - 2ab + b^2 = (a - b)^2$

EXAMPLE:

Factor $x^2 - 18x + 81$.

$x^2 - 18x + 81 = (x - 9)(x - 9)$ Recognize that half of the second term squared equals the third term. $\left(\frac{1}{2} \times 18 = 9 \text{ and } 9^2 = 81. \right)$

$= (x - 9)^2$

When you are factoring, it is a good idea to check your work by multiplying the factors to get the original polynomial. Using the FOIL method, you can quickly check that $(x - 9)(x - 9)$ does, in fact, equal $x^2 - 18x + 81$.

EXAMPLE:

Factor $x^2 + x + \dfrac{1}{4}$.

$$x^2 + x + \frac{1}{4} = \left(x + \frac{1}{2}\right)\left(x + \frac{1}{2}\right) \quad \text{Recognize that } \frac{1}{2}(1) = \frac{1}{2} \text{ and } \frac{1}{2^2} = \frac{1}{4}.$$

$$x = \left(x + \frac{1}{2}\right)^2$$

Of course, not every trinomial is a perfect square trinomial that can be expressed as a special product. For these problems, try thinking about the FOIL method and use trial and error.

$x^2 + 13x + 22 = (? + ?)(? + ?)$.

First, $x \times x = x^2$, so begin the factorization with $(x + ?)(x + ?)$.

Last, $22 = 1 \times 22$ or 2×11. Think about the factors of the last term. What two numbers will multiply to give you 22 and add to give you 13? (13 is the sum of the **O**uter an **I**nner terms.) 2 and 11 work: $(x + 2)(x + 11)$.

You're not done yet. Multiply the binomials to check your work. Since the three terms in the original trinomial are positive, both binomials contain positive terms. $(x + 2)(x + 11) = x^2 + 11x + 2x + 22 = x^2 + 13x + 22$. $(x + 2)(x + 11)$ is the correct answer.

EXAMPLE:

Factor $x^2 - 2x - 35$.

$x^2 - 2x - 35 = (x + ?)(x + ?)$	Think about the **First** terms: $x \times x = x^2$.
$35 = 1 \times 35$ or 5×7	What two numbers will multiply to give you -35 and add to give you -2? 5 and -7 work.
$= (x + 5)(x - 7)$	Check your work. Pay special attention to the positive and negative signs.

Difference of Perfect Squares

The product of the sum of two terms and the difference of the same terms is called the *difference of perfect squares*. When factoring, it is important to recognize that this is a special product.

$a^2 - b^2 = (a + b)(a - b)$

$x^2 - 1 = x^2 - 1^2 = (x + 1)(x - 1)$

EXAMPLE:

Factor $4x^2 - 9$.

$4x^2 - 9 = (2x + 3)(2x - 3)$ Answer   Since $4x^2 - 9 = (2x)^2 - 3^2$.

Since both $4x^2$ and 9 are perfect squares, this binomial is a special product. Remembering this will save you time when factoring.

EXAMPLE:

Factor $x^3 - 64x$.

$x^3 - 64x = x(x^2 - 64)$ Always factor out the greatest common factor first. Here the GCF is x. And x^2 and 64 are perfect squares.

$= x(x + 8)(x - 8)$ Answer

Note that there is not a rule called "Sums of Perfect Squares." An expression such as $x^2 + 4$ cannot be further factored.

Sum and Difference of Cubes

Factoring the sum and difference of cubes is not obvious. To save time on the SAT II, be able to recognize these equations:

1. **Sum of Cubes**

    $(a^3 + b^3) = (a + b)(a^2 - ab + b^2)$

2. **Difference of Cubes**

    $(a^3 - b^3) = (a - b)(a^2 + ab + b^2)$

EXAMPLE:

Factor $8x^3 - 125$.

Using the equation for the difference of cubes, substitute $a = 2x$ and $b = 5$.

$8x^3 - 125 = (2x - 5)(4x^2 + 10x + 25)$ Answer   Since $8x^3 = (2x)^3$ and $125 = s^3$.

Memorizing the perfect cubes ($1^3 = 1$, $2^3 = 8$, $3^3 = 27$, $4^3 = 64$, $5^3 = 125$, $6^3 = 216$, etc.) will help you when factoring the sum and difference of cubes.

QUADRATIC EQUATIONS

Factoring

Up to this point, when given a problem such as $x^2 - 8x + 9$, you would say the polynomial is unfactorable. In other words, it's prime. $x^2 - 8x + 9$ doesn't fit any of the three special products, and factoring the trinomial also doesn't work.

$x^2 - 8x + 9 = (x + ?)(x + ?)$

What two numbers will multiply to give you 9 and add to give you −8? At first glance, 9 and 1 seem to work resulting in four possibilities:

$(x + 9)(x + 1)$ $(x - 9)(x - 1)$ $(x + 9)(x - 1)$ $(x - 9)(x + 1)$

None of the four, however, give you a positive 9 constant and a negative 8 coefficient for x. The *Quadratic Formula* can be used to solve a trinomial equation (in the form of a quadratic equation) whether it's factorable or not.

Before discussing the Quadratic Formula, let's take a look at quadratic equations in general. Polynomials in the form $\boldsymbol{ax^2 + bx + c}$ ($a \neq 0$) are quadratic.

(Quadratic means "second-degree.") A quadratic equation looks like $ax^2 + bx + c = 0$. "Factorable" quadratic equations are solved by factoring and setting each factor equal to zero. The solutions are called *roots* of the quadratic, values of the variable that satisfy the equation.

EXAMPLE:

Solve $x^2 - 5x - 14 = 0$.

$x^2 - 5x - 14 = (x - 7)(x + 2) = 0$ Factor the trinomial.

$(x - 7) = 0$ or $(x + 2) = 0$ Set each factor equal to zero.

$x = 7$ or -2

The solution set is $\{7, -2\}$.   Answer

Therefore, the *roots* of the quadratic equation $x^2 - 5x - 14 = 0$ are 7 and -2, since $7^2 - 5 \times 7 - 14 = 0$ and $(-2)^2 - 5 \times (-2) - 14 = 0$.

▩ QUADRATIC FORMULA

As mentioned, the Quadratic Formula can be used to solve a quadratic equation, $ax^2 + bx + c = 0$, whether it's factorable or not. The formula uses the coefficients a, b, and c to find the solutions.

> **The Quadratic Formula**
>
> $$x = \frac{-b \pm \sqrt{b^2 - 4ac}}{2a} \qquad a \neq 0$$

Remember the trinomial equation $x^2 - 8x + 9 = 0$ that we determined was "unfactorable." Let's take a look at how to solve it using the Quadratic Formula.

EXAMPLE:

Solve $x^2 - 8x + 9 = 0$.

Substitute $a = 1$, $b = -8$, and $c = 9$ into the Quadratic Formula.

$$x = \frac{[-b \pm \sqrt{(b^2 - 4ac)}]}{2a} = \frac{[-(-8) \pm \sqrt{((-8)^2 - 4 \times 1 \times 9)}]}{2 \times 1}$$

$$x = \frac{[8 \pm \sqrt{(64 - 36)}]}{2}$$

$$x = \frac{(8 \pm \sqrt{28})}{2} \qquad \text{Simplify } \sqrt{28}.$$

$$x = \frac{(8 \pm 2\sqrt{7})}{2} \qquad \text{Divide the numerator by 2.}$$

$$x = 4 \pm \sqrt{7} \qquad \text{Answer}$$

The Quadratic Formula can also be used to solve "factorable" quadratic equations. Earlier, we determined that the equation $x^2 - 5x - 14 = 0$ had roots of 7 and −2. Let's try to solve it a different way using the Quadratic Formula.

EXAMPLE:

Solve $x^2 - 5x - 14 = 0$ using the Quadratic Formula.

$a = 1$, $b = -5$, $c = -14$

$$x = \frac{\left[-b \pm \sqrt{(b^2 - 4ac)}\right]}{2a} = \frac{\left[-(-5) \pm \sqrt{((-5)^2 - 4 \times 1 \times -14)}\right]}{2 \times 1}$$

$$x = \frac{\left[5 \pm \sqrt{(25 + 56)}\right]}{2}$$

$$x = \frac{\left(5 \pm \sqrt{81}\right)}{2}$$

$$x = \frac{(5 \pm 9)}{2}$$

$$x = \frac{(5 + 9)}{2} = \frac{14}{2} = 7$$

$$x = \frac{(5 - 9)}{2} = \frac{-4}{2} = -2$$

The solution set is $\{7, -2\}$.   Answer

Of course, the roots will be the same regardless of which method you choose to use to solve the quadratic equation.

▰ SOLVING BY SUBSTITUTION

Sometimes equations that don't look like quadratic equations can be solved by factoring or by using the Quadratic Formula. This is true if you can rewrite the equations in quadratic form using substitution.

$x^4 - 8x^2 - 11 = 0$ $\qquad \rightarrow$ Let $u = x^2$, $u^2 - 8u - 11 = 0$

$x + 2\sqrt{x} + 5 = 0$ $\qquad \rightarrow$ Let $u = \sqrt{x}$, $u^2 + 2u + 5 = 0$

$\left(\dfrac{1}{8x}\right)^2 + 3\left(\dfrac{1}{8x}\right) - 7 = 0 \rightarrow$ Let $u = \left(\dfrac{1}{(8x)}\right)$, $u^2 + 3u - 7 = 0$

As in the examples above, choose a value for u so that the equation becomes quadratic in u and fits the form $\boldsymbol{au^2 + bu + c = 0.}$

EXAMPLE:

Solve $x - 19\sqrt{x} + 48 = 0$.

Let $u = \sqrt{x}$ and the equation becomes $u^2 - 19u + 48 = 0$. Is this factorable? It turns out that it is. If you're unsure, use the Quadratic Formula to find the roots.

$$u^2 - 19u + 48 = (u - 16)(u - 3) = 0$$

$$(u - 16) = 0 \ \text{ or } \ (u - 3) = 0$$

$$u = 16 \ \text{ or } \ u = 3$$

$$\sqrt{x} = 16 \ \text{ or } \ \sqrt{x} = 3$$

$$x = 256 \ \text{ or } \ x = 9$$

You're not done yet! Substitute $\sqrt{x}$ back in for u to find x.

$\{256, 9\}$ Answer

THE DISCRIMINANT

The *discriminant* of a quadratic equation equals $b^2 - 4ac$, the radicand in the Quadratic Formula. It allows you to determine the nature of the roots of a quadratic equation without actually solving for them.

1. If $b^2 - 4ac > 0$, there are two real, unequal roots.

   When $b^2 - 4ac$ is a perfect square, there are *two real, rational roots*.

   When $b^2 - 4ac$ is not a perfect square, there are *two real, irrational roots*.

2. If $b^2 - 4ac = 0$, there is one real root. (It's called a *double root.*)

3. If $b^2 - 4ac < 0$, there are *no real roots*. (They're complex conjugate in the form $a + bi$ and $a - bi$.)

EXAMPLE:

Determine the nature of the roots of the quadratic equation $x^2 - 9x - 10 = 0$.

$$b^2 - 4ac = (-9)^2 - 4(1)(-10)$$

$$= 81 + 40 = 121 \quad \text{The discriminant is positive and a perfect square.}$$

Two real, rational roots   Answer

EQUATIONS WITH RADICALS

Radical equations contain radicals with variables in the radicand. To solve a radical equation, you must always isolate the radical first. Then raise both sides to the appropriate power to "undo" the radical—that is, square a square root, cube a cube root, and so on.

Example 1:

$$\sqrt{x} = 11$$

$$\left(\sqrt{x}\right)^2 = 11^2$$

$$x = 121$$

Example 2:

$$\sqrt{x + 1} = 3$$

$$\left(\sqrt{x + 1}\right)^2 = 3^2$$

$$x + 1 = 9, \ \text{so} \ x = 8$$

EXAMPLE:

Solve $2\sqrt{x-12} - 10 = \sqrt{x-12}$.

$$\sqrt{x-12} = 10 \qquad \text{Combine like terms.}$$

$$\left(\sqrt{x-12}\right)^2 = 10^2 \qquad \text{Isolate the radical and square both sides.}$$

$$x - 12 = 100$$

$$x = 112 \qquad \text{Answer}$$

It is crucial to go back and check your answer in the original radical equation. Sometimes squaring both sides of an equation introduces *extraneous roots* that do not satisfy the original equation. When $x = 112$, $2\sqrt{112-12} - 10$ equals $\sqrt{112-12}$, so the answer checks.

When there is more than one radical in an equation, you need to square both sides multiple times. Again, remember to isolate one radical at a time.

EXAMPLE:

Solve $\sqrt{x+4} + \sqrt{x} - 6 = 0$.

$$\sqrt{x+4} = 6 - \sqrt{x} \qquad \text{Isolate the radical } \sqrt{x+4}.$$

$$\left(\sqrt{x+4}\right)^2 = \left(6 - \sqrt{x}\right)^2 \qquad \text{Square both sides.}$$

$$x + 4 = 36 - 12\sqrt{x} + x$$

$$-32 = -12\sqrt{x} \qquad \text{Isolate the second radical.}$$

$$\frac{32}{12} = \frac{8}{3} = \sqrt{x}$$

$$\left(\frac{8}{3}\right)^2 = \left(\sqrt{x}\right)^2 \qquad \text{Square both sides a second time.}$$

$$\frac{64}{9} = x \qquad \text{Answer}$$

Remember to check your answer in the original radical equation.

Inequalities

The rules for solving equations also apply to inequalities. Remember that multiplying or dividing both sides of an inequality by a negative number reverses its sign.

$-x > 8$ becomes $x < -8$.

$-\dfrac{1}{2}x < 15$ becomes $x > -30$.

TRANSITIVE PROPERTY OF INEQUALITY

The *Transitive Property of Inequality* states that for any real numbers a, b, and c:

If $a < b$ and $b < c$, then $a < c$.

It makes sense that if $3 < 4$ and $4 < 5$, then $3 < 5$.

Sometimes the transitive property is written by combining the three inequalities:

$a < b < c$ and $3 < 4 < 5$

ADDITION AND MULTIPLICATION PROPERTIES

The addition and multiplication properties of inequality mirror those for equalities.

Addition Property of Inequality	
If $a < b$, then $a + c < b + c$.	If $40 < 50$, then $40 + 1 < 50 + 1$.

Multiplication Property of Inequality	
If $a < b$ and c is <u>positive,</u> then $ac < bc$.	If $5 < 6$, then $5(2) < 6(2)$.
If $a < b$ and c is <u>negative,</u> then $ac > bc$.	If $5 < 6$, then $5(-2) > 6(-2)$.

EXAMPLE:

Solve $2 - x > 4 + x$.

$-2 > 2x$

$-1 > x$

$\{x: x < -1\}$ Answer

This reads "the set of all x such that x is less than negative one." On a number line, the graph would begin with an open circle at -1 and extend forever in the left direction.

"AND" VS. "OR"

A *conjunction* joins two sentences with "and" and is true when *both* sentences are true. For instance:

$x > 29$ and $x < 48$

$29 < x < 48$ is an alternate way of writing this, and it's read "x is greater than 29 and less than 48."

A *disjunction* joins two sentences with "or" and is true when *at least one* of the sentences is true. For instance:

$x > 5$ or $x < -5$

EXAMPLE:

Solve the conjunction $0 < x - 2 \leq 6$.

Rewrite the inequality using "and."

$0 < x - 2$	and	$x - 2 \leq 6$
$2 < x$	and	$x \leq 8$

The solution set is $\{x: 2 < x \leq 8\}$.   Answer

On a number line, the graph would begin with an open circle at 2, extend to the right, and end with a closed circle at 8.

INEQUALITIES WITH ABSOLUTE VALUE

Inequalities involving absolute value can be thought of as either disjunctions or conjunctions.

1. $|x| < n$ is equivalent to the *conjunction* $-n < x < n$.
   $|x| < 2$ is equivalent to the conjunction $-2 < x < 2$.
2. $|x| > n$ is equivalent to the *disjunction* $x < -n$ or $x > n$.
   $|x| > 2$ is equivalent to the disjunction $x < -2$ or $x > 2$.

EXAMPLE:

Solve $8 - |3x + 7| < 2$.

$-|3x + 7| < -6$ Divide both sides by -1, reversing the sign.

$|3x + 7| > 6$ Analyze the inequality to determine if it's a conjunction or disjunction. Since the variable is on the greater than side of the inequality sign, it resembles the second example above $|x| > n$. The inequality is therefore a *disjunction*.

$3x + 7 > 6$	OR	$3x + 7 < -6$
$3x > -1$	OR	$3x < -13$
$x > -\dfrac{1}{3}$	OR	$x < -\dfrac{13}{3}$

$\left\{ x : x < -\dfrac{13}{3} \text{ or } x > -\dfrac{1}{3} \right\}$ Answer

Rational Expressions

SIMPLIFYING RATIONAL EXPRESSIONS

Rational numbers are numbers that can be expressed as $\frac{p}{q}$, a quotient of integers. Likewise, *rational expressions* are those that can be expressed as a quotient of polynomials. $\frac{(x^2 - 9)}{x}$, $\frac{(x^2 - 10x + 25)}{(x^2 + 100)}$, and $\frac{14xy}{xy^3}$ are examples of rational expressions. The principles of factoring are important when you are simplifying rational expressions. Take a moment to review some special products of polynomials:

Special Products:
$(a + b)^2 = a^2 + 2ab + b^2$
$(a - b)^2 = a^2 - 2ab + b^2$
$(a + b)(a - b) = a^2 - b^2$

E X A M P L E :

Simplify $\frac{(2x^2 - 6x)}{x^2 - 9}$.

$$\frac{(2x^2 - 6x)}{x^2 - 9} = \frac{2x(x - 3)}{(x + 3)(x - 3)}$$

Factor the numerator and denominator. Recognize that the numerator has a common factor of $2x$ and the denominator is the difference of perfect squares. Now simplify by dividing the numerator and denominator by their common factor $(x - 3)$.

$$\frac{2x}{x + 3}, x \neq 3 \qquad \text{Answer}$$

Typically, rational expressions are in simplest form when they do not contain zero or negative exponents. Recall that any number raised to a zero power equals one and any number raised to a negative one power equals its reciprocal.

MULTIPLYING AND DIVIDING RATIONAL EXPRESSIONS

Multiplying and dividing rational expressions follow the same rules as fractions.

Multiplication Rule for Fractions $\qquad \frac{a}{b} \times \frac{c}{d} = \frac{ac}{bd}, \ b, d \neq 0$

Division Rule for Fractions $\qquad \frac{a}{b} \div \frac{c}{d} = \frac{a}{b} \times \frac{d}{c}, \ b, c, d \neq 0$

EXAMPLE:

$$\frac{4}{x^2} \div \frac{x}{4}.$$

$$\frac{4}{x^2} \div \frac{x}{4} = \frac{4}{x^2} \times \frac{4}{x} \qquad \text{Multiply by the reciprocal of } \frac{x}{4}.$$

$$= \frac{16}{x^3} \qquad \text{Answer}$$

EXAMPLE:

Simplify $\dfrac{(x^4 - y^4)}{(x^2 + y^2)}(x + y)^{-2}$.

Factor the first fraction. The numerator $x^4 - y^4$ is the difference of perfect squares: $x^4 - y^4 = (x^2 + y^2)(x^2 - y^2)$. The denominator $x^2 + y^2$ is the sum of perfect squares and therefore cannot be factored. The simplified expression is

$$\frac{(x^2 + y^2)(x^2 - y^2)}{(x^2 + y^2)}(x + y)^{-2}$$

Simplify the fraction by factoring out a common factor of $x^2 + y^2$:

$$\frac{(x^2 - y^2)}{1}(x + y)^{-2}$$

Simplify the negative exponent by rewriting $(x + y)^{-2}$ as $\dfrac{1}{(x + y)^2}$. Now you have:

$$\frac{(x^2 - y^2)}{1} \times \frac{1}{(x + y)^2}$$

The numerator of the first term is the difference of perfect squares and can be factored. In factored form, you have

$$\frac{(x + y)(x - y)}{1} \times \frac{1}{(x + y)(x + y)}$$

Factor out a common factor of $(x + y)$.

$$= \frac{(x - y)}{(x + y)} \qquad \text{Answer}$$

This example is about as complex as you'll find on the Level 1 test. It incorporates many concepts reviewed thus far: factoring the difference of perfect squares, simplifying rational expressions, finding the greatest common factor, multiplying rational expressions, and simplifying negative exponents.

ADDING AND SUBTRACTING RATIONAL EXPRESSIONS

Similar to fractions, rational expressions can only be added or subtracted when they have a common denominator. The least common denominator (LCD) is the least common multiple (LCM) of the denominators.

EXAMPLE:

Simplify $\dfrac{1}{8x} - \dfrac{-1}{4x^2}$.

The LCM of $8x$ and $4x^2$ is $8x^2$. Express each fraction as an equivalent fraction with a denominator of $8x^2$.

$\dfrac{1}{8x} \times \dfrac{x}{x} - \dfrac{1}{-4x^2} \times \dfrac{2}{2}$ Now simplify. Change the subtraction to adding the opposite of the second term.

$\dfrac{x}{8x^2} + \dfrac{2}{8x^2}$

$= \dfrac{(x+2)}{8x^2}$ Answer

EXAMPLE:

Simplify $\dfrac{2}{(x-1)^2} - \dfrac{2}{(1-x^2)}$.

Recall that $1 - x^2 = -(x^2 - 1)$. The equation then becomes

$\dfrac{2}{(x-1)^2} + \dfrac{2}{(x^2-1)}$

The denominators can be factored as $(x-1)(x-1)$ and $(x+1)(x-1)$, resulting in an LCM of $(x+1)(x-1)^2$. Expressing each fraction with the LCM as its denominator gives you

$\dfrac{2(x+1)}{(x+1)(x-1)^2} + \dfrac{2(x-1)}{(x^2-1)(x-1)}$

$= \dfrac{[2(x+1) + 2(x-1)]}{(x+1)(x-1)^2}$

$= \dfrac{(2x+2+2x-2)}{(x+1)(x-1)^2}$

$= \dfrac{4x}{(x+1)(x-1)^2}$ Answer

SOLVING EQUATIONS WITH RATIONAL EXPRESSIONS

One way to solve equations involving rational expressions is to multiply both sides by the *least common denominator* (LCD) of the rational expressions.

EXAMPLE:

Solve $\dfrac{1}{(x+2)(x-7)} + 1 = \dfrac{1}{(x-7)}$.

The LCD is $(x + 2)(x - 7)$. Multiplying both sides by the LCD gives you:

$$1 + (x + 2)(x - 7) = (x + 2)$$

$$1 + x^2 - 5x - 14 = x + 2$$

$$x^2 - 6x - 15 = 0$$ Since this equation is not factorable, use the Quadratic Formula to find its roots.

$$x = \frac{-b \pm \sqrt{b^2 - 4ac}}{2a} = \frac{\left(6 \pm \sqrt{96}\right)}{2} = \frac{\left(6 \pm 4\sqrt{6}\right)}{2}$$

$$x = 3 \pm 2\sqrt{6}$$ Answer

When multiplying both sides of an equation by an LCD, extraneous roots may be introduced. Always go back and check your answer in the original equation.

Systems

A *system of linear equations* is made up of two or more linear equations in the same two variables. Examples of systems are as follows:

Example 1:
$$\begin{cases} 2x - 4y = 10 \\ 6x + y = -3 \end{cases}$$

Example 2:
$$\begin{cases} y = 8x - 14 \\ y = x \end{cases}$$

Example 3:
$$\begin{cases} a + b = 37 \\ 5a - 2b = -13 \end{cases}$$

Systems of linear equations are also called *simultaneous equations*. The *solution* of a system is any ordered pair of the variables that satisfy all equations. For instance, in Example 2 above, the ordered pair (2, 2) is a solution of the system. When $x = 2$ and $y = 2$, both equations ($2 = 8(2) - 14$ and $2 = 2$) are satisfied. *Equivalent systems* are systems that have the same solution.

Three methods to solve systems are (1) substitution, (2) linear combination, and (3) graphing. Here we'll explain the first two methods. Graphing is discussed in the Coordinate Geometry chapter.

SOLVING BY SUBSTITUTION

Just as one equation allows you to solve for one unknown variable, two equations allow you to solve for two unknowns. The substitution method involves expressing one variable in terms of the other in one equation (i.e., x in terms of y or y in terms of x) and *substituting* this value into the second equation.

EXAMPLE:

Solve the system using the substitution method:

$$\begin{cases} x + 3y = 14 \\ 3x - 2y = -2 \end{cases}$$

Choose one equation and solve for a variable. (You can choose what equation to use and for what variable to solve.) Let's solve for x in the first equation. This is the best choice, since the coefficient of x is 1.

$$\begin{cases} x = -3y + 14 \\ 3x - 2y = -2 \end{cases}$$

Substitute $-3y + 14$ for x in the second equation and solve for y:

$$3(-3y + 14) - 2y = -2$$
$$-9y + 42 - 2y = -2$$
$$-11y = -44$$
$$y = 4$$

Substitute 4 for y in either of the original equations in the system to solve for x:

$$x + 3(4) = 14$$
$$x + 12 = 14$$
$$x = 2$$

The solution is the ordered pair $(2, 4)$.   Answer

It is a good idea to check your answer by substituting $(2, 4)$ back into both of the equations.

SOLVING BY LINEAR COMBINATION

Adding two linear equations results in what's called a *linear combination* of the equations. For example:

$$\begin{array}{r} x + 2y = 7 \\ +3x + y = -8 \\ \hline 4x + 3y = -1 \end{array}$$

The linear combination method involves transforming and adding equations in order to eliminate one variable and solve for the other. The goal is to end up with one equation in one variable. Let's solve the previous example in a different way.

EXAMPLE:

Solve the system using the linear combination method:

$$x + 3y = 14$$
$$3x - 2y = -2$$

Let's try to eliminate x and solve for y. (You can choose to eliminate either variable here.) Start by multiplying the first equation by -3 so the coefficients of the x are opposites. Remember, what you do to one side of an equation you *must* do to the other, so both sides need to be multiplied by a -3 factor.

$-3(x + 3y = 14)$ becomes $-3x + -9y = -42$

This results in the equivalent system:

$$-3x + -9y = -42$$
$$3x - 2y = -2$$

Add the two equations:

$$
\begin{array}{r}
-3x + -9y = -42 \\
+\ \ \underline{3x - 2y = -2} \\
0x + 11y = -44
\end{array}
$$

It is important that one variable cancels out. If this doesn't happen, check your work for errors or try multiplying by a different number in the first step. Now that x is eliminated, you are able to solve for y.

$$-11y = -44$$

$$y = 4$$

Substitute 4 for y in either of the original equations in the system to solve for x:

$$3x - 2(4) = -2$$

$$3x - 8 = -2$$

$$3x = 6$$

$$x = 2$$

The solution is the ordered pair (2, 4).   Answer

This, of course, is the same answer you got by using the substitution method. Remember that you have a choice of what method to use when solving systems of linear equations.

NO SOLUTION VS. INFINITE SOLUTIONS

Systems of linear equations can have three possible solution sets:

1. One solution
2. No solution
3. Infinitely many solutions

Graphing systems will be discussed in the Coordinate Geometry chapter, but it is worth mentioning that one solution occurs when the two lines intersect in one point, no solution occurs when the lines are parallel, and infinitely many solutions occur when the lines are actually the same line.

When you are solving a system algebraically, *no solution* results from a *contradiction*. You end up with a statement that will never be true, such as $5 = 6$ or $-1 = 0$.

EXAMPLE:

Solve the system:

$$2y = x + 36$$

$$y = \frac{1}{2}x + 4$$

Since the second equation is already solved for y in terms of x, let's substitute that value into the first equation:

$$2\left(\frac{1}{2}x + 4\right) = x + 36$$

$$x + 8 = x + 36$$

$$8 = 36$$

Of course, $8 \neq 36$, so this contradiction shows the systems has no solution.

No solution   Answer

This example can be solved an alternate way by rewriting the first equation in slope-intercept form. This results in the system:

$$y = \frac{1}{2}x + 18$$

$$y = \frac{1}{2}x + 4$$

Immediately you can see that these lines have the same slope, $m = \frac{1}{2}$. Therefore, they must be parallel and will, by definition, never intersect.

Infinitely many solutions, on the other hand, result from an **identity.** You end up with a statement that is always true, such as $7 = 7$ or $0 = 0$.

EXAMPLE:

Solve the system:

$$y = 3x - 9$$

$$-6x + 2y = -18$$

Let's use the linear combination method to solve this system. Start by rewriting the first equation:

$$\begin{cases} -3x + y = -9 \\ -6x + 2y = -18 \end{cases}$$

Multiply the first equation by -2 so the coefficients of the y are opposites:

$$\begin{cases} 6x + -2y = 18 \\ -6x + 2y = -18 \end{cases}$$

Add the equations:

$$\begin{array}{r} 6x + -2y = 18 \\ + \quad -6x + 2y = -18 \\ \hline 0x + 0y = 0 \\ 0 = 0 \end{array}$$

Zero always equals zero, so this identity shows the system has infinitely many solutions.

Infinitely many solutions   Answer

An alternate method of solving the system is to rewrite the second equation, isolating y on the left side:

$y = 3x - 9$

$2y = 6x - 18$

Both of these lines have a slope of 3 and a y-intercept of 9, so they are, in fact, the same line. You may also notice that the second equation is equivalent to the first. It is simply a factor of 2 greater than $y = 3x - 9$.

WORD PROBLEMS WITH SYSTEMS

Word problems with two unknowns can be solved by setting up a system and then solving it using either the substitution or linear combination method.

EXAMPLE:

Tickets for the homecoming football game cost $3 for students and $5 for the general public. Ticket sales totaled $1,396, and 316 people attended the game. How many student tickets were sold?

First, define the variables. Let s = the number of student tickets and p = the number of tickets for the general public.

Since ticket sales totaled $1,396:

$3s + 5p = 1,396$

Now use the given information on attendance to get:

$s + p = 316$

The system looks like:

$$\begin{cases} 3s + 5p = 1,396 \\ s + p = 316 \end{cases}$$

Which method, substitution or linear combination, works best here? Both produce the same solution, so it is your choice. Let's try using the linear combination method. Multiply the second equation by -3 and add to get

$$\begin{array}{r} 3s + 5p = 1,396 \\ + \quad -3s + -3p = -948 \\ \hline 0s + 2p = 448 \\ p = 224 \end{array}$$

Substitute $p = 224$ into one of the original equations:

$s + 224 = 316$

$s = 92$

92 student tickets were sold.   Answer

As with all word problems, always make sure to answer the question asked. Although we solved for both p and s, the word problem asks for the number of student tickets.

EXAMPLE:

A mother is twice as old as her daughter. Twelve years ago she was three times as old as her daughter was then. Find the mother's present age.

Let m = the mother's age now and d = the daughter's age now. Since the mother is twice as old has her daughter, you have the first equation:

$m = 2d$

Twelve years ago, the mother was $m - 12$ years old and the daughter was $d - 12$ years old. This gives you the second equation:

$m - 12 = 3(d - 12)$

$m - 12 = 3d - 36$

$m = 3d - 24$

You have two equations in two unknowns, m and d. A system is needed to solve the word problem:

$m = 2d$

$m = 3d - 24$

Again, you can choose to solve by either the substitution or linear combination method. Let's try using substitution. Since the first equation is already solved for m in terms of d, substitute $m = 2d$ into the second equation and solve for d.

$2d = 3d - 24$

$24 = d$

The word problem asks for the mother's age, so substitute $d = 24$ back into one of the original equations.

$m = 2(24)$

$m = 48$

The mother is 48 years old.   Answer

CHAPTER 5

PLANE GEOMETRY

This chapter provides a review of Plane Euclidean Geometry principles. Eighteen to twenty-two percent of the Level 1 test questions relate specifically to plane geometry. By definition, plane geometry focuses on two-dimensional shapes and figures. Solid (i.e., three-dimensional) and coordinate geometry are covered in the succeeding chapters. The pie chart shows approximately how much of the Level 1 test is related to plane geometry:

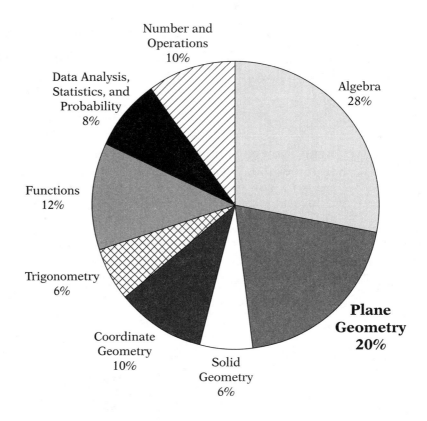

The following geometry topics are covered in this chapter:

1. Undefined Terms
    a. Points, Lines, Planes

2. Lines, Segments, Rays

3. Angles
    a. Measures of Angles
    b. Supplementary and Complementary Angles
    c. Vertical Angles
    d. Linear Pairs of Angles

4. Triangles
    a. Types of Triangles
    b. Sum of Interior Angles and Exterior Angles
    c. Medians, Altitudes, and Angle Bisectors

Undefined Terms

Three "undefined terms" make up the foundation of geometry:

1. **Point**—A location in space. A point has no size or dimension.

2. **Line**—A collection of infinitely many points extending forever in opposite directions.

3. **Plane**—A flat surface that extends forever in all directions. A plane has no thickness.

Let's review some of the basic definitions for points, lines, and planes. *Collinear points* lie on the same line. Two distinct points are always collinear, and three points may or may not be collinear. *Coplanar points* lie on the same plane, and the set of all points is called *space*.

Following are a few key things to remember about the intersection of points, lines, and planes:

- Two distinct points determine a line.
- If two distinct lines intersect, then they intersect in a point.
- If two distinct planes intersect, then they intersect in a line.
- If a plane intersects a line, then they intersect in a point. (This assumes the line is not contained in the plane.)
- Three noncollinear points determine a plane. This can be expanded upon to show that two intersecting lines determine a plane. A line and a point not on it also determine a plane.

EXAMPLE:

Each of the following sets of points could be the intersection of two planes EXCEPT:

(A) the empty set

(B) a point

(C) a line

(D) a plane

(E) cannot be determined

The intersection of two planes is the set of points that they share. If two planes do not intersect, then their intersection is the empty set. If two planes are in fact the same plane, then their intersection is a plane. If two (distinct) planes intersect, then they intersect in a line. It is not possible for two planes to intersect in a point, so the correct answer is B.

B   Answer

When in doubt, draw a picture to help solve geometry problems. Pictures allow you to visualize what's happening in a problem. The next example uses a picture to better understand how lines can be determined from four noncollinear points.

EXAMPLE:

How many lines are determined by four noncollinear points?

(A) 2

(B) 4

(C) 6

(D) 8

(E) infinitely many

Two distinct points determine a line. Draw four noncollinear points to visualize the problem.

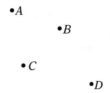

Draw lines through each pair of points as shown.

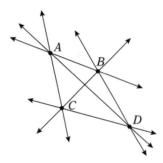

Six distinct lines are determined.   Answer

Lines, Segments, Rays

A *ray* has one endpoint and extends forever in one direction.

A *line segment* is the set of all points between two endpoints on a line.

Segments that have the same measure are called *congruent* segments. For example, if $AB = CD$, then $\overline{AB}$ is congruent to $\overline{CD}$. In a mathematical expression, congruency is written as the symbol $\cong$, $\overline{AB} \cong \overline{CD}$. Congruency is depicted as "tick marks" in diagrams as shown below:

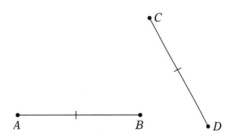

Given three collinear points *X, Y,* and *Z:*

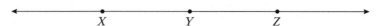

$XY + YZ = XZ$. In other words, the distance from X to Y added to the distance from Y to Z equals the total distance from X to Z. This is called the Segment Addition Postulate. Y is between X and Z by the *definition of betweeness.* If $XY = 2$ cm and $YZ = 3$ cm, for example, it makes sense that XZ should equal 5 cm.

EXAMPLE:

Points *J, K,* and *L* are collinear. *K* is between *J* and *L*. If the length of $JK = 36$ and the length of $JK = \dfrac{3}{4}JL$, what is the length of *KL*?

Drawing a diagram such as the one below will help to visualize the given information.

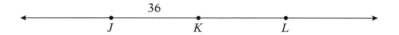

$$36 = \frac{3}{4}JL$$

$$36 \times \frac{4}{3} = JL$$

$JL = 48$ cm. You're not done yet. Now use the definition of betweeness to find the length of *KL*. Since the problem states that *K* is between *J* and *L*, you can conclude that $JK + KL = JL$.

$36 + KL = 48$

$KL = 12$ cm   Answer

The *Midpoint Theorem* states that if M is the midpoint of $\overline{XY}$, then $XM = \dfrac{1}{2}XY$. You can also say that $2XM = XY$, $2MY = XY$, $MY = \dfrac{1}{2}XY$, or $XM = MY$.

EXAMPLE:

ΔQRS is an equilateral triangle with a perimeter of 36. If line $\overleftrightarrow{RT}$ bisects $\overline{QS}$, find *QT*.

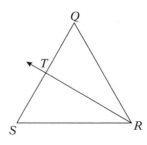

Since $\triangle QRS$ is equilateral, each side measures 12. Since $\overleftrightarrow{RT}$ is the bisector of the side $\overline{QS}$, point T must be the midpoint of the side. The Midpoint Theorem tells you that $QT = \dfrac{1}{2}QS$.

$$QT = \frac{1}{2} \times 12$$

$$QT = 6 \qquad \text{Answer}$$

Angles

An *angle* is the union of two noncollinear rays. The rays themselves are called the *sides*, and the shared endpoint is called the *vertex*. Some textbooks teach that the union of two collinear rays is called a straight angle. Since this is not a universal term, it will not appear on the SAT Level 1 test.

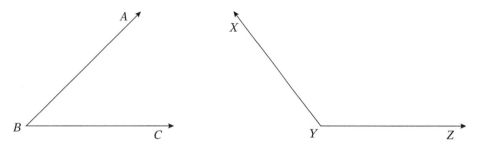

Angles are typically named using three capital letters, such as $\angle ABC$ and $\angle XYZ$. The middle letter always represents the vertex of the angle. In cases where there's one unique angle from a given vertex, the angle can be named using one letter, such as $\angle B$ and $\angle Y$.

MEASURES OF ANGLES

The *measure of an angle* is a unique number between 0° and 180°. Note that an angle's measure cannot equal 180° or 0°, since by definition an angle is the union of *noncollinear* rays. Think of a protractor when assigning a degree measure to an angle. A protractor only allows you to assign numbers between 0 and 180. The "measure of angle *ABC* equals 45 degrees" is written as $m\angle ABC = 45°$.

Angles are classified by their measure:

- **Right angles** measure 90°.

- **Acute angles** measure less than 90°.

- **Obtuse angles** measure greater than 90° but less than 180°.

If two lines intersect to form right angles, the lines are said to be *perpendicular*. The symbol for perpendicular is "$\perp$". The expression $l_1 \perp l_2$, reads "line 1 is perpendicular to line 2." In diagrams, perpendicular lines are shown by a small box in the angle.

Remember that figures are not always drawn to scale on the SAT Subject tests. Just because an angle appears to be acute or lines appear to be perpendicular, don't assume this is true. Look at the given information in the problem to clarify figures. To answer some problems, it may be helpful to draw your own diagram.

SUPPLEMENTARY AND COMPLEMENTARY ANGLES

Complementary angles are two angles whose measures add up to 90°. Complementary angles may or may not share a side. (If they do share side, they are known as *adjacent angles*.)

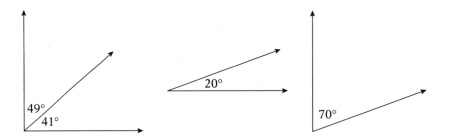

Supplementary angles are two angles whose measures add up to 180°. Similar to complementary angles, supplementary angles may or may not share a side.

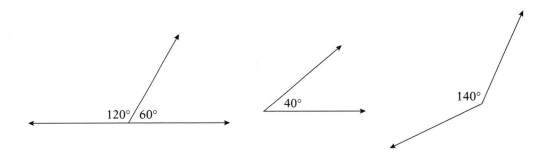

EXAMPLE:

Three times the measure of the complement of a certain angle is equal to 40° less than the measure of the supplement of that angle. What is the measure of the angle?

Let x = the measure of the angle and $90 - x$ = the measure of its complement. It is important to define the given information in terms of *one* variable if possible. If you let x = the measure of the angle and y = the measure of its complement, you're left with $x + y = 90°$, which is not enough information to solve for both variables. Remember that the sum of an angle and its complement is 90° so use that information when defining the second angle as $90 - x$. Similarly, let $180 - x$ = the measure of the angle's supplement. Set up the equation:

$3(90 - x) = (180 - x) - 40$

$270 - 3x = 140 - x$

$130 = 2x$

$x = 65°$ Answer

The complement of the angle is 25°, since 65 + 25 = 90.

The supplement of the angle is 115°, since 65 + 115 = 180.

EXAMPLE:

Each of the following statements is true EXCEPT:

(A) A complement of an acute angle is acute.

(B) A supplement of an obtuse angle is acute.

(C) The supplement of an acute angle is obtuse.

(D) The complement of a right angle is a right angle.

(E) The supplement of a right angle is a right angle.

The complement of an acute angle must always measure less than 90°, so A is true. Let's take an obtuse angle measuring 100°. Its supplement is 80°, which is an acute angle. B is true. Answer C states the opposite of B and is also true. D and E involve right angles. Since 90 + 90 = 180, a right angle and another right angle are in fact supplementary, so answer E must be true. That leaves D. A right angle does not have a complement. 90 + 0 = 90, and we've already determined that an angle cannot measure 0°.

The correct answer is D.   Answer

VERTICAL ANGLES

Vertical angles are opposite angles formed by two intersecting lines. Vertical angles are always congruent, as shown by the congruency marks in the diagram.

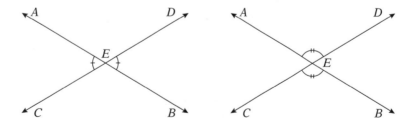

   Two pairs of vertical angles are formed when two lines intersect. ∠AEC ≅ ∠DEB and ∠AED ≅ ∠CEB.

■ LINEAR PAIRS OF ANGLES

A *linear pair of angles* is formed by two angles that share a common side and whose noncommon sides form a straight line. By definition, linear pairs of angles are always adjacent angles and are also always supplementary.

EXAMPLE:

In the figure below, $\angle ABC$ and $\angle DBE$ are right angles and the measure of $\angle EBF$ is four times the measure of $\angle DBC$. Find the measure of $\angle ABD$.

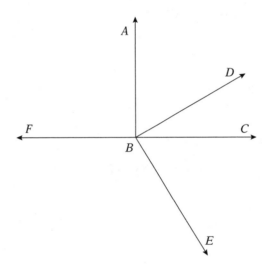

Let $m\angle DBC = x$ and $m\angle EBF = 4x$. It follows that the $m\angle ABD = 90 - x$ and $m\angle CBE = 90 - x$, since $\angle ABC$ and $\angle DBE$ are right angles. Note that $\angle CBE$ and $\angle EBF$ are a linear pair, and therefore, they are supplementary.

$$m\angle CBE + m\angle EBF = 180$$
$$(90 - x) + 4x = 180$$
$$90 + 3x = 180$$
$$3x = 90$$
$$x = 30$$

But the question asks for the measure of $\angle ABD$:

$$m\angle ABD = 90 - x = 90 - 30 = 60°$$

60°   Answer

Note that the complements of the same angle are congruent. The measure of $\angle DBC$ is 30° while both its complements, $\angle ABD$ and $\angle CBE$, measure 60°.

There's one unique number that will result in 90° when added to 30°. In fact, the complements of congruent angles are always congruent, and, likewise, the supplements of congruent angles are always congruent.

EXAMPLE:

Each of the following statements is true EXCEPT:

(A) Vertical angles could be supplementary.

(B) Vertical angles are never adjacent.

(C) If $m\angle A = 60°$, $m\angle B = 100°$, and $m\angle C = 20°$, then the angles are supplementary.

(D) Vertical angles could be complementary.

(E) The angles of a linear pair are always adjacent.

If the opposite angles formed by two intersecting lines both equal 90°, then A is true. Likewise, if the opposite angles formed by two intersecting lines both equal 45°, then D is true. Vertical angles are never adjacent; they're opposite angles. Linear pairs of angles always share a common side and are therefore adjacent, so B and E are true. On first glance, C may appear to be true, since 60 + 100 + 20 = 180. Supplementary angles must be a *pair*, however, so C is, in fact, false.

The correct answer is C.   Answer

Triangles

TYPES OF TRIANGLES

The triangle is the most common geometric figure used on the SAT Math Level 1 test. A *triangle* is a polygon with three sides. It is formed by connecting three noncollinear points.

Triangles can be classified by their angles.

- **Acute**—A triangle with three acute angles

- **Obtuse**—A triangle with one obtuse angle

- **Right**—A triangle with one right angle

- **Equiangular**—A triangle with all angles congruent

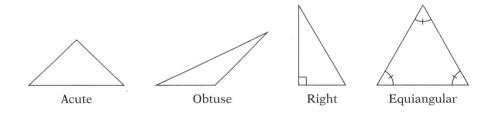

Acute   Obtuse   Right   Equiangular

Triangles can also be classified by their sides:

- **Isosceles**—A triangle with at least two congruent sides
- **Equilateral**—A triangle with all sides congruent
- **Scalene**—A triangle with no congruent sides

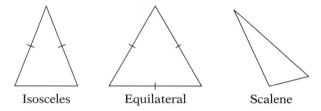

Isosceles   Equilateral   Scalene

SUM OF INTERIOR ANGLES AND EXTERIOR ANGLES

The *sum of the measures of the interior angles* in a triangle is always 180°. This is a useful theorem that is often used when solving problems involving triangles and other polygons. One way to show this concept is to draw a triangle, cut it out, and tear off each of the three angles. Now, place each angle so that it shares a side with the one next to it. The three angles of the triangle will always form a straight line.

In the figure above, $x + 100 + 20 = 180$, so $x = 60°$. Whenever you know the measures of two angles in a triangle, subtract their sum from 180° to find the measure of the missing angle. A triangle with all angles congruent is called *equiangular*. Each angle of an equiangular triangle measures 60°, since $x + x + x$ must equal 180°. Equiangular triangles are also always equilateral.

An exterior angle is an angle on the outside of a triangle formed by extending one of the triangle's sides. Each exterior angle of a triangle has two remote interior angles and an adjacent interior angle. The *remote interior angles* are the two angles inside the triangle that do not share a vertex with the exterior angle. The *measure of an exterior angle* is equal to the sum of the measures of its two remote interior angles.

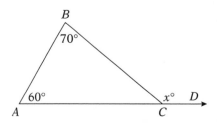

In the figure above, $\angle CAB$ and $\angle ABC$ are the remote interior angles for the exterior angle measuring $x°$. Therefore, $x = 60 + 70 = 130°$. You can check your answer by looking the *adjacent interior angle* for $\angle BCD$. $\angle BCD$ and $\angle ACB$ are a linear pair, so $m\angle ACB = 50°$. The sum of the interior angles is $50 + 60 + 70$, which does, in fact, equal $180°$.

The *sum of the measures of the exterior angles of a triangle* is always $360°$. This sum is found by including *one* exterior angle for each vertex of the triangle, not two. In fact, the sum of the measures of the exterior angles of *any* polygon is $360°$.

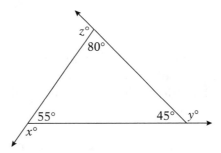

In the figure above, $x + y + z = 360°$. Solve for each exterior angle by subtracting the measure of its adjacent interior angle from $180°$.

$$x = 125°, y = 135°, \text{ and } z = 100°$$

$$125 + 135 + 100 = 360°$$

EXAMPLE:

Find the measure of $\angle SRT$ given $m\angle RTS = m\angle RST = 45°$. Then classify the triangle by its angles and sides.

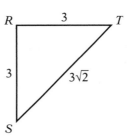

Let $x = m\angle SRT$.

$x + 45 + 45 = 180$

$x = 90°$

The triangle has one $90°$ angle, making it a right triangle.

Since the triangle has two congruent sides that measure 3, it is isosceles.

$90°$; right, isosceles triangle   Answer

EXAMPLE:

Find the measure of the missing angles. Then classify the triangle by its angles and sides.

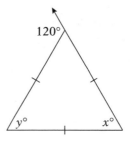

Since the sum of the measures of the two remote interior angles equals the measure of the exterior angle, $x + y = 120$. Notice that the triangle is equilateral. By definition, all equilateral triangles are equiangular. Each angle measures 60°.

$x = 60°$ and $y = 60°$; equiangular, equilateral triangle   Answer

MEDIANS, ALTITUDES, AND ANGLE BISECTORS

A *median* of a triangle is a segment extending from one vertex to the midpoint of the opposite side. Every triangle actually has three medians. $\overline{AM}$ is a median of $\triangle ABC$.

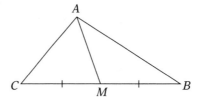

An *altitude* of a triangle is a segment extending from one vertex and is perpendicular to the opposite side (or the line containing the opposite side). Every triangle also has three altitudes. $\overline{AD}$ is an altitude of each of the triangles below.

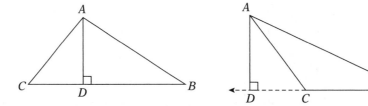

An *angle bisector* of a triangle is a segment that divides an interior angle of the triangle into two congruent angles and has an endpoint on the opposite side of the triangle. Every triangle has three angle bisectors. $\overline{CD}$ is a bisector of $\angle C$ in $\triangle ABC$.

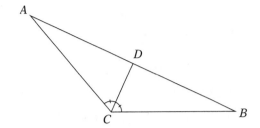

The angle bisector of the vertex angle of an isosceles triangle is also a median to the base and an altitude of the triangle.

EXAMPLE:

Given $\triangle RST$ has an exterior altitude, the triangle could be which of the following?

(A) Acute

(B) Obtuse

(C) Right

(D) Equilateral

Exterior altitudes extend from one vertex and are perpendicular to *the line containing* the opposite side. This only occurs when a triangle has an obtuse angle.

B; obtuse is the correct answer.   Answer

EXAMPLE:

Given $\triangle MNL$, the measure of $\angle NMP$ is $40°$. $\overline{MP}$ bisects $\angle M$, and $\angle N$ is congruent to $\angle LMP$. Find $m\angle L$.

Sketching a diagram of $\triangle MNL$ will help to solve for the measure of $\angle L$. Since $\angle M$ is bisected, the measures of both $\angle NMP$ and $\angle LMP$ are $40°$. The measure of $\angle N$ is also $40°$, since it is congruent to $\angle LMP$. The measure of $\angle M$ is, therefore, $80°$. $m\angle M + m\angle N + m\angle L = 180°$, so $80° + 40° + m\angle L = 180°$.

$m\angle L = 60°$.   Answer

CONGRUENT TRIANGLES

Triangles are congruent if they have the same shape and size. In other words, given two congruent triangles, if you cut out one and place it over the other, they will perfectly overlap. Congruent triangles have three pairs of congruent sides and three pairs of congruent angles.

SSS, SAS, and ASA Postulates and the AAS Theorem

It is not necessary, however, to compare all six parts of two triangles (three angles and three sides) to prove congruency. Comparing three parts, in some cases, will do. The following four postulates illustrate "shortcuts" to proving triangles congruent.

1. **Side Side Side (SSS).** If three sides of one triangle are congruent to three sides of another, then the triangles are congruent.

2. **Side Angle Side (SAS).** If two sides and the included angle of one triangle are congruent to two sides and the included angle of another, then the triangles are congruent.

3. **Angle Side Angle (ASA).** If two angles and the included side of one triangle are congruent to two angles and the included side of another, then the triangles are congruent.

4. **Angle Angle Side (AAS).** If two angles and the side not between them of one triangle are congruent to two angles and the side not between them of another, then the triangles are congruent.

An *included angle* is the angle between the given pair of sides. Likewise, an *included side* is the side between the given pair of angles. Notice that SSA and AAA are not included in the above list. Knowing two sides and an angle not between them are congruent or knowing three angles are congruent does not prove triangle congruency. Take two equilateral triangles. Equilateral triangles must also be equiangular, so each angle measures 60°. Say the first triangle has sides measuring 1 cm and the second triangle has sides measuring 10 cm. The second triangle is significantly larger. The two equilateral triangles are the same shape, but not the same size. AAA does not prove that these two triangles are congruent.

EXAMPLE:

Which of the following triangles are congruent?

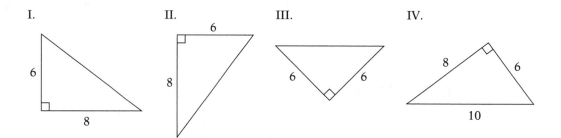

(A) I and II

(B) II and III

(C) I and IV

(D) III and IV

(E) All four are congruent.

Look for SSS, SAS, ASA, or AAS to be true for two triangles. You can immediately eliminate ASA and AAS because you do not know the measure of two angles in any triangle. That leaves SSS and SAS triangles. I has a side measuring 6, a side measuring 8, and a 90° included angle. Triangle IV has the same, so I and IV are congruent. (Using the Pythagorean Theorem, you can find that the third side of I also measures 10, so SSS also proves I and IV are congruent.)

The correct answer is C.   Answer

CPCTC

If triangles are congruent, then the corresponding parts of the triangles are congruent. *CPCTC* stands for *Corresponding Parts of Congruent Triangles are Congruent*. If $\triangle ABC \cong \triangle DEF$, six pairs of corresponding parts are congruent:

$$\overline{AB} \cong \overline{DE} \quad \angle A \cong \angle D$$
$$\overline{BC} \cong \overline{EF} \quad \angle B \cong \angle E$$
$$\overline{AC} \cong \overline{DF} \quad \angle C \cong \angle F$$

EXAMPLE:

$\triangle JHK$ is congruent to $\triangle JHI$ and the two triangles share $\overline{JH}$. $\angle K$ is congruent to $\angle I$ and $\angle JHK$ is congruent to $\angle JHI$. Is $\overline{HK}$ congruent to $\overline{HI}$?

Sketching the two triangles may help answer this question. Determine if the triangles are congruent and then use CPCTC to show the sides are congruent. Two angles and the side not between them ($\overline{JH}$) are congruent in the two triangles, making the triangles congruent by AAS. Since corresponding parts of the triangles are therefore congruent, you can conclude that $\overline{HK} \cong \overline{HI}$.

ISOSCELES TRIANGLES

Isosceles triangles have *at least* two sides congruent. By this definition, equilateral triangles are also classified as isosceles. In an isosceles triangle, the two congruent sides are the *legs*, the remaining side is the *base*, the *vertex angle* is the angle included by the two congruent sides, and the *base angles* are the angles having the base as a side.

Isosceles Triangle Theorem

The *Isosceles Triangle Theorem* states that if two sides of a triangle are congruent, then the angles opposite the congruent sides (the base angles) are congruent. Given $\triangle ABC$ is isosceles and $AB = BC$, then $\angle BAC \cong \angle BCA$.

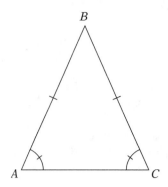

EXAMPLE:

Which of the following could be the degree measures of the angles of an isosceles triangle?

I.   40, 40, 80

II.   45, 45, 90

III. 30, 60, 90

(A) I only

(B) II only

(C) III only

(D) I and II only

(E) II and III only

At first glance, it may seem that both I and II are possible angles of an isosceles triangle. By the Isosceles Triangle Theorem, you know that two of the angles must be equal in measure. The angle measures in I, however, add up to 160°, which is not possible for a triangle. (The three angles must add up to 180°.)

B; II only is the correct answer.   Answer

TRIANGLE INEQUALITY

The *Triangle Inequality Theorem* states that the sum of the lengths of any two sides of a triangle is greater than the length of the third side. Let's assume $\triangle ABC$ is a right triangle with sides of 3, 4, and 5 cm. Using the Triangle Inequality Theorem, you can show that the following three inequalities are true:

$3 + 4 > 5$

$3 + 5 > 4$

$4 + 5 > 3$

If just one of the inequalities proves not to be true, it is impossible for a triangle to have sides of the given measures. Take a triangle of sides measuring 3, 5, and 8.

$3 + 8 > 5$

$5 + 8 > 3$

$3 + 5 > 8$ Not true

The third inequality is not valid, meaning that it is impossible to have a triangle with sides measuring 3, 5, and 8 units.

EXAMPLE:

Which sets of numbers could be the lengths of sides of a triangle?

I.   7, 24, 25

II. 7, 7, 7

III. 1, 2, 3

(A) I only

(B) II only

(C) III only

(D) I and II only

(E) II and III only

Answer II is an equilateral triangle. The Triangle Inequality Theorem is valid because $7 + 7 > 7$. Answer I also passes the Triangle Inequality Theorem because $7 + 24 > 25$, $24 + 25 > 7$, and $7 + 25 > 24$. Answer III is not a valid triangle since $1 + 2$ is not greater than 3.

D; I and II only is the correct answer.   Answer

PYTHAGOREAN THEOREM

The *Pythagorean Theorem* shows a special relationship among the sides of a right triangle. Before getting into the theorem, let's review the parts of a right triangle. The two sides adjacent to the right angle are called the *legs,* and the side opposite the right angle is called the *hypotenuse*. The Pythagorean Theorem states that the sum of the squares of the lengths of the legs equals the square of the length of the hypotenuse.

$$\text{leg}^2 + \text{leg}^2 = \text{hypotenuse}^2$$

Often, a and b are the variables used to show the lengths of the legs and c is used to show the length of the hypotenuse. The Pythagorean Theorem states that:

$$a^2 + b^2 = c^2$$

Pythagorean triples are sets of three whole numbers that work in the Pythagorean Theorem. The following table shows a few commonly used triples.

a	b	c
3	4	5
5	12	13
7	24	25
8	15	17

In fact, any multiple of a Pythagorean triple also will work in the Pythagorean Theorem. Take a 3-4-5 right triangle and multiply the sides by 2. 6-8-10 will work in the Pythagorean Theorem. Multiply 3-4-5 by 3 and you'll see that 9-12-15 also works in the Pythagorean Theorem.

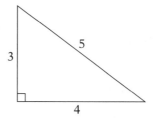

Often, the Pythagorean Theorem is applied to word problems involving triangles as parts of other figures. The next example illustrates this concept.

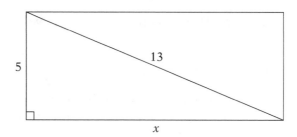

E X A M P L E :

Find the length of a rectangle whose width is 5 cm and whose diagonal measures 13 cm.

It may be helpful to sketch a diagram to show the given information in the problem. Let x represent the length of the rectangle.

$5^2 + x^2 = 13^2$

$x^2 = 13^2 - 5^2$

$x^2 = 169 - 25 = 144$

$x = 12$ cm   Answer

SPECIAL RIGHT TRIANGLES

Two special right triangles, a 45°-45°-90° and a 30°-60°-90°, occur often in mathematics and it is important to understand the relationships between their sides and angles. A *45°-45°-90°* triangle is an isosceles right triangle whose sides are in the following ratios:

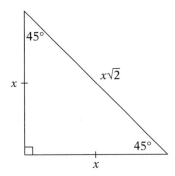

In other words, the length of the hypotenuse is $\sqrt{2}$ times longer than the lengths of its legs.

A *30°-60°-90°* triangle is a scalene right triangle whose sides are in the following ratios:

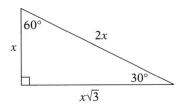

The length of the hypotenuse is two times longer than the length of the shorter leg (opposite the 30°) and the length of the longer leg (opposite the 60°) is $\sqrt{3}$ times longer than the length of the shorter leg.

EXAMPLE:

One leg of a 45°-45°-90° is 10 cm long. How long is its hypotenuse?

Using the ratios for the sides of a 45°-45°-90°, the hypotenuse is a factor of $\sqrt{2}$ bigger than the legs. Each leg measures 10 cm.

$10\sqrt{2}$ cm   Answer

EXAMPLE:

The hypotenuse of a 30°-60°-90° is 7 in. Find the length of its longer leg.

Using the ratios for the sides of a 30°-60°-90°, the shorter leg is half of the hypotenuse, $\dfrac{7}{2}$ inches. The longer leg is $\sqrt{3}$ times the shorter leg.

$\dfrac{7\sqrt{3}}{2}$ in.   Answer

EXAMPLE:

Find the length of each leg of an isosceles right triangle whose hypotenuse is 6 cm.

If a right triangle is isosceles, its angles must measure 45°-45°-90°. (Remember that the Isosceles Triangles Theorem states that if two sides are congruent, the angles opposite them are also congruent.) The hypotenuse is a factor of $\sqrt{2}$ bigger than the legs. To find the measure of the legs, *divide* 6 cm by $\sqrt{2}$. $\frac{6}{\sqrt{2}}$ is not in simplest form, though. Now, multiply the numerator and denominator by $\sqrt{2}$ to rationalize the denominator.

$$\frac{6}{\sqrt{2}} \times \frac{\sqrt{2}}{\sqrt{2}} = \frac{6\sqrt{2}}{2} = 3\sqrt{2} \quad \text{Answer}$$

Parallel Lines

Lines that do not intersect and that lie in the same plane are called *parallel*. Lines that do not intersect and lie in different planes are called *skew*. Planes, segments, and rays can also be parallel.

The expression $l_1 \| l_2$ means "line 1 is parallel to line 2." Parallel lines are marked by arrows, ">," in diagrams. A *transversal* is a line that intersects two or more distinct coplanar lines. In the figure below, line t is a transversal and $l_1 \| l_2$.

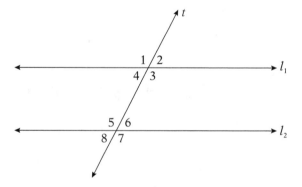

When two lines are cut by a transversal, special angles are created. Based on the figure below, the angles are as follows:

- **Corresponding angles.** $\angle 1$ and $\angle 5$, $\angle 2$ and $\angle 6$, $\angle 3$ and $\angle 7$, $\angle 4$ and $\angle 8$

  A pair of nonadjacent angles, one interior and the second exterior, on the same side of the transversal

- **Alternate interior angles.** $\angle 3$ and $\angle 5$, $\angle 4$ and $\angle 6$

  A pair of nonadjacent, interior angles on opposite sides of the transversal

- **Alternate exterior angles.** $\angle 1$ and $\angle 7$, $\angle 2$ and $\angle 8$

  A pair of nonadjacent, exterior angles on opposite sides of the transversal

- **Interior angles on the same side of the transversal.** $\angle 3$ and $\angle 6$, $\angle 4$ and $\angle 5$

- **Exterior angles on the same side of the transversal.** $\angle 1$ and $\angle 8$, $\angle 2$ and $\angle 7$

When the two lines cut by the transversal are parallel, then corresponding angles, alternate interior angles, and alternate exterior angles are *congruent*.

Interior angles on the same side of the transversal and exterior angles on the same side of the transversal are *supplementary*. If two parallel lines are cut by a transversal and the transversal is perpendicular to one of the parallel lines, you can conclude that it is also perpendicular to the second parallel line. Each of the eight angles formed measures 90°.

EXAMPLE:

Given $l_1 || l_2$ in Figure 5-35, $m\angle 1 = 2x$, and $m\angle 2 = x$, find the measure of $\angle 7$.

$\angle 1$ and $\angle 2$ are a linear pair of angles and are, therefore, supplementary.

$$m\angle 1 + m\angle 2 = 180$$
$$2x + x = 180$$
$$3x = 180$$
$$x = 60°$$

Thus, $m\angle 1 = 2(60) = 120°$. $\angle 1$ and $\angle 7$ are alternate exterior angles, and therefore, they are congruent.

$$m\angle 7 = 120° \quad \text{Answer}$$

Polygons

A *polygon* is a many-sided closed figure. It consists of line segments connected endpoint to endpoint.

The line segments are called *sides,* and each endpoint is called a *vertex.* (The plural of vertex is "vertices.") A *diagonal* is a segment that connects one vertex to another, nonconsecutive vertex. (A segment connecting one vertex to another, *consecutive* vertex is a side.) Rectangle *ABCD,* for example, has two diagonals $\overline{AC}$ and $\overline{BD}$.

A *regular polygon* is both equiangular and equilateral. A square is an example of a regular polygon.

TYPES OF POLYGONS

Polygons are named according to their number of sides.

Number of Sides	Name of Polygon
2	Doesn't exist
3	Triangle
4	Quadrilateral
5	Pentagon
6	Hexagon
7	Heptagon
8	Octagon
9	Nonagon
10	Decagon
11	Hendecagon or undecagon
12	Dodecagon
n	n-gon

EXAMPLE:

How many diagonals can be drawn from one vertex of a decagon?

Think about the problem. A decagon has 10 vertices. You can connect the given vertex to 7 nonconsecutive vertices, not including the 2 vertices next to the given one, and the given vertex itself. Therefore, 7 diagonals can be drawn. $7 = 10 - 3$. The expression $n - 3$ (where n is the number of sides) represents the number of diagonals from one vertex of any polygon.

The correct answer is 7.   Answer

EXAMPLE:

How many *total* diagonals can you draw in an octagon?

The total number of diagonals can be expressed as $\dfrac{n(n-3)}{2}$, where n is the the number of sides. A rectangle, for example, has two diagonals: $\dfrac{4(4-3)}{2} = 2$.

An octagon has $\dfrac{8(8-3)}{2} = \dfrac{40}{2} = 20$ diagonals.

20 diagonals   Answer

PERIMETER

The *perimeter* of a polygon is the sum of the lengths of its sides.

EXAMPLE:

Find the perimeter of a regular pentagon whose sides measure 13 cm.

This is a straightforward perimeter calculation. Since the pentagon is regular, it is equilateral. The perimeter is simply $13 \times 5 = 65$ cm.

65 cm   Answer

EXAMPLE:

A quadrilateral has sides x, $3x$, $4x - 1$, and $2x + 3$. Find the length of the longest side, given the perimeter is 72 cm.

Since the perimeter is the sum of the lengths of all four sides, you know that:

$$x + 3x + 4x - 1 + 2x + 3 = 72$$
$$10x + 2 = 72$$
$$10x = 70$$
$$x = 7$$

The longest side measures $4x - 1$, which is $4(7) - 1$ or 27 cm.

27 cm   Answer

SUM OF THE INTERIOR ANGLES

The sum of the measures of the angles of a triangle is 180°. The sum of the measures of the angles of a quadrilateral is 360°. The sum of the measures of the angles of a pentagon is 540°. The sum of the measures of the angles of a polygon can, therefore, be expressed as **180(n − 2)°**, where n is the number of sides.

EXAMPLE:

Find the measure of each angle in a regular decagon.

The sum of all 10 angles in a decagon is $180(10 - 2)$ or 1,440°. A *regular* decagon is equiangular, meaning that each angle has the same measure. Each angle, therefore, measures $1{,}440 \div 10$ or 144°.

144°   Answer

EXAMPLE:

Each of the following statements is true EXCEPT:

(A) The larger the number of sides of a polygon, the greater the sum of its interior angles.

(B) The sum of the interior angles of a polygon is always a multiple of 180°.

(C) There is a polygon whose interior angles add up to 900°.

(D) There is a polygon whose interior angles add up to 800°.

(E) Any interior and exterior angles of a regular polygon are supplementary.

It is possible to have a polygon whose angles add up to 900°, since 900 is a multiple of 180. 800 is not a multiple of 180, however, so it is not possible to have a polygon whose angles add up to 800°.

D is the correct answer.   Answer

SUM OF THE EXTERIOR ANGLES

The sum of the exterior angles of any polygon is 360°. This assumes that the polygon is convex and that there is one exterior angle at each vertex.

EXAMPLE:

Find the measure of each exterior angle of a regular hexagon.

The sum of all 6 exterior angles of a hexagon is 360°. A regular hexagon is equiangular, meaning that each interior angle has the same measure. Each exterior angle will also have the same measure since it forms a linear pair with its adjacent interior angle. Each exterior angle, therefore, measures $360 \div 6$ or 60°.

60°   Answer

EXAMPLE:

The measure of each interior angle of a regular polygon is 120° more than its adjacent exterior angle. How many sides does the polygon have?

Let x = the measure of the exterior angle and $120 + x$ = the measure of the interior angle. Since an interior angle of a polygon and its adjacent exterior angle are supplementary, you know that:

$$x + (120 + x) = 180$$
$$2x + 120 = 180$$
$$2x = 60$$
$$x = 30$$

Knowing the sum of the exterior angles must be 360°, solve for the number of sides using:

$$\frac{360}{n} = 30$$
$$\frac{360}{30} = n$$
$$n = 12$$

The polygon has 12 sides.   Answer

▨▨▨ SPECIAL QUADRILATERALS

A quadrilateral refers to any four-sided polygon. Quadrilaterals with special properties are named as follows:

Quadrilateral	Definition
Trapezoid	A quadrilateral with exactly one pair of parallel sides. A trapezoid can also be right or isosceles.
Parallelogram	A quadrilateral with two pairs of parallel sides.
Rhombus	An equilateral parallelogram.
Rectangle	An equiangular parallelogram.
Square	An equilateral and equiangular parallelogram. A square can also be defined as an equilateral rectangle, an equiangular rhombus, or a regular parallelogram.

Notice that rhombi, rectangles, and squares are also types of parallelograms. This means that all of the properties of a parallelogram also apply to these three shapes. A square is unique in that in can be classified as three figures: a parallelogram, a rectangle, and a rhombus.

EXAMPLE:

Given parallelogram *ABCD*, each of the following statements is true EXCEPT:

(A) A pair of opposite sides is parallel and congruent.

(B) Both pairs of opposite angles are congruent.

(C) The diagonals are perpendicular.

(D) The diagonals bisect each other.

(E) All pairs of consecutive angles are supplementary.

Diagonals of a parallelogram do bisect each other, but they are not perpendicular bisectors. (The diagonals of a rhombus and a rectangle are perpendicular bisectors, though.)

C is the correct answer.   Answer

The four true answers in the example, A, B, D, and E, are important characteristics of parallelograms. Two more characteristics can be added to this list:

1. Both pairs of opposite sides are parallel.
2. Both pairs of opposite sides are congruent.

If one of these six characteristics is true for a quadrilateral, you can conclude that the quadrilateral is a parallelogram.

Similarity

Similar figures have the same shape but different size. A square with sides of 2 cm is *similar* to a square with sides of 4 cm. Both have the same shape, but the second square is twice the size of the first. Note the difference between *congruent* figures and similar figures. Congruent figures have both the same shape and the same size.

▓▓ RATIO AND PROPORTION

The *ratio* of a to b is the quotient $\frac{a}{b}$, where b ≠ 0. Ratios can be written as "a to b," $\frac{a}{b}$, a:b. A ratio is in simplest form when it is impossible to divide the terms by a common factor bigger than 1.

EXAMPLE:

If the ratio of the lengths of segment $\overline{AB}$ to segment $\overline{CD}$ is 3:5 and $\overline{AB}$ = 15 cm, find the measure of segment $\overline{CD}$.

Let $y = \overline{CD}$. $\frac{15}{y} = \frac{3}{5}$. Cross multiply to solve for y, resulting in:

$$3y = 75$$

$$y = 25 \text{ cm} \quad \text{Answer}$$

You may also have immediately seen that 15 is 5 times larger than 3, so $5(5) = 25$.

We used a proportion to solve the previous problem. A *proportion* is an equation in which both sides are ratios. Proportions can be solved using cross multiplication:

If $\frac{a}{b} = \frac{c}{d}$, then $ad = cb$.

EXAMPLE:

The measures of the angles of a triangle are in the ratio of 2:3:4. Find the measure of the smallest angle.

You know that the sum of the angles in a triangle is 180° so:

$$2x + 3x + 4x = 180$$

$$9x = 180$$

$$x = 20$$

The smallest angle therefore measures $2(20) = 40°$.

40°   Answer

EXAMPLE:

Write the ratio $\frac{2x^2 - 18}{x - 3}$ in simplest form.

First, distribute out a common factor of 2 in the numerator.

$$\frac{2(x^2 - 9)}{x - 3}$$

The numerator is the difference of perfect squares, so it can be further factored to:

$$\frac{2(x - 3)(x + 3)}{x - 3}$$

Dividing the numerator and denominator by a factor of $x - 3$ gives you:

$$\frac{2(x + 3)}{1} \quad \text{Answer}$$

SIMILAR TRIANGLES

We've previously mentioned that similar figures have the same shape but different size. Specifically, two polygons are *similar* if their corresponding angles are congruent and their corresponding sides have proportional lengths. The statement $\triangle ABC \sim \triangle DEF$ reads, "triangle ABC is similar to triangle DEF."

E X A M P L E :

Each of the following statements is true EXCEPT:

(A) Any two equilateral triangles are similar.

(B) Any two isosceles triangles are similar.

(C) Any two congruent polygons are similar.

(D) Any two squares are similar.

(E) Any two regular pentagons are similar.

Remember that similar figures must have the same shape. Isosceles triangles may or may not have the same shape. They are similar only when the vertex angles (the angle included by the two congruent sides) are congruent.

B is the correct answer.   Answer

When you are proving two triangles similar, it is not necessary to compare all three pairs of corresponding angles and all three pairs of corresponding sides. There are "shortcuts" to proving triangles similar just as there are "shortcut" postulates, such as SAS and ASA, to prove triangles congruent.

1. **Angle Angle (AA).** If two angles of one triangle are congruent to two angles of another triangle, then the triangles are similar.

2. **Side Angle Side (SAS).** If an angle of one triangle is congruent to an angle of another triangle and the sides including those angles are proportional, then the triangles are similar.

3. Side Side Side (SSS). If the corresponding sides of two triangles are proportional, then the triangles are similar.

EXAMPLE:

Is $\triangle TUV \sim \triangle WXV$?

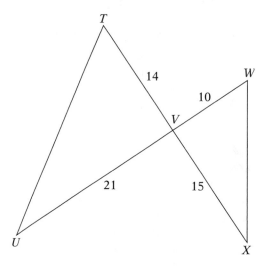

$\angle TVU$ and $\angle WVX$ are vertical angles and are, therefore, congruent. Now, take a look at the ratio of the lengths of corresponding sides:

$$\frac{WV}{TV} = \frac{10}{14} = \frac{5}{7}$$

$$\frac{XV}{UV} = \frac{15}{21} = \frac{5}{7}$$

By the Side Angle Side theorem, SAS, the two triangles are similar.

Yes, $\triangle TUV \sim \triangle WXV$.   Answer

EXAMPLE:

Given $\triangle AMN \sim \triangle ABC$, find $\overline{BC}$.

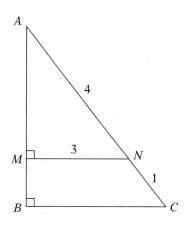

Note that $\triangle AMN \sim \triangle ABC$ by the *AA* theorem. $\angle AMN$ and $\angle ABC$ are both 90° and both triangles share a common angle, $\angle A$. Because the triangles are similar, the sides must be proportional.

$$\frac{\overline{AC}}{\overline{AN}} = \frac{5}{4}$$

$$\frac{\overline{BC}}{\overline{MN}} = \frac{\overline{BC}}{3}$$

$$\frac{\overline{BC}}{3} = \frac{5}{4} \quad \text{so } \overline{BC} \text{ must measure } \frac{15}{4} \text{ units.}$$

$$\overline{BC} = \frac{15}{4} \quad \text{Answer}$$

The *Triangle Proportionality Theorem* actually states that if a line is parallel to one side of a triangle and intersects the other two sides, then the line divides those sides proportionally. The converse of this theorem is also true. If a line divides two sides of a triangle proportionally, then it is parallel to the third side. The converse was true in the previous example, $\overline{MN} \parallel \overline{BC}$.

Circles

A *circle* is the set of all points in a plane at a given distance from given point. The given point is called the *center* and the given distance is called the *radius*. All radii in a circle must, therefore, be congruent. Circles with congruent radii are congruent.

CHORDS

A *chord* is a segment whose endpoints are on the circle. A chord that passes through the center of the circle is called the *diameter*. The diameter is the longest possible chord of a circle and measures twice the length of the radius. A *secant* is a line, ray, or segment containing a chord. Two properties of chords are as follows:

- A segment from the center of a circle perpendicular to a chord bisects the chord.
- Two chords are congruent if they are equally distant from the center of the circle.

EXAMPLE:

Each of the following statements is true EXCEPT:

(A) A chord of a circle could also be a diameter.

(B) A radius of a circle can never be a chord.

(C) If two circles are congruent, then their diameters are congruent.

(D) Concentric circles share the same center.

(E) If $\overline{XY}$ is a secant of a circle, than $\overline{XY}$ is also a chord of the circle.

By definition, answers A, B, C, and D are true statements. E could be true, but a counterexample to show that it is false is as shown below:

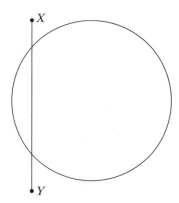

Although $\overline{XY}$ is a secant, the points X and Y do not lie on the circumference of the circle. $\overline{XY}$ is not a chord.

E is the correct answer.   Answer

TANGENTS

A *tangent* to a circle is a line that intersects a circle at exactly *one* point and that lies in the plane of the circle. At the point of tangency, the tangent forms a 90° angle with the radius. In the figure below, ray $\overline{JH}$ is a tangent and is perpendicular to radius $\overline{OH}$.

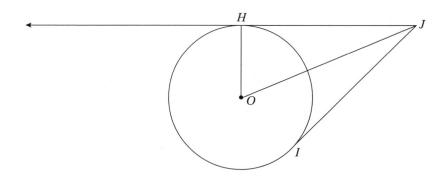

$\overline{JH}$ and $\overline{JI}$ in the figure above are called tangent segments. *Tangent segments* from a given exterior point (in this case, point J) to the circle are congruent. The ray from the exterior point J through the center O of the circle bisects $\angle HJI$, the angle formed by the tangent segments.

EXAMPLE:

In the figure below, $\overline{RS}$ and $\overline{TS}$ are tangent segments. $SO = 10$, $ST = 8$, and $m\angle TOS = 53°$. Find OT, RS, and $m\angle RSO$.

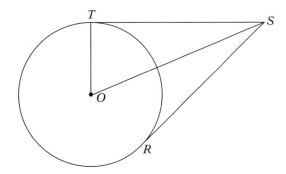

$ST = RS$ since both are tangent segments from the same exterior point S. RS must also measure 8 units. A tangent segment is perpendicular to the radius at the point of tangency, making $m\angle OTS = 90°$. This makes $\triangle OTS$ a right triangle. Use the Pythagorean Theorem to find the length of $\overline{OT}$.

$$ST^2 + OT^2 = OS^2$$

$$8^2 + OT^2 = 10^2$$

$$OT^2 = 100 - 64 = 36$$

$$OT = 6$$

$\overline{SO}$ bisects $\angle RST$. Since you know two angles in $\triangle OTS$, the third angle, $\angle OST$, equals $180 - (90 + 53) = 37°$. $\angle RSO$ and $\angle OST$ are congruent, so $m\angle RSO = 37°$.

$OT = 6$, $RS = 8$, and $m\angle RSO = 35°$.   Answer

ARCS AND ANGLES

Circles can be broken into three types of arcs:

1. **Semicircle.** An arc that represents half of the circle. A semicircle measures 180° and is named using three letters (e.g., $\overarc{ABC}$).

2. **Minor arc.** An arc that measures less than 180°. Two letters are used to name a minor arc (e.g., $\overarc{AB}$).

3. **Major arc.** An arc that measures greater than 180°. Three letters are used to name a major arc (e.g., $\overarc{ABC}$).

Arc measure is always given in degrees. Remember, a circle measures 360°, so the measure of an arc must be between 0 and 360°. Arc measure is different than "arc length," so be careful not to confuse the two terms.

A *central angle* is an angle of a circle whose vertex is the center of the circle. (In the figure below, $\angle AOB$ and $\angle COA$ are central angles.) The *measure of a*

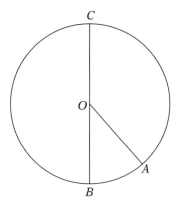

minor arc equals the measure of its central angle. Thus, the measure of $\overset{\frown}{AB}$ equals the measure of $\angle AOB$. Let $m\angle AOB = 100°$; then $m\ \overset{\frown}{AB} = 100°$. It is also important to note that:

- Two minor arcs are congruent when their central angles are congruent.
- Two minor arcs are congruent when their chords are congruent.
- Two chords are congruent if their corresponding minor arcs are congruent.

The *measure of a major arc* equals 360° minus the measure of its corresponding minor arc. In the figure above, $m\ \overset{\frown}{ABC} = 360 - m\ \overset{\frown}{AC}$. The *measure of a semicircle* always equals 180°.

An *inscribed angle* is an angle of a circle whose vertex is on the circle and whose sides include chords of the circle. The *measure of an inscribed angle* equals half the measure of its intercepted arc. In the figure below, $\angle GFH$ and $\angle GIH$ are inscribed angles.

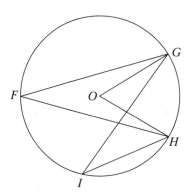

EXAMPLE:

In the figure above, $m\angle GOH = 60°$. Find $m\ \overset{\frown}{GH}$, $m\angle GFH$, and $m\angle GIH$.

$\overset{\frown}{GH}$ measures 60°, since it equals the measure of its central angle. $\angle GFH$ and $\angle GIH$ are inscribed angles, so they measure half of their intercepted $\overset{\frown}{GH}$. Both therefore measure 30°.

$m\ \overset{\frown}{GH} = 60°$, $m\angle GFH = 30°$, $m\angle GIH = 30°$ **Answer**

EXAMPLE:

Equilateral $\triangle ABC$ is inscribed in a circle. Each of the following statements is true EXCEPT:

(A) $m\ \overset{\frown}{BC} = 60°$.

(B) m minor $\overset{\frown}{AB} = m$ minor $\overset{\frown}{BC}$.

(C) m major $\overset{\frown}{CAB} = m$ major $\overset{\frown}{BCA}$.

(D) $\overline{AC}$ and $\overline{AB}$ are equidistant from the center of the circle.

(E) $m\angle ABC = 60°$.

It is helpful to draw a diagram to visualize the given information.

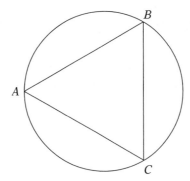

Congruent chords intercept congruent arcs. Therefore, m minor $\overset{\frown}{AB} = m$ minor $\overset{\frown}{BC}$, since $AB = BC$. B is true and, likewise, C is true. Because they are congruent chords, $\overline{AC}$ and $\overline{AB}$ must be equidistant from the center of the circle. D is also true. $\angle ABC$ is an inscribed angle and its measure is 60°, because all angles in an equilateral triangle are 60°. That leaves answer A. $\overset{\frown}{BC}$ is intercepted by inscribed angle, $\angle BAC$. Since $m\angle BAC = 60°$, $m\ \overset{\frown}{BC}$ must be 2(60) or 120°. A is the correct answer.

An alternative way of solving the problem is to realize that $\overset{\frown}{AB}$, $\overset{\frown}{BC}$, and $\overset{\frown}{AC}$ are congruent arcs. Since the whole circle measures 360°, each arc must measure $\dfrac{360}{3}$ or 120°. You can immediately deduce that A is not true.

A   Answer

CIRCUMFERENCE

Circumference is the distance around a circle. It is calculated using one of the following formulas:

$$C = 2\pi r \quad \text{or} \quad C = \pi d$$

where r = the length of the radius and d = the length of the diameter.
   Pi, written as the Greek letter π, is the ratio of the circumference of a circle to its diameter. $\pi = \dfrac{C}{d}$. π is an irrational number, meaning it's nonterminating and nonrepeating. $\pi = 3.14159\ldots$ and it is typically approximated as 3.14, or $\dfrac{22}{7}$.

EXAMPLE:

Find the circumference of a circle whose radius is 11 cm. Leave your answer in terms of π.

This problem simply involves substituting values into the circumference formula.

$C = 2\pi r$

$C = 2\pi(11)$

$C = 22\pi$ cm   Answer

EXAMPLE:

The radius of one circle is 8 cm more than the radius of a smaller circle. If the ratio of the two circles' circumferences is 3:1, find the circumference of the larger circle.

The circumference of the smaller circle is $2\pi r$, and the circumference of the larger circle is $2\pi(8 + r)$. Set up a proportion to solve for r:

$$\frac{2\pi(8 + r)}{2\pi r} = \frac{3}{1}$$

$$\frac{(8 + r)}{r} = \frac{3}{1}$$

$$3r = 8 + r$$

$$2r = 8$$

$$r = 4$$

If the radius of the smaller circle is 4 cm so the radius of the larger circle is $4 + 8 = 12$, its circumference is:

$2\pi(12) = 24\pi$

24π cm   Answer

ARC LENGTH

An *arc length* is a fraction of the circumference of a circle. Arc length is measured in units such as centimeters, inches, feet, and meters, whereas arc measure is measured in degrees. The formula for arc length is as follows:

$$l = \frac{x}{360}(2\pi r)$$

where $x° =$ the arc measure.

A semicircle, for example, has an arc length equal to half the circumference, since $\dfrac{180}{360} = \dfrac{1}{2}$.

EXAMPLE:

Find the length of $\overset{\frown}{AB}$ given $m\angle AOB = 60°$.

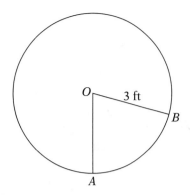

The measure of $\overset{\frown}{AB}$ is 60°, since the arc measure equals the measure of the central angle. The length of $\overset{\frown}{AB}$ is therefore:

$$l = \frac{60}{360}[2\pi(3)]$$

$$l = \frac{1}{6}(6\pi)$$

π ft   Answer

EXAMPLE:

$\angle EFD$ is inscribed in a circle and measures 70°. If the length of major $\overset{\frown}{EFD}$ is 33π inches, find the diameter of the circle.

Since $\angle EFD$ is an inscribed angle, the arc it intercepts, $\overset{\frown}{ED}$, measures 2(70) or 140°. m major $\overset{\frown}{EFD} = 360 - 140 = 220°$. Write an equation for the length of $\overset{\frown}{EFD}$ EFD and solve for r.

$$l = \frac{x}{360}(2\pi r)$$

$$33\pi = \frac{220}{360}(2\pi r)$$

$$33 = \frac{11}{18}(2r)$$

$$33 = \frac{11}{9}(r)$$

$$\frac{33(9)}{11} = r$$

27 inches $= r$

The diameter is $2(27)$ or 54 inches.   Answer

Area

AREA FORMULAS

Area is the measure of the region enclosed by a figure. Every polygon has a unique area, and congruent polygons have equal areas. Area is measured in *square units*, such as centimeters², inches², feet², and meters². Most of the formulas used for calculating area require a base and height. Recall that the height of a polygon is the length of its altitude. The base, however, can be any side of the polygon (not just the "bottom" side as some students believe). The height must measure the altitude that's perpendicular to the *given* base.

Common area formulas are as follows:

Shape	Area Formula	Variable Definitions
Rectangle	$A = bh$	b = the length of the base
		h = the height, the length of the altitude
Triangle	$A = \frac{1}{2}bh$	b = the length of the base
		h = the height, the length of the altitude
Right triangle	$A = \frac{1}{2}\text{leg}_1 \times \text{leg}_2$	leg_1 and leg_2 are the legs (the sides adjacent to the right angle)
Equilateral triangle	$A = \frac{s^2\sqrt{3}}{4}$	s = the length of a side
Square	$A = s^2$	s = the length of a side
Parallelogram	$A = bh$	b = the length of the base
		h = the height, the length of the altitude
Rhombus	$A = bh \text{ or } A = \frac{1}{2}d_1d_2$	b = the length of the base
		h = the height, the length of the altitude
		d_1 and d_2 = the length of diagonals 1 and 2
Trapezoid	$A = \frac{1}{2}(b_1 + b_2)h$	b_1 and b_2 = the length of the 2 bases, i.e., the parallel sides
		h = the height, the length of the altitude
Regular polygon	$A = \frac{1}{2}asn \text{ or } A = \frac{1}{2}ap$	a = the length of the apothem
		s = the length of a side
		n = the number of sides
		p = the perimeter
Circle	$A = \pi r^2$	r = the length of the radius
Sector	$A = \frac{x}{360}\pi r^2$	r = the length of the radius
		x = the arc measure

The shapes above should be familiar to you. A *sector* is a part of a circle that resembles a "slice" of the circle. Its edges are two radii and an arc.

EXAMPLE:

Find the area of a circle with a circumference of 108π cm.

Since $C = 2\pi r$, set up an equation for circumference and solve for r.

$$C = 2\pi r$$

$$108\pi = 2\pi r$$

$$54 = r$$

The area formula for a circle is $A = \pi r^2$, so $A = \pi(54)^2$.

$2{,}916\pi$ cm^2 Answer

EXAMPLE:

Find the area of the shaded region given that the radius is 12 m.

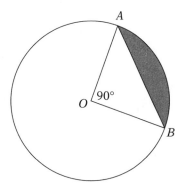

Start by looking at the area of the sector, the "slice" of the circle, which includes the shaded region. The area of the sector is as follows:

$$A = \frac{90}{360}\pi(12^2)$$

$$A = \frac{1}{4}\pi(144)$$

$$A = 36\pi \text{ cm}^2$$

The problem is asking only for the area of the shaded region, not the area of the entire sector. Subtract the area of the right triangle ΔAOB from the area of the sector. Note that the right triangle is an isosceles right triangle whose both legs are formed by radii of the circle.

Area of the sector – Area of the triangle

$$36\pi - \frac{1}{2}bh$$

$$36\pi - \frac{1}{2}(12)(12)$$

$36\pi - 72$ cm^2 Answer

EXAMPLE:

Find the area of a regular pentagon with a perimeter of 75 in and an apothem of 6 in.

Since the pentagon is *regular,* you can apply the area formula. This formula only applies to regular, equiangular, and equilateral figures. The *apothem* is the distance from a side of the polygon to the center of a circle circumscribed around it.

$$A = \frac{1}{2}ap$$

$$A = \frac{1}{2}(6)(75)$$

$$A = 225 \text{ in}^2 \quad \text{Answer}$$

EXAMPLE:

The area of a rhombus is 96 m². If the length of one diagonal is 12, find the length of the second diagonal.

Two area formulas may be used for a rhombus:

$$A = bh \text{ or } A = \frac{1}{2}d_1d_2$$

Since you are given the length of one diagonal, it makes sense to use the formula that includes diagonals.

$$96 = \frac{1}{2}(12)d_2$$

$$96 = 6d_2$$

$$d_2 = 16 \text{ m} \quad \text{Answer}$$

AREA VS. PERIMETER

Perimeter and area are NOT related. If two polygons have the same perimeter, they do not necessarily have the same area. Think of two rectangles with a perimeter of 100 cm. The dimension of the first rectangle could be 30×20 cm, while the dimensions of the second rectangle could be 25×25 cm. Which one has a greater area?

The area of the first rectangle	The area of the second rectangle
A = 30(20)	A = 25(25)
A = 600 cm²	A = 625 cm²

The rectangle measuring 25×25 cm encloses a bigger region. (You may have noticed that this "rectangle" is actually a square. Remember that squares can be thought of as equilateral rectangles.)

AREA RATIO OF SIMILAR FIGURES

Remember that similar polygons have the same shape but different size. The ratio of the length of a part of one polygon to the length of the corresponding part of another polygon is called the *scale factor*. Take a look at two equilateral triangles. All equilateral triangles are similar because they have congruent corresponding angles. (Remember, AA proves similarity.) The sides of the first triangle measure 4 cm and the sides of the second triangle measure 8 cm. The scale factor of the two triangles is 4:8, or 1:2. Now let's compare their areas:

$$\text{Area of triangle 1} = \frac{s^2\sqrt{3}}{4} \qquad\qquad \text{Area of triangle 2} = \frac{s^2\sqrt{3}}{4}$$

$$A = \frac{4^2\sqrt{3}}{4} \qquad\qquad\qquad A = \frac{8^2\sqrt{3}}{4}$$

$$A = 4\sqrt{3}\ \text{cm}^2 \qquad\qquad\qquad A = 16\sqrt{3}$$

The ratio of the areas of the two triangles is $4\sqrt{3} : 16\sqrt{3}$, which simplifies to 1:4. Note that the sides of the triangles have the same ratio as the scale factor, 1:2.

The ratio of the areas is the square of the scale factor, $1^2 : 2^2$ or 1:4. This is always the case. If the scale factor of two similar figures is *m:n*, then the ratio of their sides and perimeters is also *m:n* and the ratio of their areas is $m^2 : n^2$.

EXAMPLE:

ABCDEF ~ KLMNOP. If the perimeter of the first hexagon is 66 ft and the perimeter of the second is 72 ft, what is the ratio of their areas?

The scale factor of the two hexagons will be the same as the ratio of their perimeters.

66:72 simplifies to 11:12

The ratio of their areas is therefore $11^2 : 12^2$.

121:144   Answer

FIGURES THAT COMBINE NUMEROUS SHAPES

Of course, on the SAT Subject test, the area problems are not as straightforward as some of the examples presented in this chapter. Instead of simply being given a rectangle and asked to calculate its area using $A = bh$ or being given a triangle and asked to calculate its area using $A = \frac{1}{2}bh$, you will need to recognize common figures hidden in diagrams.

The *Area Addition Postulate* states that if a region can be divided into nonoverlapping parts, the area of the given region is the sum of the areas of its parts. This is a useful concept to use when confronted with an irregular shape whose area you may not know how to calculate.

EXAMPLE:

Find the area of the figure.

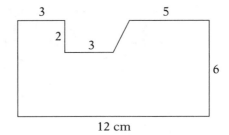

The best way to solve this problem is to recognize that the big shape is a rectangle and the missing piece is a right trapezoid. The trapezoid missing base measures $12 - (3 + 5)$, or 4 cm. To solve, find the area of the rectangle and subtract the area of the trapezoid.

$A = 12(6) - \dfrac{1}{2}(b_1 + b_2)h$

$A = 72 - \dfrac{1}{2}(4 + 3)2$

$A = 72 - 7$

$A = 65$ cm²   Answer

EXAMPLE:

WXYZ is a square of area 36 cm². What is the area of the shaded region?

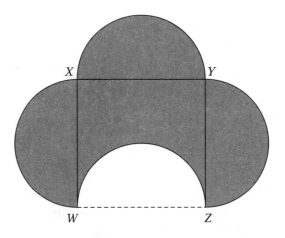

First, recognize that each side of the square measures 6 cm, since $6^2 = 36$. Before fully attacking the problem, take a look at the given information and come up with a plan. Notice that there are three semicircles included in the shaded region and one semicircle "cut out" of the square. One semicircle's area will cancel with the semicircle that is *not* included in the shaded region. You need to take the area of the square and add the area of the two remaining semicircles. Two semicircles, of course, form one circle. Simply take the area of the square and add the area of a circle with diameter 6.

$A = 36 + \pi 3^2$

$A = 36 + 9\pi$ cm^2 Answer

EXAMPLE:

What is the area of a square inscribed in a circle whose diameter is $9\sqrt{2}$ inches?

Recognize that the diameter of the circle is also a diagonal of the square. A square's diagonal creates two isosceles right triangles within the square, and isosceles right triangles have angles measuring 45°-45°-90°. Do you remember the special relationships among the sides of a 45°-45°-90° triangle? The diagonal is the hypotenuse of both right triangles, so the legs of the triangles must measure $\dfrac{9\sqrt{2}}{\sqrt{2}}$, or 9 inches. A square with sides of 9 has an area of 9^2 square inches.

81 square inches   Answer

CHAPTER 6
SOLID GEOMETRY

This chapter provides a review of solid (i.e., three-dimensional) geometry principles. Four to six percent of the Level 1 test questions relate specifically to solid geometry. By definition, solid geometry focuses on three-dimensional shapes and figures. The pie chart shows approximately how much of the Level 1 test is related to solid geometry:

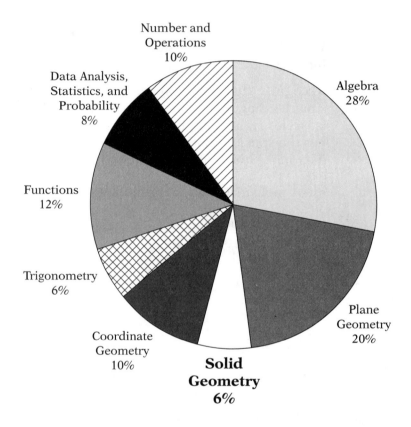

The following solid geometry topics are covered in this chapter:

1. Vocabulary for Polyhedra

2. Prisms
    a. Surface Area
    b. Lateral Surface Area
    c. Volume
    d. Distance Between Opposite Vertices of a Rectangular Prism

3. Cylinders
    a. Surface Area
    b. Lateral Surface Area
    c. Volume

4. Pyramids
   a. Surface Area
   b. Lateral Surface Area
   c. Volume

5. Cones
   a. Surface Area
   b. Lateral Surface Area
   c. Volume

6. Spheres
   a. Surface Area
   b. Volume

7. Volume Ratio of Similar Figures

The following reference information is provided during the Level 1 test. You do NOT need to memorize these formulas. Become familiar with the information below so that you can refer to it during the test, if necessary. These formulas are printed in the directions of the test.

Reference Information	
Right circular cone with radius r and height h:	Volume $= \frac{1}{3}\pi r^2 h$
Right circular cone with circumference of base c and slant height ℓ:	Lateral Area $= \frac{1}{2}c\ell$
Sphere with radius r:	Volume $= \frac{4}{3}\pi r^3$ Surface Area $= 4\pi r^2$
Pyramid with base area B and height h:	Volume $= \frac{1}{3}Bh$

Vocabulary for Polyhedra

The previous chapter focused on plane, or two-dimensional, figures. Remember the term "polygon" from plane geometry—a many-sided closed figure created by connecting line segments endpoint to endpoint. A *polyhedron* is a many-sided solid created by connecting polygons along their sides. A polyhedron encloses a single region of space, and the plural of polyhedron is polyhedra.

The parts of a polyhedron are as follows:

- **Faces.** The flat surfaces of a polyhedron that are shaped like polygons

- **Edge.** A segment where two faces intersect

- **Vertex.** The point of intersection of three or more edges

- **Base** (of a prism or cylinder). The two congruent, parallel faces

- **Base** (of a pyramid or cone). The circular (for a cone) or polygonal (for a pyramid) face that does not contain the common vertex

- **Lateral faces.** The face(s) that make up the sides of the solid (for prisms, the lateral faces are always parallelograms).

- **Altitude.** The segment perpendicular to the plane of both bases (for a prism or cylinder); the perpendicular segment joining the vertex to the plane of the base (for a pyramid or cone)

- **Height** (h). The length of the altitude

- **Slant height** (ℓ). The distance from the edge of the base to the common vertex

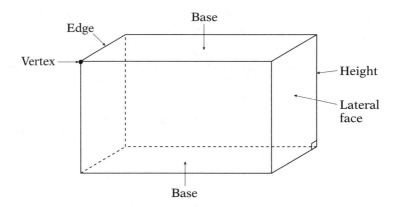

Some solids, such as prisms and pyramids, have flat faces, while others, such as cones, cylinders, and spheres, have curved faces. Solids with curved faces are not polyhedra, however, since they are not created by connecting polygons along their sides.

Let's review a few terms that are commonly used in solid geometry problems:

Volume is the amount of space enclosed by a solid.

Surface area is the sum of the area of all of the faces.

Lateral surface area is the sum of the area of only the lateral faces (or the sides). This is also referred to as simply the lateral area.

Prisms

A *prism* is a polyhedron consisting of two congruent, parallel bases connected by lateral faces shaped like parallelograms. Prisms are classified by their bases: Rectangular prisms have bases shaped like rectangles, triangular prisms have bases shaped like triangles, hexagonal prisms have bases shaped like hexagons, and so on. The rectangular prism is the most commonly used solid on the Level 1 test. A rectangular prism looks like what you would think of as a box.

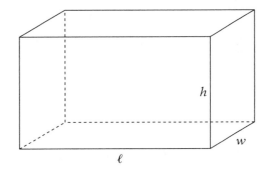

Rectangular Prism		
Surface Area	**Lateral Surface Area**	**Volume**
$S = 2\ell w + 2\ell h + 2hw$	$S = 2\ell h + 2hw$	$V = \ell wh$

In general, the formula for the volume for any prism can be written as:

$$V = Bh$$

where B = the area of the base and h = the height.

In the case of a rectangular prism, the area of the base is the product of its length and width, ℓw. Substituting ℓw for B results in $V = \ell wh$. The volume of a cube with edge s is therefore $V = Bh = (s^2)s = s^3$. Volume is measured in *cubic units,* such as centimeters³, inches³, feet³, and meters³.

EXAMPLE:

The volume of a square prism is equal to its lateral surface area. Find the length of the sides of the base.

Note that a square prism is not equivalent to a cube. The two bases of this prism must be squares, but the height may be any length. A square prism is equivalent to a rectangular prism whose length and width have equal measures. Draw a diagram to help solve this problem:

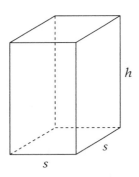

Let s equal the sides of the base and h equal the height of the prism. Use formulas for a rectangular prism and substitute s for the length and width. The volume is

$V = \ell wh = s^2h$

The lateral surface area is therefore

$S = 2\ell h + 2hw = S = 2sh + 2hs = 4sh$

Now set the volume equal to the lateral surface area and solve for s:

$s^2h = 4sh$ Divide both sides by h. This is okay to do since h is a length and cannot equal zero.

$s^2 = 4s$ Divide both sides by s, since s also cannot equal zero.

$s = 4$ Answer

EXAMPLE:

The surface area of a cube is 150 cm². Find the length of its edges.

The formula for the surface area of a cube is similar to the formula for a rectangular prism, except length, width, and height are equal in a cube. If the length of an edge of the cube is s, $s = \ell = w = h$.

$S = 2\ell w + 2\ell h + 2hw$ becomes $S = 2s^2 + 2s^2 + 2s^2 = 6s^2$.

$150 = 6s^2$

$25 = s^2$

$s = 5$ cm   Answer

DISTANCE BETWEEN OPPOSITE VERTICES OF A RECTANGULAR PRISM

Along with surface area and volume, you may be asked to determine the distance between opposite vertices of a rectangular prism. The problem is included here in the Solid Geometry chapter because it involves a prism, but it can actually be solved by using the Pythagorean Theorem *twice*.

EXAMPLE:

Find the distance from vertex P to vertex Q in the rectangular prism below.

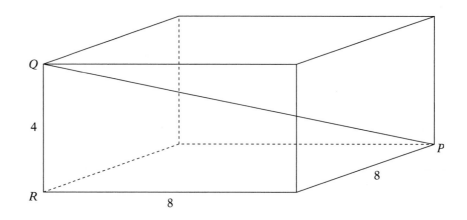

Think of $\overline{PQ}$ as the hypotenuse of a right triangle whose legs are the diagonal of the base and the edge of the prism, $\overline{QR}$. First find the length of the diagonal of the base:

$$RP^2 = 8^2 + 8^2$$

$$RP^2 = 128$$

$$RP = \sqrt{128} = 8\sqrt{2}$$

Did you recognize that $\overline{RP}$ is the hypotenuse of an isosceles right triangle? If so, you can determine the length, RP, simply by remembering the ratio of the sides of a 45°-45°-90° triangle.

Now, use the Pythagorean Theorem for a second time to determine PQ.

$$PQ^2 = \left(8\sqrt{2}\right)^2 + 4^2$$

$$PQ^2 = 64(2) + 16$$

$$PQ^2 = 128 + 16 = 144$$

$$PQ = \sqrt{144}$$

$$PQ = 12 \qquad \text{Answer}$$

Another way to find the distance between opposite vertices of a rectangular prism is to use the formula:

$$\text{Distance} = \sqrt{\ell^2 + w^2 + h^2}$$

Try using this formula for the last example to get:

$$\text{Distance} = \sqrt{8^2 + 8^2 + 4^2} = \sqrt{144} = 12$$

Cylinders

A *cylinder* is similar to a prism with circular bases. Right circular cylinders are the most commonly used cylinders on the Level 1 test. They consist of two congruent, parallel, circular bases joined by an *axis* that is perpendicular to each. The axis of a right circular cylinder is also its *altitude*.

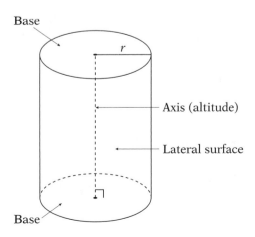

Base

r

Axis (altitude)

Lateral surface

Base

Cylinder		
Surface Area	**Lateral Surface Area**	**Volume**
$S = 2\pi r^2 + 2\pi rh$	$S = 2\pi rh$	$V = \pi r^2 h$

In general, the formula for the volume for any cylinder is the same as that for any prism and can be written as:

$$V = Bh$$

where B = the area of the base and h = the height.

In the case of a right circular cylinder, the area of the base is πr^2. Substituting πr^2 for B results in $V = \pi r^2 h$.

EXAMPLE:

Find the volume of the solid created by rotating rectangle $WXYZ$ 360° around side $\overline{XY}$.

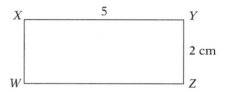

The hardest part of a problem like this is to visualize the solid formed by rotating the rectangle. Picture rectangle $WXYZ$ rotating fully around the axis $\overline{XY}$. A right circular cylinder is created whose height is 5 cm (the length $\overline{XY}$) and whose radius is 2 cm. (You may think of this cylinder as being "on its side," since the axis is not vertical.)

Using $r = 2$ cm and $h = 5$ cm, its volume is

$V = \pi(2)^2(5)$

$V = 20\pi$ cm³   Answer

EXAMPLE:

Find the total surface area of a cylinder whose volume equals its lateral surface area and whose height is 10 inches.

First, set the formula for lateral surface area equal to that of volume to solve for r. Since lateral surface area equals $2\pi rh$ and volume equals $\pi r^2 h$, the resulting equation is

$2\pi rh = \pi r^2 h$

Notice that h cancels, meaning that height is not a factor in a cylinder having equal volume and lateral surface area. One r and π also cancel to get

$2 = r$

Use the given information, $h = 10$, and the radius that you just found, $r = 2$, to get the cylinder's total surface area.

$S = 2\pi r^2 + 2\pi rh$

$S = 2\pi(2)^2 + 2\pi(2)(10)$

$S = 8\pi + 40\pi$

$S = 48\pi$ in²   Answer

Pyramids

A *pyramid* consists of one base and triangular lateral faces that connect at a common vertex. Like prisms, pyramids are classified by their base: Rectangular pyramids have a base shaped like a rectangle, triangular pyramids have a base shaped like a triangle, hexagonal pyramids have a base shaped like a hexagon, and so on.

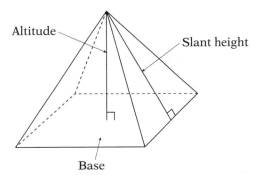

The following are formulas for a *regular pyramid*. A pyramid is regular if its base is a regular polygon (i.e., a square or equilateral triangle) and its lateral edges are congruent.

Regular Pyramid		
Surface Area	**Lateral Surface Area**	**Volume**
$S = \dfrac{1}{2}\,\ell P + B$	$S = \dfrac{1}{2}\,\ell P$	$V = \dfrac{1}{3}\,Bh$
B = area of the base	ℓ = slant height P = perimeter of the base	

In general the formula for the volume for any pyramid can be written as:

$$V = \frac{1}{3}Bh$$

where B = the area of the base and h = the height.

In the case of a rectangular pyramid, the area of the base is the product of its length and width, ℓw. Substituting ℓw for B results in $V = \dfrac{1}{3}\ell wh$.

Remember that the volume formula for a pyramid, $V = \dfrac{1}{3}Bh$, is listed in the reference information of the Level 1 test.

EXAMPLE:

Find the volume of a pyramid whose base is an equilateral triangle with sides of length 4 cm and whose height is 9 cm.

Start by finding B, the area of the base. Recall that the area of an equilateral triangle is

$$A = \frac{s^2\sqrt{3}}{4}$$

$$A = \frac{4^2\sqrt{3}}{4}$$

$$A = 4\sqrt{3} \text{ cm}^2$$

Since the volume of a pyramid is given by the formula $V = \dfrac{1}{3}Bh$ and $h = 9$ cm, the volume is

$$V = \frac{1}{3}Bh$$

$$V = \frac{1}{3}\left(4\sqrt{3}\right)(9)$$

$$V = 12\sqrt{3} \text{ cm}^3 \qquad \text{Answer}$$

Cones

A *cone* consists of one circular base and a lateral surface that comes to a common vertex. Right circular cones are the most commonly used cones on the Level 1 test. They consist of a circular base connected to a vertex by an *axis* perpendicular to the base. The axis of a right circular cone is also its *altitude*.

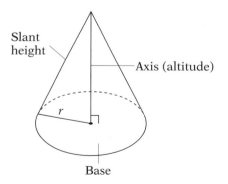

Right Circular Cone		
Surface Area	**Lateral Surface Area**	**Volume**
$S = \dfrac{1}{2}c\ell + \pi r^2$	$S = \dfrac{1}{2}c\ell$	$V = \dfrac{1}{3}\pi r^2 h$
	ℓ = slant height	
	c = circumference of the base	

In general, the formula for the volume for any cone is the same as that for any pyramid and can be written as:

$$V = \frac{1}{3}Bh$$

where B = the area of the base and h = the height.

In the case of a right circular cone, the area of the base is πr^2. Substituting πr^2 for B results in $V = \dfrac{1}{3}\pi r^2 h$.

Remember that the volume formula for a right circular cone, $V = \dfrac{1}{3}\pi r^2 h$, and the lateral surface area formula, $S = \dfrac{1}{2}c\ell$, are listed in the reference information of the Level 1 test. You don't need to memorize these!

EXAMPLE:

Find the lateral area of a cone whose diameter is 12 cm and whose height is 8 cm.

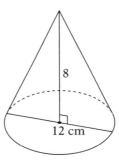

You need to solve for the circumference, c, and the slant height, ℓ, in order to use the formula for lateral surface area.

Circumference can be determined using $c = \pi d$ or $c = 2\pi r$. Since you're given the diameter, it makes sense to use the first formula:

$C = \pi(12)$

The radius is therefore half the diameter, or 6 cm. Notice that the radius and the altitude form a right triangle whose hypotenuse is the slant height. Use the Pythagorean Theorem to solve for ℓ.

$\ell^2 = 8^2 + 6^2$

$\ell^2 = 100$

$\ell = 10$

Now you have enough information to solve for the lateral area.

$S = \dfrac{1}{2}c\ell$

$S = \dfrac{1}{2}(12\pi)(10)$

$S = 60\pi$ cm^2 Answer

EXAMPLE:

A right circular cylinder and a right circular cone have the same radius and volume. If the cone has a height of 18 inches, find the height of the cylinder.

To solve for the height, set the volume of each solid equal to each other:

$\pi r^2 h = \dfrac{1}{3}\pi r^2 (18)$

$h = 6$ inches   Answer

The height of the cylinder must be one-third the height of the cone, since the volume of the cone is one-third the volume of the cylinder.

EXAMPLE:

A right circular cone can have a cross section in the shape of all of the following EXCEPT:

(A) a circle
(B) a triangle
(C) a rectangle
(D) its base
(E) an ellipse

A *cross section* of a solid is a figure formed when a plane intersects the solid. Try to visualize what happens when you cut a cone. A circle is obviously possible when the plane intersecting the cone is parallel to the base. The base is a possibility if the plane intersecting the cone is the same plane that contains the base. A triangle is possible if the plane cuts through the vertex of the cone and is perpendicular to the base. An ellipse results if the plane that intersects the cone is at an angle, creating an oval-type figure. It is not possible to have a cross-sectional area in the shape of a rectangle.

C is the correct answer.   Answer

Spheres

A *sphere* is the set of all points in space at a given distance from a given point. Rotating a circle 360° around one of its diameters creates a sphere.

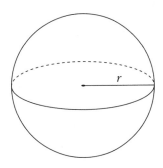

Sphere	
Surface Area	**Volume**
$S = 4\pi r^2$	$V = \dfrac{4}{3}\pi r^3$

Remember that the volume formula for a sphere, $V = \dfrac{4}{3}\pi r^3$, and the surface area formula, $S = 4\pi r^2$, are listed in the reference information of the Level 1 test. Again, you don't need to memorize these!

EXAMPLE:

Find the volume of a sphere whose surface area equals its volume.

First, set surface area equal to volume and solve for *r*.

$$4\pi r^2 = \frac{4}{3}\pi r^3$$

$$4 = \frac{4}{3}r$$

$$r = 3$$

Now use the radius to solve for volume:

$$V = \frac{4}{3}\pi(3)^3$$

$$V = 36\pi \quad \text{Answer}$$

EXAMPLE:

A ball is immersed in a cup of water and displaces 288π cubic units of water. Find the surface area of the ball.

The amount of water displaced by the ball is equivalent to its volume. Therefore, you have enough information to write an equation for the volume of the ball and solve for r.

$$\frac{4}{3}\pi r^3 = 288\pi$$

$$r^3 = \frac{3}{4}(288)$$

$$r^3 = 216$$

$$r^3 = \sqrt[3]{216}$$

$$r = 6$$

Now substitute $r = 6$ into the surface area formula to get

$$S = 4\pi(6)^2$$

$$S = 144\pi \text{ units}^2 \quad \text{Answer}$$

Volume Ratio of Similar Figures

Solids are said to be similar if their bases are similar and their corresponding parts are proportional. Just like similar polygons mentioned in the Plane Geometry chapter, *similar solids* have the same shape but different size. A square, right pyramid with a base area of 2 cm², for example, is similar to a square, right pyramid with a base area of 4 cm². The ratio of the length of corresponding parts of similar solids is called the *scale factor*.

If the scale factor of two similar solids is $m{:}n$, then the following ratios are true:

1. The ratio of their corresponding base perimeters or circumferences is also **m:n**.
2. The ratio of their base areas, total surface areas, and lateral surface areas is **m²:n²**.
3. The ratio of their volumes is **m³:n³**.

EXAMPLE:

The lateral surface areas of two similar right cylinders are 80π in³ and 120π in³, respectively. Find the ratio of their volumes.

First determine the scale factor of the similar cylinders by comparing their lateral surface areas.

$80\pi{:}120\pi$ simplifies to 8:12, which simplifies to 2:3.

Therefore, the scale factor is $\sqrt{2}{:}\sqrt{3}$.

Now, find the volume ratio by cubing the scale factor:

$$\left(\sqrt{2}\right)^3{:}\left(\sqrt{3}\right)^3$$

$$2\sqrt{2}{:}3\sqrt{3} \quad \text{Answer}$$

CHAPTER 7

COORDINATE GEOMETRY

This chapter provides a review of coordinate geometry principles. Eight to twelve percent of the Level 1 test questions relate specifically to coordinate geometry. In actuality, however, about 20 percent of the Level 1 test questions assume an understanding of coordinate geometry concepts. Coordinate geometry focuses on graphing in an *xy*-coordinate plane. The pie chart shows approximately how much of the Level 1 test is related to coordinate geometry:

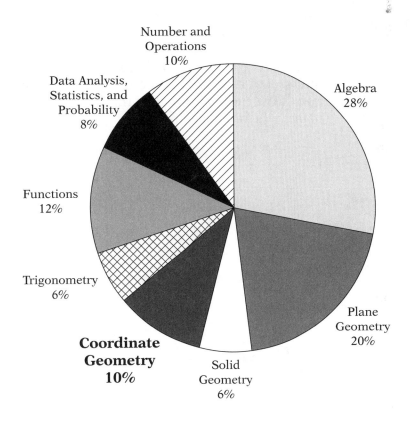

The following geometry topics are covered in this chapter:

1. Plotting Points

2. Midpoint

3. Distance

4. Slope

5. Slope of Parallel and Perpendicular Lines

Plotting Points

A *plane rectangular coordinate system* is created by drawing two axes that intersect at right angles at an origin. The horizontal axis is called the *y-axis,* and the vertical axis is called the *x-axis*. The axes create four *quadrants* in the plane, which are numbered using Roman numerals as shown:

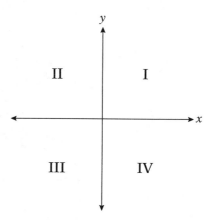

An *ordered pair* (x, y) denotes a unique point in the plane. To plot a point, simply graph the location of its x and y coordinates. The x-coordinate of a point is also referred to as the *abscissa,* while the y-coordinate is also referred to as the *ordinate*.

EXAMPLE:

Graph the following points in the same coordinate plane: $A(1, 4)$, $B(-2, -3)$, $C(-5, 1)$, $D(4, 0)$.

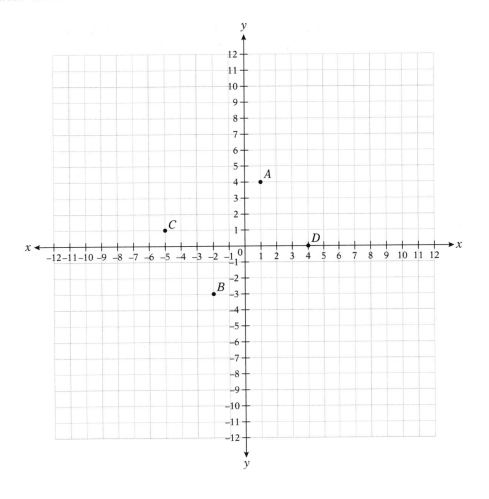

EXAMPLE:

Find three solutions of $2x + 3y = 1$.

The graph of an equation in two variables is the set of all points whose x- and y-coordinates satisfy the equation. To find three solutions to this equation, simply choose three values for x and solve for the corresponding value of y. Write y in terms of x, and create an xy-table to determine solutions of the equation.

x	$y = \dfrac{1 - 2x}{3}$	y
0	$y = \dfrac{1 - 2(0)}{3}$	$\dfrac{1}{3}$
2	$y = \dfrac{1 - 2(2)}{3}$	-1
-1	$y = \dfrac{1 - 2(-1)}{3}$	1

The graph of $2x + 3y = 1$ is a line, so there are infinitely many points that will satisfy the equation. Here three possible points are given.

$(0, \frac{1}{3})$, $(2,-1)$, and $(-1, 1)$ are three possible solutions.   Answer

Midpoint

The *midpoint* of a segment with endpoints (x_1, y_1) and (x_2, y_2) is the point:

$$\left(\frac{x_1 + x_2}{2}, \frac{y_1 + y_2}{2} \right)$$

Finding the midpoint of a line segment can also be thought of as finding the *average* of the x- and y-coordinates.

EXAMPLE:

Find the midpoint $\overline{AB}$ given the endpoints $A(1, 6)$ and $B(-3, -7)$.

Substitute the given coordinates into the midpoint formula to get

$$\left(\frac{1 + -3}{2}, \frac{6 + -7}{2} \right)$$

$$\left(\frac{-2}{2}, \frac{-1}{2} \right)$$

$$\left(1, \frac{-1}{2} \right)$$ Answer

EXAMPLE:

M is the midpoint of $\overline{AB}$. Find the coordinates of B if A has coordinates $(3, 8)$ and M has coordinates $(-4, 0)$.

Let the coordinates of B be (x_2, y_2); then:

$$\frac{3 + x_2}{2} = -4 \qquad \text{and} \qquad \frac{8 + y_2}{2} = 0$$

$$3 + x_2 = -8 \qquad\qquad\qquad 8 + y_2 = 0$$

$$x_2 = -11 \qquad\qquad\qquad\quad y_2 = -8$$

$B(-11, -8)$ Answer

Distance

The *distance* between any two points (x_1, y_1) and (x_2, y_2) is

$$d = \sqrt{(x_2 - x_1)^2 + (y_2 - y_1)^2}$$

Some aspects of coordinate geometry simply involve solving a plane geometry question by using an xy-coordinate plane. Here's an example of one.

EXAMPLE:

Find the perimeter of $\triangle ABC$ given its vertices are $A(2, 2)$, $B(-1, 5)$, and $C(-5, 2)$.

This problem requires applying the distance formula three times to find the lengths of the three sides of the triangle. Solve for AB, BC, and AC as follows:

$$AB = \sqrt{(2 - -1)^2 + (2 - 5)^2} = \sqrt{(3)^2 + (-3)^2} = \sqrt{9 + 9} = \sqrt{18} = 3\sqrt{2}$$

$$BC = \sqrt{(-1 - -5)^2 + (5 - 2)^2} = \sqrt{(4)^2 + (3)^2} = \sqrt{16 + 9} = \sqrt{25} = 5$$

$$AC = \sqrt{(2 - -5)^2 + (2 - 2)^2} = \sqrt{(7)^2 + (0)^2} = \sqrt{49} = 7$$

Notice that $\overline{AC}$ is a horizontal line segment, so the distance from A to C can be easily found be determining the change in the x coordinates. $|2 - -5| = 7$. The perimeter of the triangle is

$7 + 5 + 3\sqrt{2}$

$12 + 3\sqrt{2}$ Answer

The concept of distance can also be applied to finding the area of figures in a coordinate plane. Use the distance formula to find the length of the base and/or height of a figure and substitute these values into the appropriate area formula. (See Chapter 5, "Plane Geometry," for a review of area formulas.)

EXAMPLE:

Find the area of parallelogram $ABCD$ given its vertices are $A(3, 1)$, $B(2, -1)$, $C(-1, -1)$, and $D(0, 1)$.

Sketch a diagram to help picture the parallelogram.

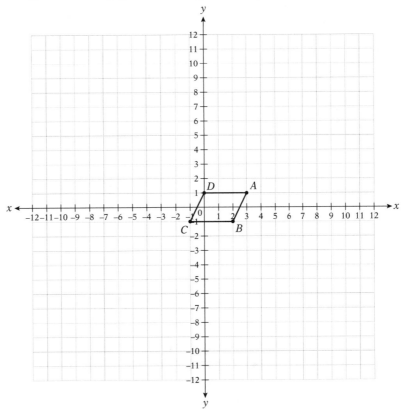

Assume $\overline{BC}$ is the base of the parallelogram and the height is the length of the perpendicular from vertex D to side $\overline{BC}$. Notice that there is no change in the y-coordinate in the segment $\overline{BC}$, so the distance from B to C can be found simply by using absolute value.

$BC = |2 - -1| = 3$

The height is $|1 - -1| = 2$

The area of the parallelogram is therefore

$A = bh = 3(2) = 6$

6 units^2 Answer

Slope

Slope is the measure of the steepness of a line. The slope of a line containing the points (x_1, y_1) and (x_2, y_2) is

$$\text{slope} = \frac{\text{rise}}{\text{run}} = \frac{\text{change in } y}{\text{change in } x} = \frac{y_2 - y_1}{x_2 - x_1}$$

Horizontal lines have no change in y, so the slope of a horizontal line is zero:

$$m = \frac{0}{\text{change in } x} = 0$$

Vertical lines have no change in x. Since you cannot divide by zero, vertical lines have an undefined slope.

$$m = \frac{\text{change in } y}{0} = \text{undefined}$$

A line having *positive slope* rises from left to right, and a line having *negative slope* falls from left to right.

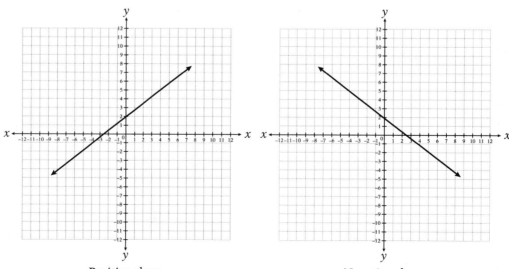

Positive slope   Negative slope

EXAMPLE:

Find the slope of the line containing the points $S(6, -9)$ and $R(-2, -5)$.

$$m = \frac{y_2 - y_1}{x_2 - x_1}$$

$$m = \frac{-5 - -9}{-2 - 6}$$

$$m = \frac{4}{-8}$$

$$m = \frac{-1}{2} \quad \text{Answer}$$

In the above example, we subtracted the coordinates of S from R. Order doesn't matter, however, as long as you choose the same order in the numerator and the denominator. We could have found the slope by subtracting the coordinates of R from S to get the same answer:

$$m = \frac{-9 - -5}{6 - -2} = \frac{-4}{8} = \frac{-1}{2}$$

Slope of Parallel and Perpendicular Lines

You can determine whether or not lines are parallel (never intersect) or perpendicular (intersect at a right angle) by examining their slope:

1. Parallel lines have the *same slope*: $m_1 = m_2$
2. Perpendicular lines have slopes that are *negative reciprocals*: $m_1 m_2 = -1$

EXAMPLE:

Find the slope of the perpendicular bisector of $\overline{AB}$ given $A(0, -2)$ and $B(3, 3)$.

The slope of $\overline{AB}$ is

$$m = \frac{y_2 - y_1}{x_2 - x_1}$$

$$m = \frac{3 - -2}{3 - 0} = \frac{5}{3}$$

The slope of *any* line perpendicular to $\overline{AB}$, including the perpendicular bisector, is the opposite reciprocal of $\frac{5}{3}$.

$$m = \frac{-3}{5} \quad \text{Answer}$$

Equations of Lines

Linear equations are equations whose graphs are straight lines. Equations containing two variables x and y raised to the first power are linear. By definition, linear equations have a constant slope.

The following equations are NOT linear:

$$3x^2 + 2y^2 = 1 \qquad \frac{3}{x} + 4y = 5$$

The following equations are linear:

Slope-Intercept Form	Point-Slope Form	Standard Form
$y = mx + b$	$y - y_1 = m(x - x_1)$	$Ax + By = C$

The three forms of the equation of a line are further explained in the succeeding paragraphs.

HORIZONTAL AND VERTICAL LINES

The most basic forms of linear equations are horizontal and vertical lines. Horizontal lines are written in the form $y = a$, where a is any constant. Vertical lines are in the form $x = a$, where, again, a is any constant.

EXAMPLE:

Find the point of intersection of the lines $y = 7$ and $x = 5$.

The graph of the two lines clearly shows their intersection.

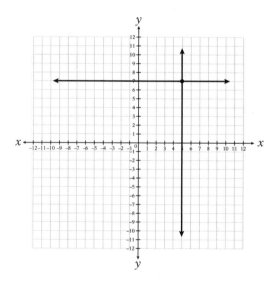

(5, 7)   Answer

STANDARD FORM

The *standard form* of the equation of a line is:

$Ax + By = C$ (where A and B are both $\neq 0$)

The *slope* of a line in standard form is $\dfrac{-A}{B}$ $(B \neq 0)$.

EXAMPLE:

Find the slope of the line $6x + 3y + 1 = 0$.

If you remember that the slope of a line in standard form is $\dfrac{-A}{B}$, this problem can be quickly solved. You may want to rewrite the equation in standard form, although this does not affect the calculation of slope.

$6x + 3y = -1$

$$m = \frac{-6}{3} = -2 \quad \text{Answer}$$

POINT-SLOPE FORM

There is exactly one line passing through a given point having a given slope. Because this is true, a line can also be written in what is called point-slope form. The *point-slope form* of a line containing the point (x_1, y_1) with a slope of m is

$$y - y_1 = m(x - x_1)$$

EXAMPLE:

Find the equation of the line in point-slope form through points $A(1, 10)$ and $B(3, 0)$.

Start by finding the slope:

$$m = \frac{y_2 - y_1}{x_2 - x_1} = \frac{0 - 10}{3 - 1} = \frac{-10}{2} = -5$$

Now, choose one of the two points and substitute its x- and y-coordinates into x_1 and y_1 in the point-slope form of a line. Let's choose point A:

$y - 10 = -5(x - 1)$ Answer

Choosing point B instead of A results in the same line. $y - 0 = -5(x - 3)$. You can compare the two equations by rewriting each in standard form:

$y - 10 = -5(x - 1)$	$y - 0 = -5(x - 3)$
$y - 10 = -5x + 5$	$y = -5x + 15$
$5x + y = 15$	$5x + y = 15$

SLOPE-INTERCEPT FORM

The *slope-intercept form* of a line with slope of m and y-intercept b is

$$y = mx + b$$

The y-intercept is the point where the line intersects the y-axis. If the y-intercept is 5, the line intersects the y-axis at the point $(0, 5)$. If the y-intercept is $\dfrac{-1}{2}$, the line intersects the y-axis at the point $\left(0, \dfrac{-1}{2}\right)$.

EXAMPLE:

Which of the following lines is parallel to the line $y = 5x - 1$?

(A) $y = 5x - \dfrac{1}{5}$

(B) $y = -5x - \dfrac{1}{5}$

(C) $y = -5x + \dfrac{1}{5}$

(D) $y = \dfrac{-1}{5}x - 1$

(E) $y = \dfrac{-1}{5}x + 1$

Recall that parallel lines have the same slope. Answers B, C, D, and E can quickly be eliminated, since their slopes do not equal 5, the x coefficient of the given line. Answer A is the only equation in which $m = 5$, so A is the correct answer.

The correct answer is A.   Answer

EXAMPLE:

Find the equation of the line with a slope of 3 containing the point (9, 7). Write your answer in slope-intercept form.

Using $m = 3$, you can write the equation of the line as:

$y = 3x + b$

Since (9, 7) is a point on the line, let $x = 9$ and $y = 7$ and solve for b.

$7 = 3(9) + b$

$7 = 27 + b$

$-20 = b$

Now you have enough information to write the slope-intercept form of the line.

$y = 3x - 20$ Answer

Since you are given the slope of the line and a point on it, you may be inclined to immediately use the point-slope form of the line. Doing so results in the equation:

$y - 7 = 3(x - 9)$

Now solve for y to get

$y - 7 = 3x - 27$

$y = 3x - 20$

Notice that you get the same final answer.

DETERMINING X- AND Y-INTERCEPTS

The y-intercept of a line is the point where $x = 0$ and the x-intercept is the point where $y = 0$.

EXAMPLE:

Determine the x- and y-intercepts of the line $3x - 4y = 12$.

Let's first determine the y-intercept by letting $x = 0$ and solving for y:

$$3(0) - 4y = 12$$
$$-4y = 12$$
$$y = -3$$

Now, let's determine the x-intercept by letting $y = 0$ and solving for x.

$$3x - 4(0) = 12$$
$$3x = 12$$
$$x = 4$$

The intercepts are $(0, -3)$ and $(4, 0)$.   Answer

EXAMPLE:

Find the equation of the line with y-intercept $(0, 4)$ and x-intercept $(-3, 0)$. Write your answer in standard form.

The slope of the line is $m = \dfrac{4 - 0}{0 - (-3)} = \dfrac{4}{3}$. Since its y-intercept is $(0, 4)$, $b = 4$.

In slope-intercept form, the equation of the line is

$$y = \frac{4}{3}x + 4$$

To determine the standard form of the equation, multiply through by 3.

$$3y = 4x + 12$$
$$-4x + 3y = 12$$ Answer

Circles

So far, we have been focused on graphing lines in an xy-coordinate plane. The Level 1 test includes questions on some curved graphs; however, they mainly involve circles and parabolas. Circle questions involve manipulating the standard form of the equation of a circle.

Recall that a circle is defined as the set of all points at a given distance from a given point. The set of all points at a distance of 2 units from the origin can be written as:

$$x^2 + y^2 = 2^2$$

In standard form, the equation of a circle with center (h, k) and radius r is:

$$(x - h)^2 + (y - k)^2 = r^2$$

The set of all points at a distance of 5 from the point (–2, 1) would, therefore, be

$$(x + 2)^2 + (y - 1)^2 = 5^2$$

EXAMPLE:

Find the x- and y-intercepts of the graph of $x^2 + y^2 = 9$.

First, recognize that this is the graph of a circle with center (0, 0) and radius 3. Picture the circle or sketch a graph to help visualize the intercepts.

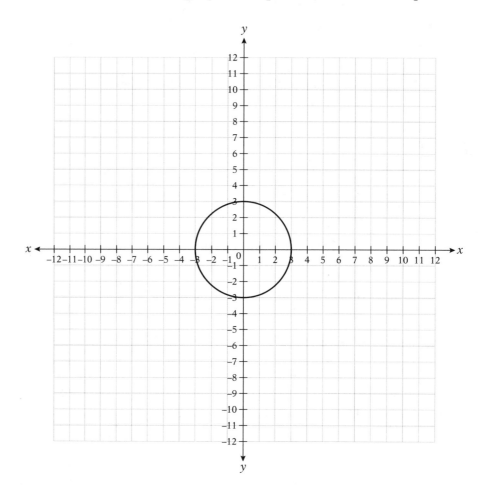

This circle is the set of all points at a distance of 3 from the origin. The intercepts can be determined by moving 3 units to the right and left of the origin, and then moving 3 units up and down from the origin.

The intercepts are (3, 0), (–3, 0), (0, 3), and (0, –3).   Answer

EXAMPLE:

Find the equation of a circle with a center in quadrant II that is tangent to both the x- and y-axis with a radius of 4.

Since the circle's center is in quadrant II, its x-coordinate must be negative and its y-coordinate must be positive. The radius is 4, which tells you that the points (0, 4) and (–4, 0) are on the circle. These are the tangent points. The circle's center must, therefore, be (–4, 4).

Now you have enough information to write the standard form of the equation of the circle:

$(x - -4)^2 + (y - 4)^2 = 4^2$

$(x + 4)^2 + (y - 4)^2 = 16$ Answer

Parabolas

A *parabola* is the second type of curved graph that you may find on the Level 1 test. The *vertex* of a parabola is a turning point where a decreasing graph begins to increase, or vice versa. The most basic parabola is $y = x^2$. This parabola has a vertex at the origin and is concave up. Similarly, the graph of $y = -x^2$ also has a vertex at the origin but is concave down.

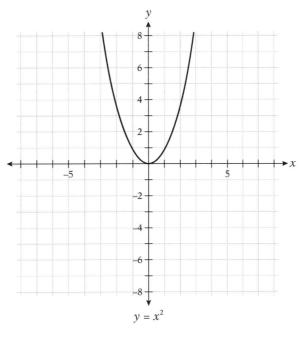

$y = x^2$

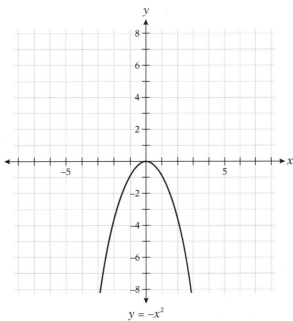

$y = -x^2$

You should know that the graph of a quadratic equation $y = ax^2 + bx + c$ is a parabola. The standard form of a parabola is

$$y - k = a(x - h)^2$$

where (h, k) is the vertex.

The graph opens upward when $a > 0$ and opens downward when $a < 0$. The greater $|a|$, the more narrow the graph becomes. Parabolas in this form have an axis of symmetry at $x = h$.

Parabolas can also be in the form $x - k = a(y - h)^2$. Parabolas in this form open right if $a > 0$, open left if $a < 0$, and have an axis of symmetry at $y = k$. The most basic parabolas in this form are $x = y^2$ and $x = -y^2$.

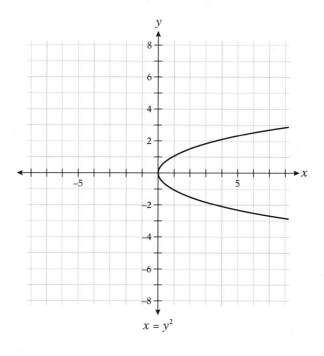

$$x = y^2$$

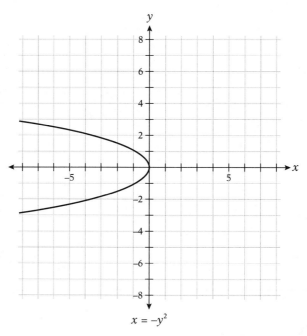

$$x = -y^2$$

Parabolas in the form $x - k = a(y - h)^2$ are NOT functions, though, since they do not pass the vertical line test. There is not a one-to-one correspondence been a given x value and its corresponding y values for these parabolas.

EXAMPLE:

Determine the vertex of the graph of $y = (x + 1)^2 + 7$.

Recognize that this is the graph of a parabola. The parabola is concave up, since $a = 1$. In standard form, the equation becomes

$y - 7 = (x + 1)^2$

The vertex is $(-1, 7)$.   Answer

As mentioned, the vertex of a parabola is a turning point where a decreasing graph begins to increase, or vice versa. Because of this, the vertex represents either the maximum or minimum value of the graph. The vertex is a *maximum* if the parabola is concave down and *minimum* if the parabola is concave up. The x-coordinate of the parabola is the x value of the maximum or minimum of the function. The *maximum value of a function* is the y-coordinate of the vertex.

EXAMPLE:

Find the minimum value of the function $f(x) = 2x + x^2$.

There are many ways to go about solving for the minimum of a function like this. Remember that the minimum value is the y-coordinate of the parabola's vertex. You could find the vertex by doing one of the following:

1. Complete the square to write the parabola in standard form.

    $y + 1 = x^2 + 2x + 1$

    $y + 1 = (x + 1)^2$

    Since the vertex is $(-1, -1)$, the minimum value of the function is -1.

2. Find its x-intercepts and determine its axis of symmetry.

    $y = x(2 + x)$

    $0 = x(2 + x)$

    $x = 0$ or $x = -2$ so the intercepts are $(0, 0)$ and $(-2, 0)$.

    The axis of symmetry is halfway between the two intercepts, so the axis is $x = -1$.

    The x coordinate of the vertex must be -1, so solve for the y value.

    $f(-1) = 2(-1) + (-1)^2 = -2 + 1 = -1$

3. Use the fact that the maximum or minimum value of a quadratic function occurs when $x = \dfrac{-b}{2a}$.

$$y = ax^2 + bx + c$$

$f(x) = 2x + x^2$, meaning that $a = 1$ and $b = 2$.

$$\frac{-b}{2a} = \frac{-2}{2(1)} = -1$$

Solve for y when $x = -1$ to get $f(x) = -1$.

4. Graph the parabola on your calculator to see where the vertex is.

The third solution above works for any parabolic function, $y = ax^2 + bx + c$. Remember that the maximum or minimum value of a function is the y value when $x = \dfrac{-b}{2a}$. The value is a maximum when $a < 0$ and a minimum when $a > 0$.

Graphing Inequalities

Graphing inequalities results in the set of all ordered pairs (x, y) that make the inequality true when substituted for the variables. The set is usually infinite and is illustrated by a region in the plane. Think of an inequality as an equation. Graph the line represented by the equation (assuming the given equation is linear), and determine what region satisfies the inequality. Then shade this region.

EXAMPLE:

Graph $y < x + 5$.

Start by graphing the line $y = x + 5$. Since y is *less than* $x + 5$ and not *less than or equal to* $x + 5$, the line is dotted. Now determine whether to shade the region above or below the line. Choose a point below the line, say, $(0, 2)$, and see if it satisfies the inequality.

$2 < 0 + 5$

$2 < 5$ This is a true statement, so the region below the line $y = x + 5$ is the solution to the inequality. The graph is as follows:

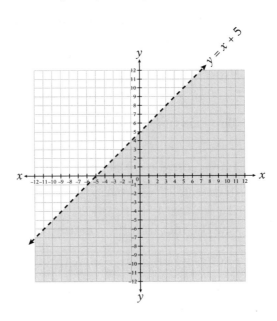

Graphing Absolute Value

Absolute value graphs are V-shaped. The most basic absolute value graphs are for $y = |x|$ and $y = -|x|$.

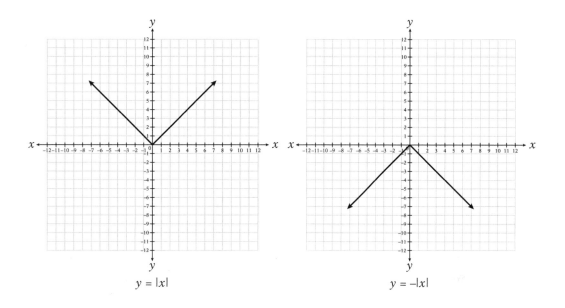

$$y = |x| \qquad\qquad y = -|x|$$

EXAMPLE

Based on the previous example, try graphing $y = |x + 5|$. When $x = -5$, you get the turning point of the V-shaped graph. The graph is

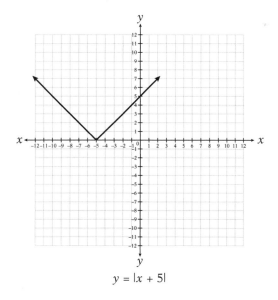

$$y = |x + 5|$$

Now try graphing an absolute value inequality $y < |x + 5|$. The graph is similar to the graph of $y = |x + 5|$ with a dotted line at $y = |x + 5|$. As with any inequality, determine whether to shade above or below the line. Choose a point, say, $(-8, 1)$, and see if it satisfies the inequality.

$1 < |-8 + 5|$

$1 < |-3|$

$1 < 3$ This is a true statement, so the region below the graph satisfies the inequality. The graph is as follows:

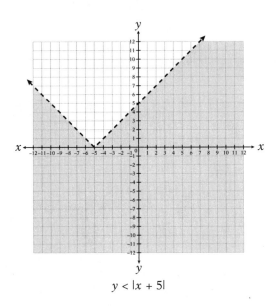

$$y < |x + 5|$$

CHAPTER 8
TRIGONOMETRY

This chapter provides a review of basic trigonometry principles. Six to eight percent of the Level 1 test questions relate to trigonometry. The 6 to 8 percent works out to be 3 or 4 questions, which are usually grouped with the more difficult questions toward the end of the Level 1 test. The pie chart shows approximately how much of the Level 1 test is related to trigonometry:

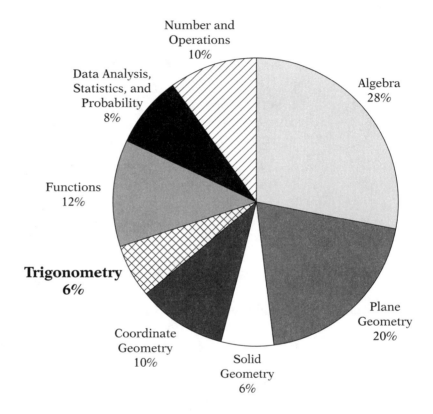

The following trigonometry topics are covered in this chapter:

1. Right Triangle Trigonometry

2. Relationships Among Trigonometric Ratios
    a. Secant, Cosecant, Cotangent
    b. Cofunction Identities
    c. Inverse Functions

3. Special Right Triangles

4. Trigonometric Identities

Right Triangle Trigonometry

Trigonometry means "the measurement of triangles," and one aspect of trigonometry relates to the study of the relationships between the sides and angles of right triangles. Those three ratios are presented below. They are true when focusing on one acute angle in a right triangle. Take ΔABC, for example:

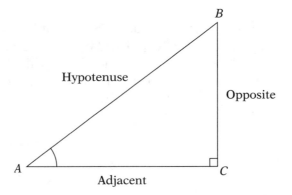

$\overline{BC}$ is the side opposite the given angle (in this case ∠A). $\overline{AC}$ is the side adjacent, or next to, ∠A. $\overline{AB}$ is the hypotenuse, since it's the side opposite the 90° angle. The three trigonometric ratios for ∠A are

$$\text{sine } \angle A = \frac{\text{opposite}}{\text{hypotenuse}} = \frac{BC}{AB}$$

$$\text{cosine } \angle A = \frac{\text{adjacent}}{\text{hypotenuse}} = \frac{AC}{AB}$$

$$\text{tangent } \angle A = \frac{\text{opposite}}{\text{adjacent}} = \frac{BC}{AC}$$

The abbreviation **SOH CAH TOA** is used to remember the ratios shown above. Typically sine, cosine, and tangent are abbreviated as *sin, cos,* and *tan,* as they are on the your calculator's buttons.

EXAMPLE:

In the right triangle below, $m\angle XZY = 35°$. Find the length of $\overline{XY}$. Round your answer to the nearest hundredth.

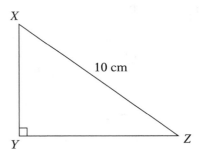

You know the length of the hypotenuse and you're missing the length of $\overline{XY}$, the side opposite ∠XYZ. The sine ratio will enable you to determine XY, since

$$\text{sine} = \frac{\text{opposite}}{\text{hypotenuse}}.$$

$$\sin 35° = \frac{XY}{10}$$

$$10(\sin 35°) = XY$$

$$10(0.57358) = XY$$

$XY = 5.74$ cm   Answer

Make sure your calculator is set to *degree mode* to do the trigonometry problems on the Level 1 test, because all angles will be in degrees. (Angle measures on the Level 2 test may, however, be given in radians.) To check the setting of your calculator, determine $\sin 30°$. In degree mode, $\sin 30° = 0.5$. If your calculator is incorrectly set to radian mode, $\sin 30° = -0.98803$. Change your mode to degree if this is the case.

EXAMPLE:

At a distance of 45 feet from a flagpole, the angle from the ground to the top of the flagpole is 40°. Find the height of the flagpole. Round your answer to the nearest hundredth.

It may help to sketch a diagram to solve this problem.

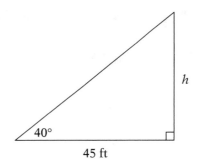

Now, determine which trigonometric ratio could be used to solve for h. You don't have enough information to use sine or cosine, since you don't know the length of the hypotenuse. Tangent $= \dfrac{\text{opposite}}{\text{adjacent}}$, so

$$\tan 40° = \frac{h}{45}$$

$$45(\tan 40°) = h$$

$$45(0.83910) = h$$

$$h = 37.76 \text{ feet} \quad \text{Answer}$$

EXAMPLE:

A 15-foot ladder leans against the side of a building, creating an angle of 28° with the building. How far is the base of the ladder from the side of the building?

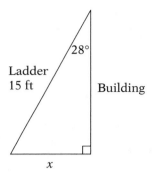

The ladder problem is commonly used in right triangle trigonometry problems. First, determine which trigonometric ratio to use. Since you know the hypotenuse and are trying to solve for the side opposite the 28° angle, it makes sense to use sine.

$$\sin 28° = \frac{x}{15}$$

$$15(\sin 28°) = x$$

$$x = 7.04 \text{ feet} \quad \text{Answer}$$

Relationships Among Trigonometric Ratios

SECANT, COSECANT, COTANGENT

There are three other trigonometric functions that are *reciprocal functions* of those already mentioned—sine, cosine, and tangent. Again, take a look at $\triangle ABC$:

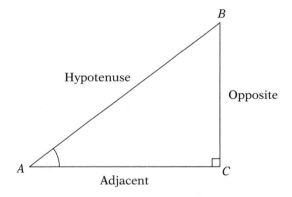

$\overline{BC}$ is the side opposite $\angle A$. $\overline{AC}$ is the side adjacent to $\angle A$. $\overline{AB}$ is the hypotenuse. The three remaining trigonometric ratios for $\angle A$ are

$$\text{cosecant } \angle A = \frac{1}{\sin A} = \frac{\text{hypotenuse}}{\text{opposite}} = \frac{AB}{BC}$$

$$\text{secant } \angle A = \frac{1}{\cos A} = \frac{\text{hypotenuse}}{\text{adjacent}} = \frac{AB}{AC}$$

$$\text{cotangent } \angle A = \frac{1}{\tan A} = \frac{\text{adjacent}}{\text{opposite}} = \frac{AC}{BC}$$

The cosecant, secant, and cotangent functions are abbreviated as *csc, sec,* and *cot* respectively. As with any reciprocal, a function multiplied by its reciprocal equals 1.

$$\sin x \csc x = 1 \quad \cos x \sec x = 1 \quad \tan x \cot x = 1$$

It is worth mentioning that the tangent and cotangent functions can be written in terms of sine and cosine as follows:

$$\tan x = \frac{\sin x}{\cos x} \quad \cot x = \frac{\cos x}{\sin x}$$

EXAMPLE:

Given ΔLMN is a right triangle with a right angle at vertex *M,* find the secant of $\angle N$.

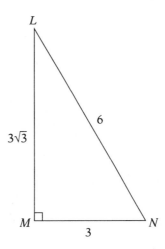

The hypotenuse of ΔLMN measures 6 and the leg adjacent to $\angle N$ measures 3. Write an equation for the secant of $\angle N$:

$$\sec N = \frac{\text{hypotenuse}}{\text{adjacent}}$$

$$= \frac{6}{3}$$

$$= 2 \quad \text{Answer}$$

EXAMPLE:

Simplify $\cot \theta \cos \theta + \sin \theta$.

Write the cotangent function in terms of sine and cosine to get

$$\frac{\cos \theta}{\sin \theta}(\cos \theta) + \sin \theta$$

$$= \frac{(\cos^2 \theta + \sin^2 \theta)}{\sin \theta}$$

$$= \frac{1}{\sin \theta}$$

$$= \csc \theta \quad \text{Answer}$$

COFUNCTION IDENTITIES

Sine and cosine, tangent and cotangent, and secant and cosecant are called *cofunctions*. Notice that in $\triangle ABC$, $\angle A$ and $\angle B$ are complementary. The acute angles of any right triangle are actually complementary, since the sum of all three angles in triangle must be $180°$.

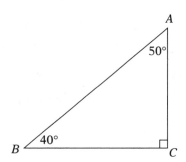

The complementary angles in $\triangle ABC$ result in the following relationships:

$\sin \angle A = \cos \angle B$		$\sin 50° = \cos 40°$
$\tan \angle A = \cot \angle B$	or	$\tan 50° = \cot 40°$
$\sec \angle A = \csc \angle B$		$\sec 50° = \csc 40°$

Knowing that $m\angle A + m\angle B = 90°$, you can write $\angle B$ in terms of $\angle A$: $m\angle B = 90° - m\angle A$. Substituting this new value of $m\angle B$ into the previous relationships gives you the following *cofunction identities:*

$\sin \angle A = \cos (90 - \angle A)$	$\cos \angle A = \sin (90 - \angle A)$
$\tan \angle A = \cot (90 - \angle A)$	$\cot \angle A = \tan (90 - \angle A)$
$\sec \angle A = \csc (90 - \angle A)$	$\csc \angle A = \sec (90 - \angle A)$

In general, the cofunction identities show that the sine of an angle is the cosine of its complement, and vice versa, the cosine of an angle is the sine of its complement. The same is true for secant and cosecant and tangent and cotangent.

EXAMPLE:

If $\csc x = \sec 70°$, then solve for x.

Remember that cosecant and secant are cofunctions:

$\csc x = \sec (90 - x)$

Set $\sec (90 - x)$ equal to $\sec 70°$ to determine x.

$90 - x = 70$

$x = 20°$ Answer

To check your answer, notice $\csc 20° = \sec (90 - 20)°$.

▨ INVERSE FUNCTIONS

Trigonometry can also be used to determine the measures of angles. Sin^{-1} x denotes the inverse sine of x, or the *arcsine.*

Sin^{-1} (0.707) means "the angle whose sine is 0.707."

To solve for the angle measure, use the sin^{-1} function on your calculator. (On most graphing calculators, this is accessed by pressing the second button and then the sin button.) Try calculating sin^{-1} (0.707) using your calculator. It should equal approximately 45°.

Similarly, cos^{-1} x denotes the inverse cosine of x, or the *arccosine,* and tan^{-1} x denotes the inverse tangent of x, or the *arctangent.* Both inverse functions can be solved in the same manner as arcsine by using the cos^{-1} and tan^{-1} function on your calculator.

Using your calculator, find the value of each of the following:

1. sin^{-1} (0.5)   (You're solving for "the angle whose sine is 0.5.")
2. cos^{-1} (0.8)   (You're solving for "the angle whose cosine is 0.8.")
3. tan^{-1} (1)   (You're solving for "the angle whose tangent is 1.")

The answers are, in order, 30°, 36.9°, and 45°. If you didn't get these solutions, check to make sure your calculator is set in degree mode.

EXAMPLE:

Given $\triangle JET$ is a 3-4-5 right triangle with a right angle at vertex E. Determine the measures of the two acute angles. Round answers to the nearest tenth.

Let's use arcsine to solve for both angles. Remember that $\sin = \dfrac{\text{opposite}}{\text{hypotenuse}}$ and the hypotenuse of $\triangle JET$ is its longest side. The sine of one of the acute angles is, therefore, $\dfrac{3}{5}$, while the sine of the second acute angle is $\dfrac{4}{5}$. Write two expressions using arcsine:

$\sin^{-1}\left(\dfrac{3}{5}\right)$ $\sin^{-1}\left(\dfrac{4}{5}\right)$

$= \sin^{-1}(0.6)$ $= \sin^{-1}(0.8)$

$= 36.9°$ $= 53.1°$

The two acute angles measure 36.9° and 53.1°.   Answer

EXAMPLE:

The diagonals of a rhombus measure 12 and 16 inches. What is the measure of the larger angle of the rhombus?

Recall that the diagonals of a rhombus are perpendicular, bisect each other, bisect the vertex angles of the rhombus, and form four congruent right triangles. Let x and y equal the measures of the acute angles of the right triangles.

Let x = the measure of the angle adjacent to the side measuring 8 units.

Let y = the measure of the angle adjacent to the side measuring 6 units.

$$\tan x = \frac{6}{8}$$

$$x = \tan^{-1}\frac{6}{8} = 36.87°$$

$$\tan y = \frac{8}{6}$$

$$y = \tan^{-1}\frac{8}{6} = 53.13°$$

One angle of the rhombus measures $2(36.87) \approx 73.7°$, while the other angle measures $2(53.13) \approx 106.3°$. Since the problem asks for the greater of the two angles, $106.3°$ is the correct answer.

$106.3°$ Answer

Special Right Triangles

Recall the two special right triangles mentioned in the Plane Geometry chapter, 45°-45°-90° and 30°-60°-90° triangles. Here they are mentioned again, because the ratios of their sides occur often in right triangle trigonometry. A *45°-45°-90°* triangle is an isosceles right triangle whose sides are in the ratio $x{:}x{:}x\sqrt{2}$, while a *30°-60°-90°* triangle is a scalene right triangle whose sides are in the ratio $x{:}x\sqrt{3}{:}2x$.

For each special right triangle below, identify the sine, cosine, and tangent of the acute angles:

$$\sin\angle T = \frac{1}{\sqrt{2}} = \frac{1}{\sqrt{2}}\left(\frac{\sqrt{2}}{\sqrt{2}}\right) \qquad\qquad \sin\angle V = \frac{1}{\sqrt{2}} = \frac{1}{\sqrt{2}}\left(\frac{\sqrt{2}}{\sqrt{2}}\right)$$

$$= \frac{\sqrt{2}}{2} \qquad\qquad\qquad\qquad\qquad = \frac{\sqrt{2}}{2}$$

$$\cos\angle T = \frac{1}{\sqrt{2}} = \frac{1}{\sqrt{2}}\left(\frac{\sqrt{2}}{\sqrt{2}}\right) \qquad\qquad \cos\angle V = \frac{1}{\sqrt{2}} = \frac{1}{\sqrt{2}}\left(\frac{\sqrt{2}}{\sqrt{2}}\right)$$

$$= \frac{\sqrt{2}}{2} \qquad\qquad\qquad\qquad\qquad = \frac{\sqrt{2}}{2}$$

$$\tan\angle T = \frac{1}{1} = 1 \qquad\qquad\qquad\qquad \tan\angle V = \frac{1}{1} = 1$$

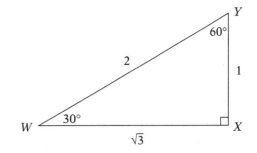

$$\sin \angle W = \frac{1}{2} \qquad\qquad\qquad \sin \angle Y = \frac{\sqrt{3}}{2}$$

$$\cos \angle W = \frac{\sqrt{3}}{2} \qquad\qquad\qquad \cos \angle Y = \frac{1}{2}$$

$$\tan \angle W = \frac{1}{\sqrt{3}} = \frac{1}{\sqrt{3}}\left(\frac{\sqrt{3}}{\sqrt{3}}\right) \qquad \tan \angle Y = \frac{\sqrt{3}}{1} = \sqrt{3}$$

$$= \frac{\sqrt{3}}{3}$$

Trigonometric Identities

Aside from the cofunction identities and reciprocal identities (i.e., cosecant, secant, and cotangent) previously mentioned, you may encounter problems involving one key trigonometric identity on the Level 1 test:

$$\sin^2 x + \cos^2 x = 1$$

An identity is an equation true for every value of the domain. Try substituting any number in for x and see what happens. Let's try $x = 25°$.

$$\sin^2(25°) + \cos^2(25°) = 1$$

$$0.422618^2 + 0.906308^2 = 1$$

EXAMPLE:

Simplify $(4\sin x)(3\sin x) - (\cos x)(-12\cos x)$.

First, multiply the terms:

$12\sin^2 x - -12\cos^2 x$

Notice that this resembles the identity $\sin^2 x + \cos^2 x = 1$. Now, simply factor out a 12.

$$= 12(\sin^2 x + \cos^2 x)$$

$$= 12(1)$$

$$= 12 \quad \text{Answer}$$

EXAMPLE:

Simplify $(1 + \sin \alpha)(1 - \sin \alpha)$.

Recall that $\sin^2 \alpha + \cos^2 \alpha = 1$, so $\cos^2 \alpha = 1 - \sin^2 \alpha$.

$$(1 + \sin \alpha)(1 - \sin \alpha) =$$

$$1 - \sin \alpha + \sin \alpha - \sin^2 \alpha =$$

$$1 - \sin^2 \alpha =$$

$$\cos^2 \alpha \quad \text{Answer}$$

CHAPTER 9
FUNCTIONS

This chapter provides a review of functions, focusing on algebraic functions. Thirty-eight to forty-two percent of the Level 1 test questions relate to Algebra and Functions combined. That translates to about 12 percent of the Level 1 test questions relating specifically to functions. Logarithmic, piecewise, recursive, parametric, and trigonometric functions are topics on the Level 2 test and are not covered here. The pie chart shows approximately how much of the Level 1 test is related to functions:

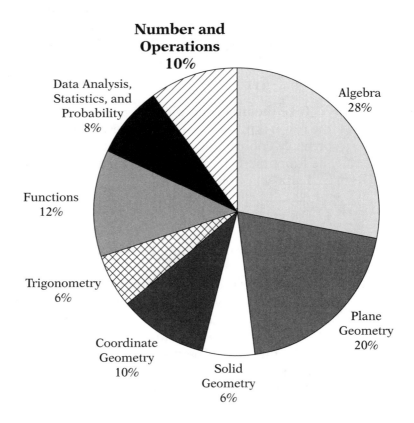

The following topics are covered in this chapter:

1. Functional Notation

2. Functions vs. Relations
   a. Graphing Functions

3. Composition of Functions
   a. Identity, Zero, and Constant Functions

4. Determining the Maximum or Minimum

5. The Roots of a Quadratic Function

6. Inverse Functions

Functional Notation

A *function* is a set of ordered pairs of real numbers. A function is often described by a rule that creates a one-to-one correspondence between sets of input and output values. The set of all input values is called the *domain* of the function, and the set of all output values is called the *range*. Unless otherwise noted on the SAT II test, the domain and range are assumed to be the set of all real numbers. Typically, a function is denoted by $f(x)$ and is read "f of x" or "the value of the function f at x." Functions can be represented by any letter, not just f, though. It is common to use f, F, g, G, h, and H to represent different functions. The following are examples of functions:

$$f(x) = x^2 \qquad\qquad F(x) = 3x \qquad\qquad g(x) = (x - 4)^2 + 1$$

Take the first example, $f(x) = x^2$. When the function is evaluated for $x = 2$, the result is $f(2) = 2^2 = 4$. $f(x)$ represents the y value when a function is graphed on an xy-coordinate plane. The point $(2, 4)$ would be included in the graph of the function $f(x) = x^2$ because when $x = 2$, $f(x) = 4$.

For a set of ordered pairs to be a function:

1. For each domain value of a function, there *must* be an associated range value.
2. A domain value cannot be matched with more than one range value.

When determining the domain of a function, look for two common restrictions: dividing by zero and identifying when the radicand is negative. You want to ensure that both cases do not happen.

A *linear function* is a function in the form $f(x) = mx + b$, where x, m, and b are real numbers. The graph of a linear function is a straight line with slope m and y-intercept b.

A *quadratic function* is a function in the form $f(x) = ax^2 + bx + c$, where $a \neq 0$. The graph of a quadratic function is a parabola.

EXAMPLE:

Which of the following mapping diagrams depicts a function?

I. 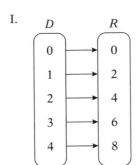   II.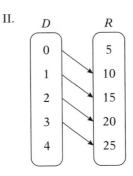

III. 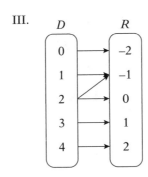   IV.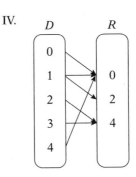

(A) I and II

(B) II and III

(C) III and IV

(D) I only

(E) II and IV

Remember that there must be a range associated with each domain value. II is not a function because 4 doesn't have an associated range. III cannot be a function because 2 is matched with both –1 and 0. IV cannot be a function because 1 is matched with both 0 and 2. I is the only function. D is the correct answer.

D   Answer

EXAMPLE:

Find the domain of $f(x) = \sqrt{100 - x^2}$.

The domain is the set of x values for which the function is defined. In other words, it the set of values allowed for x. We are assuming that the domain of the function is the set of real numbers. (On the SAT Subject test, you can assume this unless told otherwise.) The radicand, $100 - x^2$, must therefore be positive.

$100 - x^2 \geq 0$

$100 \geq x^2$

$10 \geq x$ and $10 \geq -x$

$10 \geq x$ and $-10 \leq x$

$-10 \leq x \leq 10$ Answer

EXAMPLE:

Given $f(x) = 2x - 5$, find $f(x - 3)$.

Replace x in the original function with the expression $x - 3$.

$f(x - 3) = 2(x - 3) - 5$

$f(x - 3) = 2x - 6 - 5$

$f(x - 3) = 2x - 11$ Answer

EXAMPLE:

Determine the domain of the function $g(x) = \dfrac{1}{x(x + 3)}$.

The fraction $\dfrac{1}{x(x + 3)}$ is not defined when the denominator $x(x + 3)$ equals zero. Dividing by zero is a common restriction of the domain of a function.

$x(x + 3) \neq 0$

$x \neq 0$ or $x \neq -3$

The domain is the set of all real numbers except 0 and -3.   Answer

EXAMPLE:

Find the domain and range of the function shown in the graph:

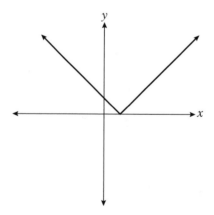

Although it is not asked in this question, do you know the equation associated with this graph? It is useful to know that "V-shaped" graphs are associated with absolute value, and this is the graph of $y = |x - 1|$. The domain is the set of x for which the function is defined. Are there any restrictions on x in this example? The graph shows that x is defined at zero and at all positive and negative values. The domain is the set of all real numbers. What about the range? Looking at the equation, you see that $y = |x - 1|$. Since y equals the absolute value of an expression and absolute value, by definition, is always positive, y must be greater than or equal to zero. You can determine this from the graph since there are no points in either quadrant III or IV where y is negative.

D = {all real numbers}, R = {y:$y \geq 0$}   Answer

Functions vs. Relations

You can test for a function algebraically or by using the vertical line test. The *vertical line test* states that any vertical line intersects the graph of a function at, at most, one point. Both tests determine if there is one and only one range (y value) associated with a given domain (x value).

EXAMPLE:

Is $y^2 = 5 + x$ a function?

Let's test this algebraically. Start by solving for y.

$y^2 = 5 + x$

$y = \pm\sqrt{5 + x}$

You can immediately see that for one value of x there are two corresponding values of y. Let $x = 4$, for example. $y = \pm\sqrt{(5 + 4)}$, so $y = \pm3$.

$y^2 = 5 + x$ is not a function.   Answer

EXAMPLE:

Is $x^2 + y^2 = 4$ a function?

Let's test this one using the vertical line test. You may be able to recognize that the graph is a circle, since $x^2 + y^2 = 4$ fits into the standard form of the equation of a circle: $(x - h)^2 + (y - k)^2 = r^2$. It center is (0, 0) and its radius is 2. A vertical line intersects the circle at two points as shown:

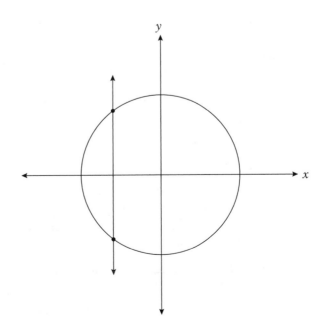

The equation does not pass the vertical line test.

$x^2 + y^2 = 4$ is not a function.   Answer

An equation that is not a function is called a relation. By definition, a *relation* is any set of ordered pairs. A function, therefore, is simply a type of relation consisting of ordered pairs with different x-coordinates. The two parabolas below show the difference between a relation and a function.

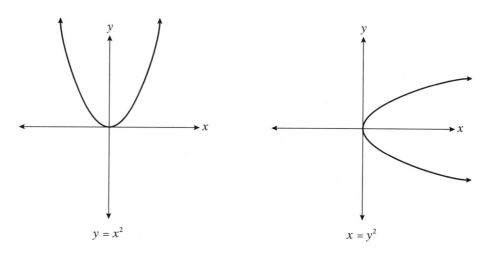

$$y = x^2 \qquad\qquad\qquad\qquad x = y^2$$

The graph of $y = x^2$ passes the vertical line test, so it is a function. The graph of $x = y^2$ does not pass the vertical line test (when $x = 4$, $y = 2$ or $y = -2$), so it is a relation.

EXAMPLE:

Which of the following is NOT a function?

(A) $\{(x, y): y = x\}$

(B) $\{(x, y): x = |y|\}$

(C) $\{(x, y): x^2 = y\}$

(D) $\{(x, y): y = \sqrt{x}\}$

(E) $\{(x, y): y = x^3\}$

Each answer is written in set notation and represents a set of ordered pairs. Answer A, for example, is read "the set of all ordered pairs (x, y) such that $y = x$."

(A) $y = x$ is a linear equation and passes the vertical line test.

(B) $x = |y|$ is a "V-shaped" graph that is concave left and does not pass the vertical line. When $x = 5$, for example, $y = \pm 5$.

(C) $x^2 = y$ is a parabola whose vertex is the origin and is concave up.

(D) $y = \sqrt{x}$ is a curve starting at the origin and moving upwards in the positive x direction. Since it is a square root equation, it is not defined when x is negative. The range, y, is restricted to positive values because y equals a square root.

(E) $y = x^3$ is a cubic curve that passes through the origin. The domain is the set of all real numbers, and each x has one y associated with it.

B is not a function.   Answer

GRAPHING FUNCTIONS

The most straightforward way to graph a function is to create an xy-table and find the coordinates of points for which the function is true. Start with the intercepts; set $y = 0$ and solve for x, then set $x = 0$ and solve for y. Knowing the graphs of a few common functions may save you time on the SAT Subject test. Be familiar with graphing the following functions:

- Identify function $f(x) = x$
- Constant function $f(x) = c$
- Absolute value function $f(x) = |x|$
- Squaring function $f(x) = x^2$
- Square root function $f(x) = \sqrt{x}$
- Cubing function $f(x) = x^3$

Composition of Functions

Two functions can be combined to form a *composition*. $f(g(x))$ is read as "the composition of f with g." Let $f(x) = x^2$ and $g(x) = x + 1$, and evaluate the following:

$$f(g(x)) = f(x + 1) = (x + 1)^2$$

$$g(f(x)) = g(x^2) = x^2 + 1$$

$$f(f(x)) = f(x^2) = x^4$$

$$f(g(2)) = f(3) = 9$$

Notice that $f(g(x))$ is not equivalent to $g(f(x))$ in this example.

EXAMPLE:

Given $g(x) = x + 3$, $h(x) = 9 - x^2$, and $g(h(x)) = 8$, find x.

$g(h(x)) = g(9 - x^2) = 9 - x^2 + 3 = 12 - x^2$

You're given that $g(h(x)) = 8$, so set $12 - x^2$ equal to 8 and solve for x.

$12 - x^2 = 8$

$4 = x^2$

$x = \pm 2$ Answer

EXAMPLE:

Given $f(x) = x^{\frac{2}{3}}$ and $g(x) = x^6$. Find $f(g(8x))$.

Start by finding $g(x)$.

$g(8x) = (8x)^6$

Now find $f((8x)^6)$.

$f((8x)^6) = [(8x)^6]^{\frac{2}{3}} = 8^{6\left(\frac{2}{3}\right)} x^{6\left(\frac{2}{3}\right)}$

$= 8x^4$

$= 4096\, x^4$ Answer

IDENTITY, ZERO, AND CONSTANT FUNCTIONS

The *identity function* is the function for which $y = x$. $f(x) = x$. Its graph is a diagonal line passing through the origin whose slope is 1.

The *zero function* is the function that assigns 0 to every x. $f(x) = 0$. Its graph is the horizontal line in which $y = 0$, otherwise known as the x-axis.

A *constant function* is any function that assigns a constant value c to every x. $f(x) = c$. Its graph is a horizontal line, $y = c$, whose y-intercept is the point $(0, c)$.

EXAMPLE:

Which of the following graphs represent(s) a constant function?

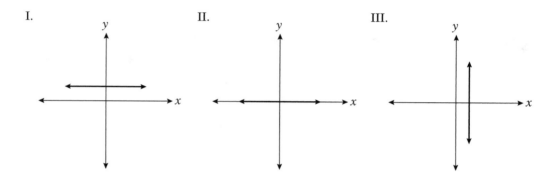

(A) I only

(B) II only

(C) III only

(D) I and II

(E) II and III

III is not a function since it does not pass the vertical line test. I represents the constant function, $y = c$. II represents the zero function, $y = 0$, but the zero function is also a constant function.

D is the correct answer.   Answer

Determining the Maximum or Minimum

The graph of a function can be increasing, decreasing, or constant for intervals of its domain. A function is

- **Decreasing** if the y value decreases from left to right
- **Increasing** if the y value increases from left to right
- **Constant** if the y value remains unchanged from left to right

Take parabola $y = x^2$, for example. The graph decreases when $x < 0$ and increases when $x > 0$. The *maximum or minimum* value of a function is often the point where the function changes behavior from decreasing to increasing.

The Maximum or Minimum of a Quadratic Function

Let $f(x) = ax^2 + bx + c$ where $a \neq 0$.

If $a < 0$, the parabola is concave down and has a maximum value.

If $a > 0$, the parabola is concave up and has a minimum value.

The maximum or minimum is $f(x)$ when $x = \dfrac{-b}{2a}$. In other words, it's

the y value of the parabola's vertex. It's $f\left(\dfrac{-b}{2a}\right)$.

EXAMPLE:

Find the maximum value of the function $f(x) = -4x^2 + 3x + 1$.

Notice a is less than zero, so the function does, in fact, have a maximum value. Solve for the x-coordinate of the function's vertex:

$$x = \frac{-b}{2a} = \frac{-3}{2(-4)} = \frac{3}{8}$$

Now find the value of the function when $x = \dfrac{3}{8}$.

$$f\left(\frac{3}{8}\right) = -4\left(\frac{3}{8}\right)^2 + 3\left(\frac{3}{8}\right) + 1$$

$$= -\frac{9}{16} + \frac{9}{8} + 1 = \frac{-9 + 18 + 16}{16} = \frac{25}{16}$$

The maximum value is $\dfrac{25}{16}$ or ≈ 1.563 Answer

EXAMPLE:

A gardener has 60 feet of fencing to enclose a rectangular garden. Find the greatest possible area of the garden.

Let $w =$ the width of the garden and $l =$ the length of the garden.

$2w + 2l = 60$

$w + l = 30$

Write l in terms of $w : l = 30 - w$. The area of the garden is $A = lw$, so substitute $30 - w$ in for l.

$A = (30 - w)w$

Notice that this results in a quadratic equation.

$A = 30w - w^2$ where $a = -1$ and $b = 30$.

The maximum value occurs when $w = \dfrac{-b}{2a} = \dfrac{-30}{2(-1)} = 15$.

When $w = 15$, $l = 30 - 15 = 15$, so the area is $15(15)$ or 225 square feet.

225 square feet   Answer

The Roots of a Quadratic Function

The *roots,* or solutions, of a quadratic equation are values of the variable that satisfy the equation. For example, factoring $x^2 + 2x - 15 = 0$ results in $(x + 5)(x - 3) = 0$. $x = -5$ and $x = 3$ are the roots of the equation. When dealing with functions, the roots are the x values that result when $f(x) = 0$. You can also think of the roots as the x-intercepts of the graph of a function or the *zeros* of the function.

If you're given the roots of a quadratic equation, you can use them to determine the equation itself. A quadratic equation can be thought of as:

$$a[x^2 - (\text{sum of the roots})x + (\text{product of the roots})] = 0$$

EXAMPLE:

The product of the roots of a quadratic equation is -14 and their sum is -3. Find a quadratic equation whose roots have the given product and sum.

Since the sum of the two roots is -3 and the product is -14, substitute these values into the equation.

$a[x^2 - (\text{sum of the roots})x + (\text{product of the roots})] = 0$

$a[x^2 - (-3)x + (-14)] = 0$

Setting a equal to 1 results in one possible answer:

$x^2 + 3x - 14 = 0$ Answer

EXAMPLE:

Find a quadratic equation with integral coefficients having roots 6 and 2.

The sum of the roots is 8 and their product is 12.

$a[x^2 - (\text{sum of the roots})x + (\text{product of the roots})] = 0$

$a(x^2 - 8x + 12) = 0$

Again, setting a equal to 1 results in one possible answer:

$x^2 - 8x + 12 = 0$ Answer

EXAMPLE:

Find a quadratic equation with integral coefficients having roots $-\sqrt{2}$ and $\sqrt{2}$.

The sum of the roots is 0 and their product is –2.

$a[x^2 - 0x + (-2)] = 0$

Setting a equal to 1 results in one possible answer:

$x^2 - 2 = 0$ Answer

Inverse Functions

The *inverse of a function* is denoted by f^{-1} and satisfies the compositions $f(f^{-1}(x)) = x$ and $f^{-1}(f(x)) = x$. f^{-1} is not necessarily a function (i.e., it doesn't have to pass the Vertical Line Test). A function has an inverse, however, if it passes the *Horizontal Line Test*. This means that if every horizontal line intersects the graph of a function in *at most* one point, then an inverse of the function exists.

If (a, b) is a point on the graph of f, then (b, a) is a point on the graph of f^{-1}. In other words, the domain of f equals the range of f^{-1}, and the range of f equals the domain of f^{-1}. Because of this property, the graphs of f and f^{-1} are reflections of each other with respect to the line $y = x$. Some examples of functions and their inverse are as follows:

$f(x) = x + 2$ $\qquad\qquad$ $f^{-1}(x) = x - 2$

$g(x) = \dfrac{(x + 3)}{2}$ $\qquad\qquad$ $g^{-1}(x) = 2x - 3$

$h(x) = x^3 - 1$ $\qquad\qquad$ $h^{-1}(x) = \sqrt[3]{x + 1}$

$f(x) = x^2$ $\qquad\qquad$ no inverse

$g(x) = \dfrac{1}{x}$ $\qquad\qquad$ $g^{-1}(x) = \dfrac{1}{x}$

$h(x) = \sqrt[4]{x}$ $\qquad\qquad$ $h^{-1}(x) = x^2$

On your graphing calculator, graph $y_1 =$ one of the given functions above, $y_2 =$ its inverse function, and $y_3 = x$ to see that the function and its inverse are reflections, or "mirror images," of each other over the line $y = x$. Notice that the squaring function, $f(x) = x^2$, does not have an inverse, since it doesn't pass the Horizontal Line Test. The square root function, $h(x) = \sqrt[4]{x}$, does, however, have an inverse because its domain is restricted to $x \geq 0$.

To algebraically solve for the inverse of a function, interchange y and x and solve for the new y value. This is the inverse function, if an inverse exists.

For example, take $f(x) = \dfrac{x + 4}{2}$. Replacing $f(x)$ by y results in $y = \dfrac{x + 4}{2}$.

Now interchange x and y and solve for y:

$$x = \frac{y + 4}{2}$$

$$2x = y + 4$$

$$2x - 4 = y$$

$$f^{-1} = 2x - 4$$

Check your answer by graphing f and f^{-1} to see that they are reflections over the line $y = x$.

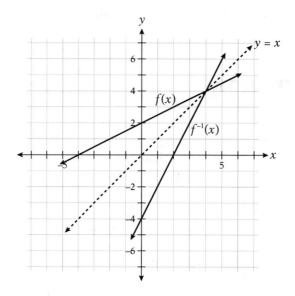

EXAMPLE:

If $f(x) = \dfrac{x + 6}{3}$ and f^{-1} is the inverse function of f, what is $f^{-1}(-1)$?

$$f(x) = \dfrac{x + 6}{3}$$

$$y = \dfrac{x + 6}{3}$$

$$x = \dfrac{y + 6}{3}$$

$$3x = y + 6$$

$$3x - 6 = y$$

$$f^{-1} = 3x - 6$$

$$f^{-1}(-1) = 3(-1) - 6 = -9 \qquad \text{Answer}$$

EXAMPLE:

If $f(x) = 4x - 1$, then what is $f^{-1}(x)$?

Interchange the x and y values in the function $f(x) = 4x - 1$ and solve for y.

$$y = 4x - 1$$

$$x = 4y - 1$$

$$x + 1 = 4y$$

$$f(x)^{-1} = \dfrac{x + 1}{4} \qquad \text{Answer}$$

EXAMPLE:

If $g(x) = x^4$, then what is $g^{-1}(x)$?

$$y = x^4$$

$$x = y^4$$

$\pm\sqrt[4]{x} = y$ There is not a one-to-one correspondence between x and y values.

No inverse   Answer

RATIONAL FUNCTIONS

A *rational function* is defined by a rational (i.e., fractional) expression in one variable and can be written as $f(x) = \dfrac{p(x)}{q(x)}$. Unlike the linear and quadratic functions that have been discussed thus far in this chapter, rational functions are not necessarily continuous. They contain a break in the graph at the point where the denominator equals zero. (Limits of rational functions are discussed in the Number and Operations chapter.) The graph of a rational function f has *vertical asymptotes* at the zeros of the denominator $q(x)$.

EXAMPLE:

Find the domain of $f(x) = \dfrac{x^2 - 4}{x^2 - 4x}$.

The domain is the set of x values for which the function is defined, so $x^2 - 4x$ cannot equal zero.

$$x^2 - 4x = 0$$

$$x(x - 4) = 0$$

$$x = 0 \text{ or } x = 4$$

The domain is all real numbers except $x = 0$ and $x = 4$.   Answer

Note that the graph of $f(x) = \dfrac{x^2 - 4}{x^2 - 4x}$ has vertical asymptotes at $x = 0$ and $x = 4$.

Many graphing calculators do not handle asymptotes well, so you may get a graph that appears to be continuous with "zigzags" at $x = 0$ and $x = 4$. The graph should be discontinuous at $x = 0$ and $x = 4$, since the function is undefined at these domain values. On a TI graphing calculator, try changing the Mode to Dot, instead of Connected, to better view the graph.

EXAMPLE:

Find the zeros of $f(x) = \dfrac{x^3 - 3x}{x^2 - 9}$.

The zeros of the function occur when $f(x) = 0$, or, in other words, at the x-intercepts of the graph.

$$0 = \frac{x^3 - 3x}{x^2 - 9}$$

$$0 = x^3 - 3x \qquad (x \neq \pm 3)$$

$$0 = x(x^2 - 3)$$

$$0 = x \quad \text{or} \qquad x^2 = 3$$

$$x = \pm\sqrt{3}$$

The zeros are: 0, $-\sqrt{3}$, and $\sqrt{3}$.   Answer

EXAMPLE:

What are the equations of the asymptotes of $f(x) = \dfrac{x^3}{x^2 - 1}$?

Vertical asymptotes occur at the zeros of the denominator.

$$x^2 - 1 = 0$$

$$x = \pm\sqrt{1} = \pm 1$$

Note there are no horizontal asymptotes, since the degree of the numerator is greater than the degree of the denominator.

$x = 1$ and $x = -1$ Answer

Higher-Degree Polynomial Functions

A *polynomial function* of x with degree n is given by:

$$f(x) = a_n x^n + a_{n-1} x^{n-1} + \cdots + a_2 x^2 + a_1 x^1 + a_0$$

where n is a nonnegative number, the coefficients of the x terms are real numbers, and $a_n \neq 0$.

A first-degree polynomial function is a *linear function: $f(x) = ax + b$ ($a \neq 0$).*

A second-degree polynomial function is a *quadratic function: $f(x) = ax^2 + bx + c$ ($a \neq 0$).*

The graphs of polynomial functions share the following properties:

1. They are continuous.
2. They have rounded curves.
3. If n (the highest exponent) is odd and $a_n > 0$, the graph falls to the left and rises to the right.
4. If n (the highest exponent) is odd and $a_n < 0$, the graph rises to the left and falls to the right.
5. If n (the highest exponent) is even and $a_n > 0$, the graph rises to the left and right.
6. If n (the highest exponent) is even and $a_n < 0$, the graph falls to the left and right.

Properties 3 through 6 describe what is known as the *Leading Coefficient Test,* which describes the right and left behavior of the graphs of functions.

EXAMPLE:

Determine the right and left behavior of the graph of $f(x) = -x^3 + 7x$.

The degree of the function is odd ($n = 3$) and its leading coefficient is -1.

The graph rises to the left and falls to the right.   Answer

The *zeros of a polynomial function* are the x values when $f(x) = 0$. A function of degree n has at most n real zeros.

EXAMPLE:

Find the real zeros of $f(x) = x^3 - 2x^2 - 8x$.

Since $f(x)$ is a third-degree function, it can have, at most, three zeros.

$x^3 - 2x^2 - 8x = 0$

$x(x^2 - 2x - 8) = 0$

$x(x - 4)(x + 2) = 0$

$x = 0$, $x = 4$, and $x = -2$ Answer

EXAMPLE:

Find the real zeros of $f(x) = -x^4 + 2x^3 - x^2$.

Since $f(x)$ is a fourth-degree function, it can have, at most, four zeros.

$-x^4 + 2x^3 - x^2 = 0$

$-x^2(x^2 - 2x + 1) = 0$

$-x^2(x - 1)^2 = 0$

$x = 0$ and $x = 1$ Answer

Note that both $x = 0$ and $x = 1$ are *repeated zeros*. Since the exponent on the factors is even, the graph touches the x-axis at these points, but it does not cross the x-axis. (If the exponent on the factors were odd, the graph would cross the x-axis at the repeated zeros.)

Long division and synthetic division are also useful in factoring and finding the zeros of polynomial functions.

EXAMPLE:

Divide $2x^3 - 9x^2 + 7x + 6$ by $x - 2$.

Let's divide using synthetic division:

```
2 | 2  -9    7    6
  |      4  -10   -6
  ‾‾‾‾‾‾‾‾‾‾‾‾‾‾‾‾‾‾‾
    2  -5   -3    0
```

The rightmost digit, 0, is the remainder. This means that $x - 2$ divides evenly into $2x^3 - 9x^2 + 7x$.

The quotient is $2x^2 - 5x - 3$.   Answer

The Division Algorithm states that:

$$f(x) = d(x)q(x) + r(x)$$

where $d(x)$ is the divisor, $q(x)$ is the quotient, and $r(x)$ is the remainder.

Applying this algorithm to the last example results in:

$$f(x) = (x - 2)(2x^2 - 5x - 3)$$

You can further factor $2x^2 - 5x - 3$ to get

$$f(x) = (x - 2)(2x + 1)(x - 3)$$

Using synthetic division helps to factor polynomials that are not special products and easily factorable.

Exponential Functions

An exponential function f with base a is given by:

$$f(x) = a^x$$

where x is a real number, $a > 0$, and $a \neq 1$.

The graphs of $y = a^x$ and $y = a^{-x}$ are as follows:

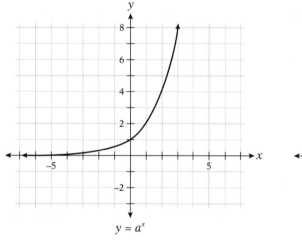

$y = a^x$

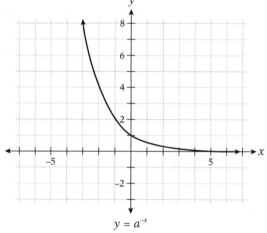

$y = a^{-x}$

Notice that both have a y-intercept of 1 and a horizontal asymptote at $y = 0$. The graph of $y = a^{-x}$ is a reflection of the graph of $y = a^x$ over the y-axis.

EXAMPLE:

Use the properties of exponents to determine if the functions $f(x) = 27(3^{-x})$ and $g(x) = \left(\dfrac{1}{3}\right)^{x-3}$ are the same.

Review the properties of exponents given in the Algebra chapter if you're unsure of how to solve this problem.

$$f(x) = 27(3^{-x}) = 3^3(3^{-x}) = 3^{3-x}$$

$$g(x) = \left(\frac{1}{3}\right)^{x-3} = (3^{-1})^{x-3} = 3^{-x+3} = 3^{3-x}.$$

$f(x)$ and $g(x)$ are the same functions.   Answer

EXAMPLE:

If $f(x) = 2^x$ and $g(x) = 3^x$, then determine when $3^x < 2^x$.

Both functions have a y-intercept of 0. Graph the functions on your graphing calculator (use the $^\wedge$ button to raise 2 and 3 to the x power) to compare the curves. When $x > 0$, $3^x > 2^x$.

$3^x < 2^x$ when $x < 0$.   Answer

CHAPTER 10

DATA ANALYSIS, STATISTICS, AND PROBABILITY

This chapter provides a review of elementary statistics. Six to ten percent of the Level 1 test questions relate specifically to data analysis, statistics, and probability. The statistics on the Level 1 test focuses on measures of central tendency, graphs and plots, linear regression and basic probability, and counting problems. Permutations, combinations, and standard deviation are included on the Level 2 test. The pie chart shows approximately how much of the Level 1 test is related to data analysis, statistics, and probability:

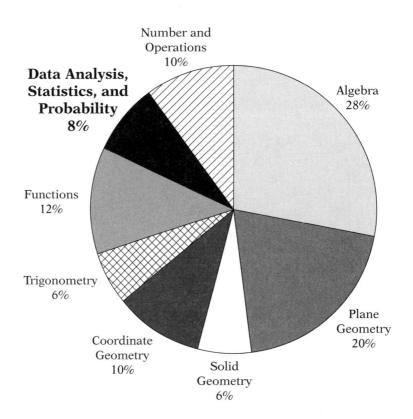

The following topics are covered in this chapter:

1. Counting Problems
2. Probability
3. Mean, Median, Mode
4. Data Interpretation

Counting Problems

The *Fundamental Counting Principle* states that if one action can be done in *a* ways, and for each of these a second action can be done in *b* ways, the number of ways the two actions can be done in order is $a \times b$.

For example, if an automobile manufacturer produces 4 different models of cars and each one is available in 5 different colors, there are

$$4 \times 5 = 20$$

20 different combinations of car model and color can be created.

Mutually exclusive events are events that cannot occur at the same time. For example, when you roll a die, you either roll a 1, 2, 3, 4, 5, or 6. 1, 2, 3, 4, 5, and 6 are mutually exclusive events. When you flip a coin, you get either heads or tails. Heads and tails are also mutually exclusive. If the possibilities being counted are mutually exclusive, then the total number of possibilities is the *sum* of the number of possibilities in each group.

EXAMPLE:

How many positive integers between 0 and 100 can be created using the digits 1, 2, 3, 4, and 5?

Consider all the possible 1-digit and 2-digit integers that can be created using 1, 2, 3, 4, or 5. These are *mutually exclusive* events.

1-digit integers:	5 possibilities for the ones digit
2-digit integers:	(5 possibilities for the tens digit)(5 possibilities for the ones digit)

Since the possibilities being counted are mutually exclusive, find the sum of the number of possibilities in each group.

$$5 + 5(5) = 30$$

30 integers can be created.   Answer

EXAMPLE:

John's high school offers 6 math courses, 4 English courses, and 3 science courses to students in his grade level. How many schedules are possible if John chooses a course in each subject?

Use the Fundamental Counting Principle to get

$$6 \times 4 \times 3 = 72 \text{ schedules}$$

72 schedules   Answer

EXAMPLE:

In how many different ways can a 15-question true or false quiz be answered? Assume every question must be answered.

There are 15 "events" and each one has two possible outcomes. Using the Fundamental Counting Principle, you get

$2 \times 2 \times 2 \times 2 \times 2 \times 2 \times 2 \times 2 \times 2 \times 2 \times 2 \times 2 \times 2 \times 2 \times 2 = 2^{15} = 32,768$

32,768 possible combinations of answers   Answer

Now, try the previous example assuming that you can leave questions blank. The number of true/false questions doesn't change, but now you have 3 possible outcomes for each question—true, false, or blank. The answer becomes 3^{15} or 14,348,907 possible combinations.

EXAMPLE:

Rosemarie wears a uniform to work. As part of her uniform, she can wear one of 3 pairs of pants, one of 4 shirts, and one of 2 hats. How many pant-shirt-hat combinations are possible?

Again, use the Fundamental Counting Principle to get

$3 \times 4 \times 2 = 24$

24 possible pant-shirt-hat combinations   Answer

EXAMPLE:

A certain state makes license plates consisting of 6 symbols (letters and numbers), and it is a requirement that the letters always come before the numbers. How many license plates of 6 symbols (letters and numbers) can be made using at least one letter in each?

There are 6 mutually exclusive events possible—license plates with 1, 2, 3, 4, 5, or 6 letters. Recognize that there are 26 possibilities for choosing a letter and 10 possibilities for choosing a number (the digits 0 through 9) and its okay to use a number or letter more than once.

1 Letter and 5 Numbers:	$26 \times 10 \times 10 \times 10 \times 10 \times 10 = 2,600,000$
2 Letters and 4 Numbers:	$26 \times 26 \times 10 \times 10 \times 10 \times 10 = 6,760,000$
3 Letters and 3 Numbers:	$26 \times 26 \times 26 \times 10 \times 10 \times 10 = 17,576,000$
4 Letters and 2 Numbers:	$26 \times 26 \times 26 \times 26 \times 10 \times 10 = 45,697,600$
5 Letters and 1 Number:	$26 \times 26 \times 26 \times 26 \times 26 \times 10 = 118,813,760$
6 Letters:	$26 \times 26 \times 26 \times 26 \times 26 \times 26 = 308,915,776$

The total number of possible license plates is the sum of the 6 mutually exclusive events:

$2,600,000 + 6,760,000 + 17,576,000 + 45,697,600 + 118,813,760 + 308,915,776 = 500,363,136$

500,363,136 possible license plates   Answer

EXAMPLE:

How many different seating arrangements can be made for 5 students in a row of 5 desks?

This problem is different from the previous ones, since order matters. Choose the student to sit in the first desk. There are 5 possibilities for choosing that student. Once one student is seated, he or she cannot be chosen again, so there are only 4 possible students who can be chosen to sit in the second desk. Using that logic, there are 3 possible students to choose for the third desk, 2 for the fourth, and 1 for the fifth. The problem can be solved using multiplication:

$5 \times 4 \times 3 \times 2 \times 1 = 120$

Notice that $5 \times 4 \times 3 \times 2 \times 1 = 5!$. You can use a *factorial* to solve problems in which order matters. A *permutation* is an ordered arrangement of elements. The number or permutations of n objects is $n!$. Hence there are $5!$ possible permutations in this problem.

120 seating arrangements   Answer

Probability

An experiment is an occurrence in which you do not necessarily get the same results when it is repeated under similar conditions. The *sample space* is the set of all possible outcomes of an experiment. When you toss a coin, the possible outcomes are heads, H, or tails, T. The sample space of a coin toss is written as {H, T}. The sample space for rolling a die, for example, is {1, 2, 3, 4, 5, 6}. An *event* is a set of outcomes and is a subset of the sample space.

If all outcomes are equally likely, the *probability* that an event, E, occurs is

$$P(E) = \frac{\text{the number of possible outcomes of E}}{\text{the total number of possible outcomes}}$$

EXAMPLE:

Two dice are rolled. Find the probability that the sum of the two numbers is less than 4.

When the two dice are rolled there are

$6 \times 6 = 36$ total possible outcomes

The sum of the two dice must, however, be less than 4. If the first die is a 1, the second could be 1 or 2. If the first die is 2, the second die could be a 1. If the first die is a 3, 4, 5, or 6, there are no possibilities that the second roll will result in a sum of less than 4. The possible outcomes are therefore

$\{(1, 1), (1, 2), (2, 1)\}$

the probability is $\dfrac{\text{the number of possible outcomes}}{\text{the total number of possible outcomes}} = \dfrac{3}{36} = \dfrac{1}{12}$.

$\dfrac{1}{12}$ Answer

EXAMPLE:

The are 12 pieces of colored chalk in a package—3 white, 3 yellow, 3 orange, and 3 green. If two pieces are selected at random, find the probability that both will be yellow.

The probability of choosing the first yellow piece of chalk is

$P(Y_1) = \dfrac{3}{12} = \dfrac{1}{4}$

Once one piece is chosen, there are only 11 pieces left in the package. The probability of choosing the second piece of yellow chalk is

$$P(Y_2) = \frac{2}{11}$$

The answer is therefore

$$\frac{1}{4}\left(\frac{2}{11}\right) = \frac{2}{44} = \frac{1}{22}$$

$$\frac{1}{22} \quad \text{Answer}$$

Notice that in the previous problem the first piece of chalk is *not replaced* before the second is drawn. This decreases the total number of outcomes to 11 when the second piece of chalk is selected.

EXAMPLE:

The probability of passing this week's math test is 70 percent, and the probability of passing this week's English test is 80 percent. What is the probability of failing both tests?

To get the probability that an event will NOT occur, subtract the probability that the event *will* occur from 1.

The probability of not passing this week's math test is $1 - 70\% = 30\%$.

The probability of not passing this week's English test is $1 - 80\% = 20\%$.

Notice that these are *independent events*, meaning that passing the math test is not dependent on how you do on the English test and vice versa. Multiply the probability of not passing both tests to get

$$30\%(20\%) = 6\%$$

6%   Answer

Mean, Median, Mode

Three different statistics are commonly used to measure central tendency. They are

> **Mean**—The average of the numbers
> **Median**—The middle number (when the data is ordered)
> **Mode**—The number that occurs the most

The mean is calculated by finding the sum of all the terms and dividing by the total number of terms. After the data is ordered, the median is simply the middle value of an odd number of terms or the average of the two middle values for an even number of terms. The mode is the most frequent value. It is possible for data to have more than one mode.

EXAMPLE:

The ages of the starting players on a high school soccer team are as follows:

14, 15, 15, 16, 16, 16, 17, 17, 17, 17, 18

Find the mean, median, and mode of the data.

1. Mean—Calculate the mean by finding the sum of all the ages and dividing that by the number of ages in question.

   The mean is $\dfrac{14 + 15 + 15 + 16 + 16 + 16 + 17 + 17 + 17 + 17 + 18}{11}$

   $= \dfrac{178}{11} \approx 16.18$

2. Median—The sixth term of 11 total terms is the middle number.

   The median is 16.

3. Mode—17 occurs 4 times in the given data.

   The mode is 17.

   Mean ≈ 16.18, Median = 16, Mode = 17   Answer

EXAMPLE:

Sarah has test scores of 65, 78, 81, 82, and 90. What must she score on her sixth test to maintain an average score of 80?

Let x be Sarah's sixth test score. Since you know the average, or mean, of the data, set up an equation equal to 80 and solve for x.

$80 = \dfrac{65 + 78 + 81 + 82 + 90 + x}{6}$

$80 = \dfrac{396 + x}{6}$

$480 = 396 + x$

$84 = x$

Sarah must score 84 on her sixth test.   Answer

EXAMPLE:

Find the median and mode of the following distribution:

0, 0, 1, 4, 6, 8, 8, 9

The mode is the number that occurs the most. Since both 0 and 8 occur twice, each number is a mode.

The median is the middle number. Since there's an *even* number of terms in the given distribution, the median cannot be one of the given terms. Instead, find the median by adding the fourth and fifth terms and dividing by 2. (In essence, you're finding the average of the two terms, since the middle occurs between them.) The median is

$\dfrac{4 + 6}{2} = 5$

The mode is 0 and 8, and the median is 5.   Answer

Data Interpretation

Data interpretation problems involve reading data from a histogram, pie chart, frequency distribution, bar graph, or other type of data display.

EXAMPLE:

The following histogram shows students' scores on a given test:

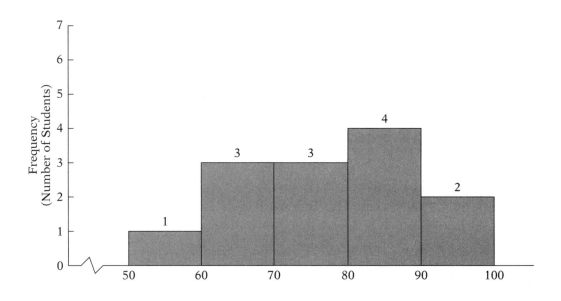

Each of the following is true EXCEPT:

(A) The interval 80–89 contains the most scores.

(B) The median score is in the interval 70–79.

(C) 9 students scored 70 or above.

(D) 13 students took the test.

(E) One student got 100 percent.

The most number of students scored in the interval between 80 and 89, since it is the highest bar in the histogram, making answer A correct. There's not enough information to find the exact median of the data, but you can see that the middle term, the seventh term, falls in the interval between 70 and 79. Answer B is therefore also correct. Nine (3 + 4 + 2) students scored higher than 70 and 13 students (1 + 3 + 3 + 4 + 2) students took the test, so answers C and D are correct. That leaves E. On quickly looking at the graph, you may mistakenly think that the highest score on the test was 100 percent. A histogram represents *intervals* of data, however. Two students scored in the highest interval, but you don't know enough information to conclude that a student received 100 percent.

E is the correct answer.   Answer

E X A M P L E :

The frequency distribution of the average daily temperatures in June is shown below. Determine the mean temperature. Round your answer to the nearest integer.

Temperature	Frequency
59	2
60	5
61	6
62	6
63	5
64	3
65	2
66	1

The mean is the sum of all the temperatures divided by the total number of days in question. Adding up the frequencies results in:

$2 + 5 + 6 + 6 + 5 + 3 + 2 + 1 = 30$ days

June actually has 30 days, so this number makes sense. Now find the sum of the 30 given temperatures and divide by 30.

$$\frac{59(2) + 60(5) + 61(6) + 62(6) + 63(5) + 64(3) + 65(2) + 66(1)}{30}$$

$$= \frac{1,859}{30}$$

$$\approx 61.97$$

62 degrees   Answer

CHAPTER 11

NUMBER AND OPERATIONS

This chapter provides a review of number sense and operations. Ten to fourteen percent of the Level 1 test questions relate to Number and Operations (formerly called Miscellaneous topics). These questions cover items outside the realm of the algebra, geometry, trigonometry, and statistics found on the rest of the test. Number and Operations questions on the Level 1 test tend to focus on logic, number theory, and sequences.

The College Board claims that students are not expected to have studied every topic on the SAT Math Level 1 test. You should expect some test questions, especially those under the Number and Operations category, to seem unfamiliar to you. In the practice tests at the end of this book, miscellaneous problems involving complex numbers, exponential functions, and logarithms are categorized under Number and Operations because they do not fit under any other category.

The pie chart shows approximately how much of the Level 1 test is related to Number and Operations:

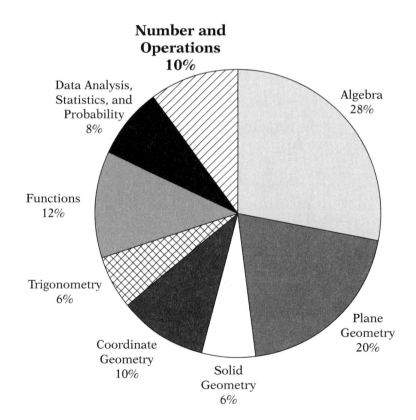

The following topics are covered in this chapter:

1. Invented Operations
2. "In Terms Of" Problems

   3. Sequences
      a. Arithmetic Sequences
      b. Geometric Sequences

   4. Logic

   5. Number Theory

Invented Operations

"Invented operations" appear often in standardized tests. This type of question introduces a new symbol that represents a made-up mathematical operation. Think back to learning what the symbols +, −, ×, ÷, and $\sqrt{}$ represent. When presented with a plus sign, +, you learned to add the number on the left of the symbol to the number on the right. Don't panic when the symbol presented in one of these problems looks unfamiliar. It should, since the symbol is made up for the problem.

EXAMPLE:

The operation ◙ is defined for all real numbers x and y by the equation:

$x ◙ y = 4x + \dfrac{y^2}{2}$. If $n ◙ 4 = 12$, find the value of n.

Remember that ◙ should NOT look familiar to you. Don't panic because you don't know what the symbol means! The question defines the symbol for you:

$x ◙ y = 4x + \dfrac{y^2}{2}$

When $x = n$ and $y = 4$, the result is 12. Substitute n and 4 into the equation for x and y, and solve for n.

$n ◙ 4 = 4n + \dfrac{4^2}{2} = 12$

$4n + 8 = 12$

$4n = 4$

$n = 1$ Answer

EXAMPLE:

The operation ▼ is defined for all real numbers a and b by the equation:

$a ▼ b = |a|^b$. If $-6 ▼ n = 216$, find the value of n.

Just like the previous example, the question defines the symbol ▼ for you:

$a ▼ b = |a|^b$

When $a = -6$ and $b = n$, the result is 216. Substitute -6 and n into the equation for a and b, and solve for n.

$-6 ▼ n = |-6|^n = 216$

$6^n = 216$

6 raised up to some power n equals 216. You know that $6^1 = 6$ and $6^2 = 36$. You may or may not know off the top of your head what 6^3 equals. $6 \times 6 \times 6 = 36 \times 6 = 216$. (On a graphing calculator, type 6 ^ 3.)

$n = 3$ Answer

"In Terms Of" Problems

Sometimes on the Level 1 test, you may be faced with one equation with more than one unknown variable. You don't have enough information to solve for an unknown, but you can solve for one variable *in terms of* the other variables.

EXAMPLE:

Given $2x - 3y = x - 6y + 9$, solve for y in terms of x.

Your goal is to isolate y on one side of the equation. This will give you the solution for y *in terms of* x.

$2x - 3y = x - 6y + 9$

$2x + 3y = x + 9$

$3y = -x + 9$

$y = \dfrac{-x + 9}{3}$ Answer

EXAMPLE:

Given $a + b = \dfrac{x}{d} + \dfrac{x}{c}$, find the value of x in terms of a, b, c, and d.

Again, your goal is to isolate x on one side of the equation. Start by multiplying both sides by the LCD, cd.

$a + b = \dfrac{x}{d} + \dfrac{x}{c}$

$cd(a + b) = cx + dx$

$cd(a + b) = x(c + d)$

$\dfrac{cd(a + b)}{(c + d)} = x$ Answer

Sequences

A *sequence* is a set of numbers listed in a certain order. You can also think of a sequence as a function whose domain is the set of consecutive positive integers. a_n is a term in the sequence and n is the number of the term. *Finite sequences* have a limited number of terms, while *infinite sequences* continue indefinitely. Some examples of infinite sequences are as follows:

$$1, 2, 3, 4, 5, \ldots n, \ldots$$

$$2, 4, 6, 8, 10, \ldots 2n, \ldots$$

$$3, 9, 27, 81, 243, \ldots 3^n, \ldots$$

$$1, 4, 9, 16, 25, \ldots n^2, \ldots$$

$$1, 4, 7, 10, 13, \ldots 3n - 2, \ldots$$

In general, infinite sequences are in the form: $a_1, a_2, a_3, a_4, a_5, a_n, \ldots$.

Arithmetic Sequences

If the difference between consecutive terms in a sequence is a constant, the sequence is an *arithmetic sequence*. The constant difference between terms is called the *common difference* and is represented by d. In a given arithmetic sequence $a_1, a_2, a_3, a_4, a_5, \ldots$, the difference between any two consecutive terms must equal d: $a_2 - a_1 = d$, $a_3 - a_2 = d$, $a_4 - a_3 = d$, and so on.

The *nth term of an arithmetic sequence* can be found using the equation $a_n = dn + c$, where d is the common difference, n is the number of the term, and c is a constant. Alternately, the equation $a_n = a_1 + (n - 1)d$ (where a_1 is the first term of the sequence) also represents the nth term of an arithmetic sequence.

The *sum of a finite arithmetic sequence* is: $S_n = \dfrac{n}{2}(a_1 + a_n)$.

EXAMPLE:

Find the nth term of the arithmetic sequence 6, 10, 14, 18, 22, ...

Since the sequence is arithmetic, there is a common difference between consecutive terms. $d = 10 - 6 = 4$. The nth term must be in the form:

$a_n = dn + c$

$a_n = 4n + c$

Because $a_1 = 6$, you can write an expression for the first term and solve for c.

$6 = 4(1) + c$

$2 = c$

The formula for the nth term is $a_n = 4n + 2$.   Answer

Notice the last example can also be solved using the equation $a_n = a_1 + (n - 1)d$. Substituting $a_1 = 6$ and $d = 4$ results in:

$a_n = 6 + (n - 1)4$

$a_n = 6 + 4n - 4 = 4n + 2$

EXAMPLE:

Find the sum of the terms in the sequence 2, 4, 6, 8, 10, 12, 14, 16, 18, 20, 22, 24, 26, 28, 30.

Of course, you could simply add these 15 terms to get an answer. A better way is to recognize that this is, in fact, an arithmetic sequence. $n = 15$, $a_1 = 2$, and $a_n = 30$. Substitute these values into the formula for the sum of a finite arithmetic sequence to get

$$S_n = 2 + 4 + 6 + 8 + 10 + 12 + 14 + 16 + 18 + 20 + 22 + 24 + 26 + 28 + 30$$

$$S_n = \frac{n}{2}(a_1 + a_n)$$

$$S_n = \frac{15}{2}(2 + 30)$$

$$S_n = \frac{15}{2}(32)$$

$$S_n = 15(16) = 240$$

240   Answer

EXAMPLE:

Find the sum of the integers from 1 to 200.

The integers from 1 to 200 form an arithmetic sequence having 200 terms. $n = 200$, $a_1 = 1$, and $a_n = 200$. Substitute these values into the formula for the sum of a finite arithmetic sequence to get

$$S_n = 1 + 2 + 3 + 4 + 5 + \cdots + 200$$

$$S_n = \frac{n}{2}(a_1 + a_n)$$

$$S_n = \frac{200}{2}(1 + 200)$$

$$S_n = 100(201) = 20,100$$

20,100   Answer

Geometric Sequences

If the ratio between consecutive terms in a sequence is a constant, the sequence is a *geometric sequence*. The constant ratio between terms is called the *common ratio* and is represented by r. In a given geometric sequence a_1, $a_2, a_3, a_4, a_5, \ldots$, the ratio between any two consecutive terms must equal r:

$\frac{a_2}{a_1} = r$, $\frac{a_3}{a_2} = r$, $\frac{a_4}{a_3} = r$, and so on, and r cannot equal zero.

The *nth term of a geometric sequence* can be found using the equation $a_n = a_1 r^{n-1}$, where r is the common ratio, n is the number of the term, and a_1 is the first term of the sequence. Using this formula, every geometric sequence can be written as follows:

$a_1, a_2, a_3, a_4, a_5, \ldots a_n, \ldots$ or $a_1, a_1 r^1, a_1 r^2, a_1 r^3, a_1 r^4, \ldots a_1 r^{n-1}, \ldots$

The *sum of a finite geometric sequence* is

$$S_n = a_1 \left(\frac{1 - r^n}{1 - r} \right) \quad \text{where } r \neq 1$$

The *sum of an infinite geometric sequence* is

$$S = \frac{a_1}{1-r} \quad \text{where} \ -1 < r < 1$$

EXAMPLE:

Find the nth term of the geometric sequence: $3, \dfrac{3}{2}, \dfrac{3}{4}, \dfrac{3}{8}, \dfrac{3}{16}, \ldots$

This is a geometric sequence because there is a common ratio.

$$r = \frac{\frac{3}{2}}{3} = \frac{3}{6} = \frac{1}{2}$$

Substitute the values $r = \dfrac{1}{2}$ and $a_1 = 3$ into the formula for the nth term to get

$$a_n = a_1 r^{n-1}$$

$$a_n = 3\left(\frac{1}{2}\right)^{n-1} \quad \text{Answer}$$

EXAMPLE:

The second term of a geometric sequence is $\dfrac{1}{2}$ and the fifth term is $\dfrac{1}{28}$. Find the common ratio.

Start by writing the two given terms in $a_n = a_1 r^{n-1}$ form.

$$a_2 = a_1 r^1 = \frac{1}{2} \quad \text{and} \quad a_5 = a_1 r^4 = \frac{1}{128}$$

You can then write a_5 in terms of a_2.

$$a_2 \times r \times r \times r = a_5$$

$$\frac{1}{2} \times r \times r \times r = \frac{1}{128}$$

$$\frac{1}{2} r^3 = \frac{1}{128}$$

$$r^3 = \frac{2}{128} = \frac{1}{64}$$

$$r = \sqrt[3]{\frac{1}{64}} = \frac{1}{4}$$

$$\frac{1}{4} \quad \text{Answer}$$

EXAMPLE:

Find the sum of the geometric sequence: $1, \dfrac{7}{10}, \dfrac{49}{100}, \ldots$

Divide the second term by the first terms to determine the common ratio,

$r = \dfrac{7}{10}$. Since this is an infinite geometric sequence, find its sum by using the formula:

$$S = \dfrac{a_1}{1 - r}$$

$$S = \dfrac{1}{1 - \dfrac{7}{10}}$$

$$S = \dfrac{1}{\dfrac{3}{10}}$$

$$S = \dfrac{10}{3} \quad \text{Answer}$$

Logic

The logic questions on the Level 1 test have to do with conditional statements, converses, inverses, and contrapositives. A *conditional statement* is an if-then statement that may or may not be true. Some examples of conditional statements are as follows:

> If two lines are perpendicular, then they intersect at a 90° angle.
>
> If given two points, then there is one and only one line determined by them.
>
> If today is Saturday, then it is the weekend.
>
> If today is the weekend, then it is Saturday.

Notice that the first three conditional statements are true, but the forth one is not. If today is the weekend, then it could also be Sunday. The *negation* of an if-then statement is formed by inserting the word *not* into the statement. Negating the third example above results in: "If today is not Saturday, then it is not the weekend." In general, if an if-then statement is given as "if p, then q," then the negation of the statement is "if not p, then not q."

Three other if-then statements are created by switching and/or negating the if and then parts of a given conditional statement.

Name	General Form	Example	True or False?
Conditional	If p, then q.	If $\angle Y$ measures 100°, then it is obtuse.	True
Converse	If q, then p.	If $\angle Y$ is obtuse, then it measures 100°.	False
Inverse	If not p, then not q.	If $\angle Y$ does not measure 100°, then it is not obtuse.	False
Contrapositive	If not q, then not p.	If $\angle Y$ is not obtuse, then it does not measure 100°.	True

Let's take a look at what happens when the given conditional statement is false.

Name	General Form	Example	True or False?
Conditional	If p, then q.	If two angles are supplementary, then they are right angles.	False
Converse	If q, then p.	If two angles are right angles, then they are supplementary.	True
Inverse	If not p, then not q.	If two angles are not supplementary, then they are not right angles.	True
Contrapositive	If not q, then not p.	If two angles are not right angles, then they are not supplementary.	False

Notice that when the given conditional statement is true, the contrapositive is also true. When the given conditional statement is false, the contrapositive is also false. This means that the contrapositive is *logically equivalent* to the conditional statement, and because of this, logic questions on the Level 1 test often ask about the contrapositive.

EXAMPLE:

The statement "If John lives in Boston, then he lives in Massachusetts" is logically equivalent to which of the following?

I.   If John lives in Massachusetts, then he lives in Boston.

II. If John does not live in Boston, then he does not live in Massachusetts.

III. If John does not live in Massachusetts, then he does not live in Boston.

(A) I only

(B) II only

(C) III only

(D) I and II only

(E) I, II, and III

The given statement is a conditional in the form "if *p*, then *q*" and it is a true statement. If you recall the properties of converse, inverse, and contrapositive statements, you can immediately determine that the contrapositive will also be true. The contrapositive is in the form "if not *q*, then not *p*" and coincides with answer III above.

If you don't recall the properties of converse, inverse, and contrapositive statements, take a look at each statement individually. I and II are false statements, so they cannot be logically equivalent to the given statement. The only possible answer is III.

The correct answer is C.   Answer

Number Theory

Number theory questions have to do with such concepts as properties of positive and negative numbers, properties of prime numbers, properties of integers, and properties of odd and even numbers. The following examples show possible number theory questions found on the Level 1 test.

EXAMPLE:

If *a* and *b* are both positive, *a* is odd, and *b* is even, which of the following must be odd?

(A) $b + 2a$

(B) ab

(C) $\dfrac{b}{a}$

(D) a^b

(E) b^a

Think of the terms in the expressions as being odd or even. The table below illustrates whether the answers are odd or even and gives a numeric example for each.

Answer	In Words	Example	Even or Odd?
$b + 2a$	even + 2(odd)	$4 + 2(3) = 10$	Even
ab	odd $\times$ even	$3(2) = 6$	Even
$\dfrac{b}{a}$	even $\div$ odd	$\dfrac{12}{3} = 4$ $\dfrac{20}{3} \approx 6.67$	Even (if it is an integer)
a^b	odd raised to an even power	$3^2 = 9$	Odd
b^a	even raised to an odd power	$2^3 = 8$	Even

The correct answer is D.

EXAMPLE:

If a is positive and b is negative, which of the following must be negative?

(A) $a + b$

(B) $a + |b|$

(C) $a - |b|$

(D) $|ab|$

(E) $|a|b$

Answers B and D are always positive because of the absolute value. Answers A and C could result in a positive or a negative value, so you cannot say that the expressions *must* result in a negative value. In answer E, $|a|$ is positive and b is negative. The product of a positive number and a negative number is always negative.

The correct answer is E.

PART III
SIX PRACTICE TESTS

PRACTICE TEST 1

Treat this practice test as the actual test and complete it in one 60-minute sitting. Use the following answer sheet to fill in your multiple-choice answers. Once you have completed the practice test:

1. Check your answers using the Answer Key.
2. Review the Answer Explanations.
3. Fill in the "Diagnose Your Strengths and Weaknesses" sheet and determine areas that require further preparation.

PRACTICE TEST 1

MATH LEVEL 1

ANSWER SHEET

Tear out this answer sheet and use it to complete the practice test.

Determine the BEST answer for each question. Then fill in the appropriate oval using a No. 2 pencil.

1. Ⓐ Ⓑ Ⓒ Ⓓ Ⓔ	21. Ⓐ Ⓑ Ⓒ Ⓓ Ⓔ	41. Ⓐ Ⓑ Ⓒ Ⓓ Ⓔ
2. Ⓐ Ⓑ Ⓒ Ⓓ Ⓔ	22. Ⓐ Ⓑ Ⓒ Ⓓ Ⓔ	42. Ⓐ Ⓑ Ⓒ Ⓓ Ⓔ
3. Ⓐ Ⓑ Ⓒ Ⓓ Ⓔ	23. Ⓐ Ⓑ Ⓒ Ⓓ Ⓔ	43. Ⓐ Ⓑ Ⓒ Ⓓ Ⓔ
4. Ⓐ Ⓑ Ⓒ Ⓓ Ⓔ	24. Ⓐ Ⓑ Ⓒ Ⓓ Ⓔ	44. Ⓐ Ⓑ Ⓒ Ⓓ Ⓔ
5. Ⓐ Ⓑ Ⓒ Ⓓ Ⓔ	25. Ⓐ Ⓑ Ⓒ Ⓓ Ⓔ	45. Ⓐ Ⓑ Ⓒ Ⓓ Ⓔ
6. Ⓐ Ⓑ Ⓒ Ⓓ Ⓔ	26. Ⓐ Ⓑ Ⓒ Ⓓ Ⓔ	46. Ⓐ Ⓑ Ⓒ Ⓓ Ⓔ
7. Ⓐ Ⓑ Ⓒ Ⓓ Ⓔ	27. Ⓐ Ⓑ Ⓒ Ⓓ Ⓔ	47. Ⓐ Ⓑ Ⓒ Ⓓ Ⓔ
8. Ⓐ Ⓑ Ⓒ Ⓓ Ⓔ	28. Ⓐ Ⓑ Ⓒ Ⓓ Ⓔ	48. Ⓐ Ⓑ Ⓒ Ⓓ Ⓔ
9. Ⓐ Ⓑ Ⓒ Ⓓ Ⓔ	29. Ⓐ Ⓑ Ⓒ Ⓓ Ⓔ	49. Ⓐ Ⓑ Ⓒ Ⓓ Ⓔ
10. Ⓐ Ⓑ Ⓒ Ⓓ Ⓔ	30. Ⓐ Ⓑ Ⓒ Ⓓ Ⓔ	50. Ⓐ Ⓑ Ⓒ Ⓓ Ⓔ
11. Ⓐ Ⓑ Ⓒ Ⓓ Ⓔ	31. Ⓐ Ⓑ Ⓒ Ⓓ Ⓔ	
12. Ⓐ Ⓑ Ⓒ Ⓓ Ⓔ	32. Ⓐ Ⓑ Ⓒ Ⓓ Ⓔ	
13. Ⓐ Ⓑ Ⓒ Ⓓ Ⓔ	33. Ⓐ Ⓑ Ⓒ Ⓓ Ⓔ	
14. Ⓐ Ⓑ Ⓒ Ⓓ Ⓔ	34. Ⓐ Ⓑ Ⓒ Ⓓ Ⓔ	
15. Ⓐ Ⓑ Ⓒ Ⓓ Ⓔ	35. Ⓐ Ⓑ Ⓒ Ⓓ Ⓔ	
16. Ⓐ Ⓑ Ⓒ Ⓓ Ⓔ	36. Ⓐ Ⓑ Ⓒ Ⓓ Ⓔ	
17. Ⓐ Ⓑ Ⓒ Ⓓ Ⓔ	37. Ⓐ Ⓑ Ⓒ Ⓓ Ⓔ	
18. Ⓐ Ⓑ Ⓒ Ⓓ Ⓔ	38. Ⓐ Ⓑ Ⓒ Ⓓ Ⓔ	
19. Ⓐ Ⓑ Ⓒ Ⓓ Ⓔ	39. Ⓐ Ⓑ Ⓒ Ⓓ Ⓔ	
20. Ⓐ Ⓑ Ⓒ Ⓓ Ⓔ	40. Ⓐ Ⓑ Ⓒ Ⓓ Ⓔ	

PRACTICE TEST 1
Time: 60 Minutes

Directions: Select the BEST answer for each of the 50 multiple-choice questions. If the exact solution is not one of the five choices, select the answer that is the best approximation. Then fill in the appropriate oval on the answer sheet.

Notes:

(1) A calculator will be needed to answer some of the questions on the test. Scientific, programmable, and graphing calculators are permitted. It is up to you to determine when and when not to use your calculator.

(2) All angles on the Level 1 test are measured in degrees, not radians. Make sure your calculator is set to degree mode.

(3) Figures are drawn as accurately as possible and are intended to help solve some of the test problems. If a figure is not drawn to scale, this will be stated in the problem. All figures lie in a plane unless the problem indicates otherwise.

(4) Unless otherwise stated, the domain of a function f is assumed to be the set of real numbers x for which the value of the function, $f(x)$, is a real number.

(5) Reference information that may be useful in answering some of the test questions can be found below.

Reference Information	
Right circular cone with radius r and height h:	Volume $= \dfrac{1}{3}\pi r^2 h$
Right circular cone with circumference of base c and slant height ℓ:	Lateral Area $= \dfrac{1}{2}c\ell$
Sphere with radius r:	Volume $= \dfrac{4}{3}\pi r^3$ Surface Area $= 4\pi r^2$
Pyramid with base area B and height h:	Volume $= \dfrac{1}{3}Bh$

GO ON TO THE NEXT PAGE

1. If $a = 2b - 10$ and $b = 3a - 5$, then $a =$

(A) 3
(B) 4
(C) 7
(D) -4
(E) -3

2. $\sqrt{\sin^2 9\theta + \cos^2 9\theta} =$

(A) -1
(B) $\sin 3\theta + \cos 3\theta$
(C) $\sin 9\theta + \cos 9\theta$
(D) 1
(E) $\sec 3\theta$

3. A fax machine sends n pages per minute. In terms of n, how many minutes will it take to fax a 25-page document?

(A) $\dfrac{n}{25}$
(B) $25 - n$
(C) $\dfrac{25}{n}$
(D) $25n$
(E) n

4. It is possible to have a triangle with all of the following sets of sides EXCEPT

(A) 1, 1, 1
(B) 1, 2, 2
(C) 3, 4, 5
(D) 9, 9, 18
(E) 7, 10, 16

5. If $x > 0$, then $\dfrac{x^{\frac{3}{4}}}{x^{-\frac{1}{4}}} =$

(A) $x^{\frac{1}{2}}$
(B) 1
(C) x
(D) $-x$
(E) x^{-1}

GO ON TO THE NEXT PAGE

6. In Figure 1, $\overline{XY} \parallel \overline{WZ}$. What is c in terms of a and b?

   (A) $a + b$
   (B) $a - b$
   (C) $b - a$
   (D) $180 - a - b$
   (E) $180 - a + b$

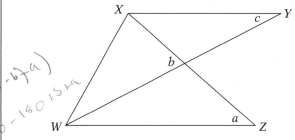

Figure 1

7. What is the slope of the line parallel to the line segment with endpoints $(0, -4)$ and $(2, 4)$?

   (A) 4
   (B) $\dfrac{1}{4}$
   (C) $-\dfrac{1}{4}$
   (D) -4
   (E) 0

8. In Figure 2, $m\angle ABC = 29°$ and $\overline{AB} = 12$. What is the length of AC?

   (A) 10.5
   (B) 6.7
   (C) 24.8
   (D) 5.8
   (E) 0.49

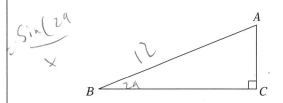

Figure 2

9. If $g(f(x)) = 2x + 1$ and $f(x) = \dfrac{1}{4}x - 1$, then $g(x) =$

   (A) $-\dfrac{8}{7}$
   (B) $8x + 9$
   (C) $\dfrac{1}{4}(2x + 1)$
   (D) $8x - 8$
   (E) $8x$

10. If $i^2 = -1$ and $7 - xi = x + y + 2i$, then $y =$

   (A) $9 - 2i$
   (B) $2 + 2i$
   (C) 7
   (D) 5
   (E) 9

11. If $|x - 8| < 5$, then

   (A) $0 < x < 14$
   (B) $x > 3$
   (C) $0 < x < 13$
   (D) $x < 13$
   (E) $3 < x < 13$

GO ON TO THE NEXT PAGE

12. What is the area of the base of a triangular pyramid with a volume of 88 cm³ and a height of 16 cm?

    (A) 5.5 cm²
    (B) 11 cm²
    (C) 8 cm²
    (D) 16.5 cm²
    (E) 22 cm²

USE THIS SPACE AS SCRATCH PAPER

13. Which of the following is the *y*-intercept of the line determined by the equation $6x + 7y - 15 = 0$?

    (A) $\dfrac{15}{7}$

    (B) $\dfrac{5}{2}$

    (C) $-\dfrac{15}{7}$

    (D) $-\dfrac{5}{2}$

    (E) 15

14. In which of the following quadrants could the point $(a, |b|)$ lie?

    (A) I only
    (B) I or II
    (C) II only
    (D) II or III
    (E) III or IV

15. $\dfrac{\sqrt{a+b}}{\sqrt{a-b}} =$

    (A) 1

    (B) $\dfrac{\sqrt{a^2 + b^2}}{a - b}$

    (C) $\dfrac{\sqrt{a^2 - b^2}}{a - b}$

    (D) $\sqrt{a - b}$

    (E) −1

16. $|-7.5| + |-8.6| - |5.2| =$

    (A) 10.9
    (B) −21.3
    (C) 16.1
    (D) 21.3
    (E) −6.3

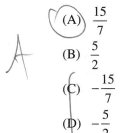

GO ON TO THE NEXT PAGE

17. The cost of 2 candy bars and 4 sodas is $6.00. If the cost of 3 sodas is $3.30, then what is the cost of 1 candy bar?

   (A) $1.10
   (B) $2.70
   (C) $1.35
   (D) $0.80
   (E) $1.60

18. If each exterior angle of a regular polygon measures 40°, how many sides does it have?

   (A) 1,260
   (B) 10
   (C) 18
   (D) 9
   (E) 8

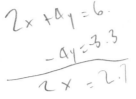

19. John spends 25 percent of his monthly salary on rent and puts 25 percent of the remaining amount into a savings account. If he puts $420 a month into his savings account, how much is his monthly salary?

   (A) $6,720
   (B) $2,240
   (C) $840
   (D) $560
   (E) $2,420

20. The cube root of twice a number, n, is $\frac{3}{4}$. $n =$

   (A) 0.422
   (B) 0.211
   (C) 0.909
   (D) 0.454
   (E) 0.563

21. A cube with an edge of 3 cm has the same volume as a sphere with a radius of what length?

   (A) 1.86 cm
   (B) 6.45 cm
   (C) 2.25 cm
   (D) 1.29 cm
   (E) 11.46 cm

22. The perimeter of a rectangle is 48 cm. If the ratio of its width to length is 1:3, then what is its length?

   (A) 6
   (B) 16
   (C) 8
   (D) 18
   (E) 12

GO ON TO THE NEXT PAGE

23. If $\log_x y = n$, then which of the following is true?

    (A) $x^n = y$
    (B) $y^x = n$
    (C) $n^x = y$
    (D) $y^x = n$
    (E) $x^y = n$

USE THIS SPACE AS SCRATCH PAPER

24. If a circle has a radius of 5 and is tangent to both the x- and y-axis, then which of the following is a possible equation for the circle?

    (A) $x^2 + y^2 = 25$
    (B) $x^2 + y^2 = 5$
    (C) $x^2 + (y - 5)^2 = 5$
    (D) $(x + 5)^2 + y^2 = 25$
    (E) $(x - 5)^2 + (y - 5)^2 = 25$

25. What is the axis of symmetry of the graph of $y = -5(x + 1)^2 + 9$?

    (A) $y = -1$
    (B) $x = -1$
    (C) $y = 9$
    (D) $x = 9$
    (E) $x = 1$

26. Which of the following is the solution set of $8x^3 + 8x^2 - 16x = 0$?

    (A) $\{-2, 1\}$
    (B) $\{-2, 0, 1\}$
    (C) $\{-2, 0, -1\}$
    (D) $\{8, 1\}$
    (E) $\{-2, 1, 8\}$

27. What is the measure of $\angle ABC$ in Figure 3?

    (A) $30°$
    (B) $85°$
    (C) $65°$
    (D) $75°$
    (E) $80°$

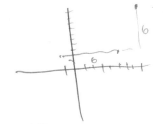

Figure 3

28. What is the area, in square units, of a triangle with vertices $(-1, 1)$, $(5, 1)$, and $(8, 8)$?

    (A) 42
    (B) 21
    (C) 48
    (D) 24
    (E) 14

GO ON TO THE NEXT PAGE

29. If the distance from $A(1, 6)$ to $B(x, -2)$ is 10, then what is a possible value for x?

    (A) 11
    (B) −5
    (C) −7
    (D) 8
    (E) 6

30. In Figure 4, $\overline{WX} = \overline{WZ}$ and $\overline{XY} = \overline{ZY}$. $n =$

    (A) 50°
    (B) 142°
    (C) 25°
    (D) 26°
    (E) 168°

31. What is the maximum value of $f(x) = -x^2 + 3x - 11$?

    (A) $\frac{3}{2}$
    (B) −11
    (C) $-\frac{35}{4}$
    (D) $-\frac{3}{2}$
    (E) $-\frac{53}{4}$

32. The diagonal of a square is 12. What is the length of a side?

    (A) $\frac{12}{\sqrt{3}}$
    (B) 14.1
    (C) 8.5
    (D) 6.9
    (E) 17

33. In Figure 5, what is the length of $\overline{OQ}$?

    (A) 3
    (B) 5
    (C) 4
    (D) 9
    (E) 8

USE THIS SPACE AS SCRATCH PAPER

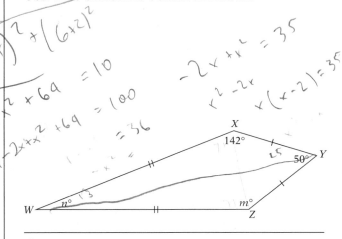

Figure 4

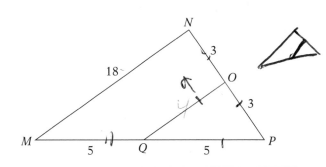

Figure 5

GO ON TO THE NEXT PAGE

34. When $f(x)$ is divided by $2x + 1$, the quotient is $x^2 - x + 4$ and the remainder is 6. What is $f(x)$?

    (A) $2x^3 - x^2 + 9x + 6$
    (B) $2x^3 - 2x^2 + 8x + 6$
    (C) $x^2 - x + 10$
    (D) $2x^3 - x^2 + 7x + 4$
    (E) $2x^3 - x^2 + 7x + 10$

35. If $f(x) = x^2 + 1$, then $f(f(x)) =$

    (A) $x^4 + 1$
    (B) $x^4 + 2x^2 + 1$
    (C) $x^4 + 2x^2 + 2$
    (D) $x^4 + x^2 + 1$
    (E) $x^4 + 2$

36. If $\dfrac{4^n}{4^3} = 2^{10}$, then $n =$

    (A) 13
    (B) 8
    (C) 7
    (D) 5
    (E) 2

37. If $xy = 7$, then which of the following must be true statements?
    I. x and y cannot both be integers.
    II. x and y have the same sign.
    III. $y \neq 0$

    (A) II only
    (B) III only
    (C) I and III only
    (D) II and III only
    (E) I, II, and III

38. In Figure 6, $FGHIJK$ is a regular hexagon with a perimeter of 36. What is the length of $\overline{KG}$?

    (A) 10.4
    (B) 8.5
    (C) 6
    (D) 5.2
    (E) 7.1

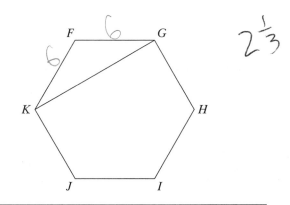

Figure 6

GO ON TO THE NEXT PAGE

39. Which of the following is NOT a true statement?

    (A) $3^2(3^3) = 3^5$
    (B) $2^3(3^3) = 6^3$
    (C) $(64)^{\frac{1}{2}} = 8$
    (D) $2^2 + 2^3 = 2^5$
    (E) $2^2(2^{-3}) = \dfrac{1}{2}$

40. A jar contains 4 red, 1 green, and 3 yellow marbles. If 2 marbles are drawn from the jar without replacement, what is the probability that both will be yellow?

    (A) $\dfrac{3}{8}$
    (B) $\dfrac{3}{28}$
    (C) $\dfrac{1}{4}$
    (D) $\dfrac{3}{56}$
    (E) $\dfrac{5}{56}$

41. If $f(x) = \sqrt{4x^2 - 9}$, then what is the domain of the function?

    (A) All x such that $x \geq 0$
    (B) All x such that $x \geq \dfrac{3}{2}$
    (C) All x such that $-\dfrac{3}{2} \leq x \leq \dfrac{3}{2}$
    (D) All x such that $x \leq -\dfrac{3}{2}$ or $x \geq \dfrac{3}{2}$
    (E) All real numbers

42. The width of a rectangular prism is doubled, its length is tripled, and its height is cut in half. If the volume of the original prism was V, what is its new volume?

    (A) $2V$
    (B) $4V$
    (C) $16V$
    (D) $6V$
    (E) $3V$

43. If $\cos x° = 0.788$, then $\cos (x + 0.5)° =$

    (A) 0.623
    (B) 1.29
    (C) 0.793
    (D) 38
    (E) 0.783

GO ON TO THE NEXT PAGE

44. The probability that Claire passes chemistry is 0.75, and the probability that she passes history is 0.88. If passing one course is independent of passing the other, what is the probability that she does not pass chemistry and passes history?

    (A) 0.22
    (B) 0.66
    (C) 0.13
    (D) 0.25
    (E) 0.03

45. A comedian has rehearsed 10 different jokes. During a given act, he performs any 5 of these jokes. How many different acts can he perform assuming the order of the jokes in an act is not important?

    (A) 10
    (B) 252
    (C) 42
    (D) 84
    (E) 126

46. What is the maximum value of the function $y = 3 + 2(\sin \pi x)$?

    (A) 3
    (B) 2
    (C) 5
    (D) 1
    (E) 6

47. If $f(x) = \dfrac{|x|}{x}$, then what is the range of the function?

    (A) $y > 0$
    (B) All real numbers except $y = 0$
    (C) $y = -1$ or $y = 1$
    (D) $y = 1$
    (E) All real numbers

48. Assuming each factor has only real coefficients, which of the following is the completely factored form of $2x^4 - 18$?

    (A) $2(x^4 - 9)$
    (B) $2(x^2 + 3)(x^2 - 3)$
    (C) $(2x + 6)(x - \sqrt{3})(x + \sqrt{3})$
    (D) $2(x^2 + 3)(x - 3)(x + 3)$
    (E) $2(x^2 + 3)(x - \sqrt{3})(x + \sqrt{3})$

GO ON TO THE NEXT PAGE

49. If n = the number of the term, the nth term of the sequence 1, 0, 1, 4, 9, . . . is which of the following?

   (A) $n - 1$
   (B) n^2
   (C) $(n - 1)^2$
   (D) $(n - 2)^2$
   (E) $n^2 - 1$

50. $\dfrac{\left(\dfrac{-6 + 2x}{x - 3}\right)}{\left(\dfrac{x^2 + 6x + 9}{x^2 - 9}\right)} =$

   (A) $\dfrac{2(x - 3)}{x + 3}$

   (B) $\dfrac{2x}{x + 3}$

   (C) $-\dfrac{2(x - 3)}{x + 3}$

   (D) 2

   (E) $\dfrac{-6 + 2x}{x - 3}$

USE THIS SPACE AS SCRATCH PAPER

S T O P

IF YOU FINISH BEFORE TIME IS CALLED, GO BACK AND CHECK YOUR WORK.

ANSWER KEY

1. B	11. E	21. A	31. C	41. D
2. D	12. D	22. D	32. C	42. E
3. C	13. A	23. A	33. D	43. E
4. D	14. B	24. E	34. E	44. A
5. C	15. C	25. B	35. C	45. B
6. C	16. A	26. B	36. B	46. C
7. A	17. D	27. C	37. D	47. C
8. D	18. D	28. B	38. A	48. E
9. B	19. B	29. B	39. D	49. D
10. E	20. B	30. D	40. B	50. A

ANSWERS AND SOLUTIONS

1. **B** Substitute $b = 3a - 5$ into the equation for a.

$$a = 2(3a - 5) - 10$$
$$a = 6a - 10 - 10$$
$$a = 6a - 20$$
$$20 = 5a$$
$$a = 4$$

2. **D** Remember the trigonometric identity $\sin^2 x + \cos^2 x = 1$. Here $x = 9\theta$, so

$$\sqrt{\sin^2 9\theta + \cos^2 9\theta} = \sqrt{1} = 1$$

3. **C** Since the fax machine sends n pages <u>per</u> minute, divide 25 by n. It will take $\dfrac{25}{n}$ minutes to send the entire 25-page document.

4. **D** The Triangle Inequality Theorem states that the sum of the length of any two sides of a triangle must be greater than the length of the third side. $9 + 9$ is not greater than 18, so sides in Answer D cannot create a triangle.

5. **C** The base in the numerator and denominator is the same, so subtract the denominator's exponent from that of the numerator.

$$\frac{x^{\frac{3}{4}}}{x^{-\frac{1}{4}}} = x^{\left(\frac{3}{4} - \left(-\frac{1}{4}\right)\right)} = x^1 = x$$

6. **C** Since $\overline{XY} \parallel \overline{WZ}$, $\angle WZX$ and $\angle YXZ$ are alternate interior angles and are, therefore congruent. $m\angle YXZ = a$. b is an exterior angle to the triangle containing the angles a and c, so b equals the sum of the two remote interior angles.

$$b = a + c$$
$$c = b - a$$

7. **A** The slope of the line segment is

$$\frac{-4 - 4}{0 - 2} = \frac{-8}{-2} = 4$$

Any line parallel to the segment must have the same slope, so 4 is the correct answer.

8. **D** You're trying to determine the length of the side opposite $\angle ABC$ and you know the length of the hypotenuse. Use sine to get

$$\sin 29° = \frac{\overline{AC}}{12}$$

$$12(\sin 29°) \approx 5.8$$

9. **B** The composition of the two functions, g and f, is $2x + 1$. Since $f(x) = \frac{1}{4}x - 1$, you know

$$g\left(\frac{1}{4}x - 1\right) = 2x + 1$$

The function g is a rule that will result in an output of $2x + 1$ when the input equals $\frac{1}{4}x - 1$.

$$8\left(\frac{1}{4}x - 1\right) + 9 = 2x - 8 + 9 = 2x + 1$$

10. **E** If $a + bi = c + di$ then $a = c$ and $b = d$. In this example:

$$-xi = 2i$$
$$-x = 2$$
$$x = -2$$

Now, look at the real parts of the expressions:

$$7 = x + y$$

Letting $x = -2$ results in

$$7 = -2 + y$$
$$y = 9$$

11. **E** Since $|x - 8| < 5$, then

$$-5 < x - 8 < 5$$

$$-5 < x - 8 \quad \text{and} \quad x - 8 < 5$$
$$3 < x \qquad\qquad\qquad x < 13$$
$$3 < x < 13$$

12. **D**

$$V = \frac{1}{3}BH \text{ where } B \text{ equals the area of the base.}$$

$$88 = \frac{1}{3}B(16)$$

$$\frac{88(3)}{16} = B$$

$$B = 16.5 \text{ cm}^2$$

13. **A** To find the y-intercept, let $x = 0$ and solve for y.

$$6(0) + 7y - 15 = 0$$
$$7y = 15$$
$$y = \frac{15}{7}$$

14. **B** Since the absolute value of b must result in a positive number, the y-coordinate of the point must be positive. a could be a positive or negative value, so the point could lie in either quadrant I (where both the x- and y-coordinates are positive) or quadrant II (where the x-coordinate is negative and the y-coordinate is positive).

15. **C** To rationalize the denominator, multiply the fraction by

$$\frac{\sqrt{a - b}}{\sqrt{a - b}}$$

$$\frac{\sqrt{a + b}}{\sqrt{a - b}} \times \frac{\sqrt{a - b}}{\sqrt{a - b}}$$

$$= \frac{\sqrt{(a + b)(a - b)}}{a - b}$$

$$= \frac{\sqrt{a^2 - b^2}}{a - b}$$

16. **A**

$$|-7.5| + |-8.6| - |5.2|$$
$$= 7.5 + 8.6 - 5.2$$
$$= 16.1 - 5.2$$
$$= 10.9$$

17. **D** Let $c =$ the cost of a candy bar and $s =$ the cost of a soda.

$$2c + 4s = 6.00 \quad \text{and} \quad 3s = 3.30$$

Solving for s in the second equation gives you $s = \$1.10$. Then substitute this value of s into the first equation:

$$2c + 4(1.10) = 6.00$$
$$2c = 1.60$$
$$c = 0.80$$

18. **D** The sum of the exterior angles of any polygon is $360°$. If each exterior angle measures $40°$, then the polygon has

$$\frac{360}{40} = 9 \text{ sides}$$

19. **B** Since 25 percent of John's monthly salary is spent on rent, he has 75 percent remaining. Let m = John's monthly salary.

$$0.25(0.75m) = 420$$

$$0.1875m = 420$$

$$m = \frac{420}{0.1875} = \$2,240$$

20. **B**

$$\sqrt[3]{2n} = \frac{3}{4}$$

$$2n = \left(\frac{3}{4}\right)^3$$

$$2n = (0.75)^3 \approx 0.4219$$

$$n \approx 0.2109$$

21. **A** The volume of the cube is e^3 or $3^3 = 27$ cm³. Remember that the formula for the volume of a sphere is given in the Reference Information.

$$\text{Volume} = \frac{4}{3}\pi r^3 = 27$$

$$r^3 = \frac{27(0.75)}{\pi} = 6.44318$$

$$r = (6.44318)^{\frac{1}{3}} = 1.86 \text{ cm}$$

22. **D** Let the width = x and the length = $3x$. The perimeter, therefore, equals

$$x + 3x + x + 3x = 48$$

$$8x = 48$$

$$x = 6 \text{ cm}$$

The length is 3(6) cm or 18 cm.

23. **A** By the definition of a logarithm, $\log_x y = n$ is equivalent to $x^n = y$. For example, $\log_2 8 = 3$ is equivalent to $2^3 = 8$.

24. **E** Radii of the circle will be perpendicular to both the x- and y-axis at the points of tangency. The center of the circle cannot be on either the x- or y-axis or the circle will intersect the axes at more than one point. The only possible solution, therefore, is $(x - 5)^2 + (y - 5)^2 = 25$, a circle with center $(5,5)$ and radius of 5.

25. **B** The graph of the equation $y = -5(x + 1)^2 + 9$ is a parabola. It is concave down and has a vertex of $(-1, 9)$. The axis of symmetry is the vertical line passing through the vertex, making $x = -1$ the correct answer.

26. **B**

$$8x^3 + 8x^2 - 16x = 0$$

$$8x(x^2 + x - 2) = 0$$

$$8x(x + 2)(x - 1) = 0$$

$$8x = 0 \text{ or } (x + 2) = 0 \text{ or } (x - 1) = 0$$

$$x = 0 \text{ or } x = -2 \text{ or } x = 1$$

$$\{-2, 0, 1\}$$

27. **C** The measure of the exterior angle of a triangle equals the sum of the two remote interior angles.

$$150 = x + x - 20$$

$$170 = 2x$$

$$x = 85°$$

The measure of $\angle ABC = 85 - 20 = 65°$.

28. **B** The base of the triangle measures $|-1 - 5| = 6$ units and the height measures $|8 - 1| = 7$ units. The area of the triangle is

$$A = \frac{1}{2}bh$$

$$A = \frac{1}{2}(6)(7) = 21 \text{ units}^2$$

29. **B** Use the distance formula to solve for x.

$$d = \sqrt{(x_2 - x_1)^2 + (y_2 - y_1)^2} = 10$$

$$\sqrt{(1 - x)^2 + (6 - -2)^2} = 10$$

$$\sqrt{(1 - x)^2 + (8)^2} = 10$$

$$(1 - x)^2 + (8)^2 = 10^2$$

$$(1 - x)^2 = 100 - 64 = 36$$

$$1 - x = \pm 6$$

$$1 - x = 6 \text{ or } 1 - x = -6$$

$$x = -5 \text{ or } x = 7$$

$x = -5$ is the only valid answer given in the problem.

As an alternative solution using geometry, sketch a right triangle with vertices $A(1, 6)$, $C(1, -2)$, and $B(x, -2)$. The hypotenuse of the triangle must measure 10 units. One leg measures 8 units, so $\overline{BC} = 6$. $x = 7$ or -5.

30. **D** *WXYZ* is a kite, so $m\angle WZY = 142°$ since the nonvertex angles of a kite are congruent. The sum of the four angles of the kite must add up to 360°.

$$n + 142 + 142 + 50 = 360$$

$$n = 26°$$

31. **C** The graph of this function is a parabola that is concave down. The maximum value is the *y*-coordinate of its vertex. The *x*-coordinate of the vertex is found by

$$x = -\frac{b}{2a}$$

$$x = -\frac{3}{2(-1)} = \frac{3}{2}$$

$$f\left(\frac{3}{2}\right) = -\left(\frac{3}{2}\right)^2 + 3\left(\frac{3}{2}\right) - 11$$

$$= -\frac{9}{4} + \frac{9}{2} - 11$$

$$= \frac{9}{4} - \frac{44}{4} = -\frac{35}{4}$$

32. **C** The diagonal of a square splits it into two 45°-45°-90° right triangles. The hypotenuse of each triangle is 12, so each leg measures

$$\frac{12}{\sqrt{2}} \approx 8.5 \text{ units}$$

33. **D** $\overline{OQ}$ is a midsegment of ΔNPM, since it connects the midpoint of $\overline{NP}$ to the midpoint of $\overline{MP}$. Midsegments are parallel to the third side of the triangle and half their length, so $OQ = \frac{1}{2}(18) = 9$.

34. **E** Using the given quotient and remainder, you know that

$$f(x) = (2x + 1)(x^2 - x + 4) + 6$$

$$f(x) = 2x^3 - 2x^2 + 8x + x^2 - x + 4 + 6$$

$$f(x) = 2x^3 - x^2 + 7x + 10$$

35. **C**

$$f(f(x)) = f(x^2 + 1)$$

$$= (x^2 + 1)^2 + 1$$

$$= x^4 + 2x^2 + 1 + 1$$

$$= x^4 + 2x^2 + 2$$

36. **B**

$$\frac{4^n}{4^3} = \frac{2^{2n}}{2^{2(3)}} = 2^{10}$$

$$\frac{2^{2n}}{2^6} = 2^{10}$$

$$2n - 6 = 10$$

$$2n = 16$$

$$n = 8$$

37. **D** Neither *x* nor *y* can equal zero for their product to equal a nonzero number, so III is a true statement. *x* and *y* can be integers, i.e., $(7)(1) = 7$, so I is not true. *x* and *y* must both be positive or both be negative to result in a positive 7 product. Both II and III are true statements.

38. **A** ΔKFG is an isosceles triangle with two sides measuring 6. Each angle of a regular hexagon measures 120°, so $\angle F = 120°$. Draw the altitude from $\angle F$ to create two congruent 30°-60°-90° right triangles. Since the side opposite the 90° angle is 6, the side opposite the 30° angle must measure 3 units. The sides opposite the 60° angles in both triangles measure $3\sqrt{3}$.

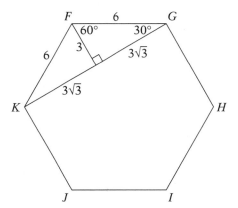

$$KG = 3\sqrt{3} + 3\sqrt{3} = 6\sqrt{3} \approx 10.4$$

39. **D** $2^2 + 2^3 = 4 + 8 = 12$, which is not equal to 2^5, so D is NOT a true statement. The other four answers are true statements.

(A) $3^2(3^3) = 3^{2+3} = 3^5$

(B) $2^3(3^3) = (2 \cdot 3)^3 = 6^3$

(C) $(64)^{\frac{1}{2}} = \sqrt{64} = 8$

(D) $2^2(2^{-3}) = 2^{-1} = \frac{1}{2}$

40. **B** There are eight marbles in the jar. The probability of choosing the first yellow marble is $\frac{3}{8}$. The probability that your second marble will also be yellow is $\frac{2}{7}$. The probability that both will be yellow is therefore

$$\frac{3}{8} \times \frac{2}{7} = \frac{6}{56} = \frac{3}{28}$$

41. **D**

$4x^2 - 9$ must be positive or equal to zero.

$$4x^2 - 9 \geq 0$$

$$4x^2 \geq 9$$

$$x^2 \geq \frac{9}{4}$$

$$x \leq -\frac{3}{2} \text{ or } x \geq \frac{3}{2}$$

42. **E** The volume of the original prism was

$$V = \ell \times w \times h$$

The volume of the new prism is

$$V = 2\ell \times 3w \times \frac{1}{2}h$$

$$= 3\ell \times w \times h$$

$$= 3V$$

43. **E**

$\cos^{-1}(0.788) = 38°$, so $x = 38$.

$\cos(x + 0.5)° = \cos(38 + 0.5)°$

$= \cos(38.5)° = 0.783$

44. **A** The probability that Claire does NOT pass chemistry is

$$1 - 0.75 = 0.25$$

The probability that she does NOT pass chemistry and she does pass history is then

$$0.25(0.88) = 0.22$$

45. **B** The order that he performs the jokes does not matter in this problem. Set up a combination for "10 choose 5" jokes.

$$\frac{10!}{5!}(10 - 5)! = \frac{10!}{5!5!}$$

$$= \frac{6(7)(8)(9)(10)}{1(2)(3)(4)(5)}$$

$$= 7(2)(9)(2)$$

$$= 252$$

46. **C**

$$y = 3 + 2(\sin \pi x)$$

The maximum value of $2(\sin \pi x)$ is $2(1)$ or 2. The 3 shifts the sine curve upward 3 units, so the maximum value for y is 5.

47. **C** Since the numerator of the function is an absolute value expression, the function can be written as two distinct expressions—one for when $x > 0$ and one for when $x < 0$. (The function is undefined when $x = 0$.)

When $x > 0$,

$$f(x) = \frac{x}{x} = 1$$

When $x < 0$,

$$f(x) = \frac{-x}{x} = -1$$

48. **E**

$$2x^4 - 18$$

$$= 2(x^4 - 9)$$

$$= 2(x^2 + 3)(x^2 - 3)$$

$$= 2(x^2 + 3)(x - \sqrt{3})(x + \sqrt{3})$$

49. **D** The sequence: 1, 0, 1, 4, 9, . . . is equivalent to $(-1)^2, 0^2, 1^2, 2^2, 3^2, \ldots$. Since n is the number of the term, this translates to: $(1-2)^2, (2-2)^2, (3-2)^2, (4-2)^2, (5-2)^2, \ldots$, so the nth term is $(n-2)^2$.

50. **A**

$$\frac{\left(\dfrac{-6 + 2x}{x - 3}\right)}{\left(\dfrac{x^2 + 6x + 9}{x^2 - 9}\right)} \times \frac{x^2 - 9}{x^2 - 9}$$

$$= \frac{(-6 + 2x)(x + 3)}{x^2 + 6x + 9}$$

$$= \frac{2(x - 3)(x + 3)}{(x + 3)^2}$$

$$= \frac{2(x - 3)}{(x + 3)}$$

Diagnose Your Strengths and Weaknesses

Check the number of each question answered correctly and "X" the number of each question answered incorrectly.

Algebra	1	3	5	11	15	16	17	19	20	26	36	37	39	48	50	Total Number Correct
15 questions																

Plane Geometry	4	6	18	22	27	28	30	32	33	38	Total Number Correct
10 questions											

Solid Geometry	12	21	42	Total Number Correct
3 questions				

Coordinate Geometry	7	13	14	24	25	29	Total Number Correct
6 questions							

Trigonometry	2	8	43	46	Total Number Correct
4 questions					

Functions	9	31	34	35	41	47	Total Number Correct
6 questions							

Data Analysis, Statistics, and Probability	40	44	45	Total Number Correct
3 questions				

Number and Operations	10	23	49	Total Number Correct
3 questions				

Number of correct answers − $\frac{1}{4}$ (Number of incorrect answers) = Your raw score

_____ − $\frac{1}{4}$ (_____) = _____

Compare your raw score with the approximate SAT Subject test score below:

	Raw Score	**SAT Subject test Approximate Score**
Excellent	46–50	750–800
Very Good	41–45	700–750
Good	36–40	640–700
Above Average	29–35	590–640
Average	22–28	510–590
Below Average	< 22	<510

PRACTICE TEST 2

Treat this practice test as the actual test and complete it in one 60-minute sitting. Use the following answer sheet to fill in your multiple-choice answers. Once you have completed the practice test:

1. Check your answers using the Answer Key.
2. Review the Answer Explanations.
3. Fill in the "Diagnose Your Strengths and Weaknesses" sheet and determine areas that require further preparation.

PRACTICE TEST 2

MATH LEVEL 1

Tear out this answer sheet and use it to complete the practice test.

Determine the BEST answer for each question. Then fill in the appropriate oval using a No. 2 pencil.

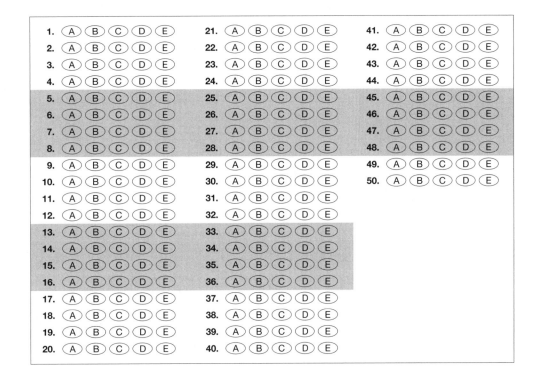

PRACTICE TEST 2

Time: 60 Minutes

Directions: Select the BEST answer for each of the 50 multiple-choice questions. If the exact solution is not one of the five choices, select the answer that is the best approximation. Then fill in the appropriate oval on the answer sheet.

Notes:

(1) A calculator will be needed to answer some of the questions on the test. Scientific, programmable, and graphing calculators are permitted. It is up to you to determine when and when not to use your calculator.

(2) All angles on the Level 1 test are measured in degrees, not radians. Make sure your calculator is set to degree mode.

(3) Figures are drawn as accurately as possible and are intended to help solve some of the test problems. If a figure is not drawn to scale, this will be stated in the problem. All figures lie in a plane unless the problem indicates otherwise.

(4) Unless otherwise stated, the domain of a function f is assumed to be the set of real numbers x for which the value of the function, $f(x)$, is a real number.

(5) Reference information that may be useful in answering some of the test questions can be found below.

Reference Information	
Right circular cone with radius r and height h:	Volume $= \dfrac{1}{3}\pi r^2 h$
Right circular cone with circumference of base c and slant height ℓ:	Lateral Area $= \dfrac{1}{2}c\ell$
Sphere with radius r:	Volume $= \dfrac{4}{3}\pi r^3$ Surface Area $= 4\pi r^2$
Pyramid with base area B and height h:	Volume $= \dfrac{1}{3}Bh$

GO ON TO THE NEXT PAGE

1. The cost to rent a DVD is $4.50 for the first five days, with a $2.50 late fee for each succeeding day. Which of the following represents the cost of renting the DVD for d days if d is greater than 5?

(A) $4.50d + 2.50d$
(B) $4.50 + 2.50(d - 5)$
(C) $7d$
(D) $4.50 + 2.50d$
(E) $4.50 + (2.50d - 5)$

2. If $x \neq 0$, then $\dfrac{1}{2x^{-\frac{3}{2}}} =$

(A) $-\dfrac{1}{2x^{\frac{3}{2}}}$

(B) $2x^{\frac{3}{2}}$

(C) $\dfrac{x^{\frac{2}{3}}}{2}$

(D) $\dfrac{x^{\frac{3}{2}}}{2}$

(E) x^3

3. What are all values of x for which $x - 3 > 9 - x^2$?

(A) $x > 3$
(B) $x < -3$
(C) $x < -4$ or $x > 3$
(D) $x < -4$
(E) $-4 < x < 3$

4. What is the distance between the points $(5, 6)$ and $(-3, 0)$?

(A) 9
(B) 100
(C) 10
(D) 6
(E) 8

5. At what point does the graph of $4x - 6y = -1$ intersect the x-axis?

(A) 4
(B) 6
(C) $\dfrac{2}{3}$
(D) $\dfrac{1}{6}$
(E) $-\dfrac{1}{4}$

USE THIS SPACE AS SCRATCH PAPER

GO ON TO THE NEXT PAGE

6. If $4x^3 = -64$, then $x =$

   (A) −1
   (B) 1
   (C) −2$\sqrt[3]{2}$
   (D) 2$\sqrt[3]{2}$
   (E) 4

7. If the fourth root of the square of a number is 2, then what is the number?

   (A) 2
   (B) 4
   (C) 8
   (D) 16
   (E) 32

8. If a line is perpendicular to the line $2x + 6y = 18$, what is its slope?

   (A) $-\dfrac{1}{3}$

   (B) $\dfrac{1}{3}$

   (C) −3

   (D) 3

   (E) $\dfrac{1}{2}$

9. If $x - y = 8$ and $2x + 3y = 16$, then $x =$

   (A) 8
   (B) 0
   (C) 10
   (D) 4
   (E) −8

10. If $f(x) = \dfrac{x^2 - 16}{x - 4}$ and $h(x) = x + 4$, which of the following is true about their graphs?

   (A) They are the same.
   (B) They are the line $x - y = 4$.
   (C) They are the same except when $x = 4$.
   (D) They are the same except when $x = -4$.
   (E) They do not share any points.

11. $(2^2 \times 2^3)^4 =$

   (A) 2^5
   (B) 2^9
   (C) 2^{20}
   (D) 2^{24}
   (E) 2^{96}

GO ON TO THE NEXT PAGE

12. If the lines ℓ_1 and ℓ_2 are parallel and are intersected by a transversal t, then what is the sum of the exterior angles on the same side of t?

  (A) 45°
  (B) 90°
  (C) 180°
  (D) 360°
  (E) Cannot be determined

13. Of the following, which has the greater value?

  (A) 2^8
  (B) $2^5 \times 2^2$
  (C) $\dfrac{2^{10}}{2^2}$
  (D) $(2^5)^2$
  (E) $2^8 + 2^4$

14. In Figure 1, if $\theta = 48°$, then what is the value of a?

  (A) 14.4
  (B) 17.5
  (C) 19.4
  (D) 9.7
  (E) 11.7

15. Line ℓ_1 has a negative slope and a positive y-intercept. If ℓ_2 is perpendicular to ℓ_1 and has a positive y-intercept, then which of the following must be true of the x-intercepts of the two lines?

  (A) Both are negative.
  (B) Both are positive.
  (C) They are equal.
  (D) The x-intercept of ℓ_1 is greater than the x-intercept of ℓ_2.
  (E) The x-intercept of ℓ_1 is less than the x-intercept of ℓ_2.

16. In a given high school, 60 percent of the teachers reported an annual salary greater than or equal to $50,000 a year. Which of the following must be greater than or equal to $50,000?

  (A) The mean salary
  (B) The median salary
  (C) The mode of their salaries
  (D) The mean and the median of their salaries
  (E) Neither the mean, median, nor mode

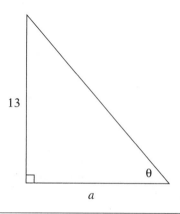

Figure 1

GO ON TO THE NEXT PAGE

17. If $2x^2 + 15x + k = 0$ has $\dfrac{1}{2}$ as one of its solutions, what is the value of k?

(A) -8

(B) 8

(C) $\dfrac{1}{2}$

(D) $-\dfrac{1}{2}$

(E) 6

18. Assuming you are factoring over the real numbers, which of the following is the completely factored form of $x^4 - 16$?

(A) $(x^2 - 4)(x^2 + 4)$

(B) $(x - 2)(x + 2)(x^2 + 4)$

(C) $(x^2 - 4)^2$

(D) $(x - 2)^2(x^2 + 4)$

(E) $(x^2 - 8)(x^2 + 2)$

19. In Figure 2, $\triangle ABE$ is similar to $\triangle ACD$. What is the value of x?

(A) 3

(B) 3.5

(C) 3.75

(D) 4

(E) 13.75

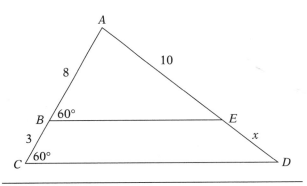

Figure 2

20. If the supplement of an angle is four times the measure of its complement, then the measure of the angle's complement is

(A) 30°

(B) 60°

(C) 20°

(D) 120°

(E) 150°

21. If $f(x) = \dfrac{4x - 1}{2}$, then $f^{-1}(x) =$

(A) $\dfrac{4x - 1}{2}$

(B) $\dfrac{2}{4x - 1}$

(C) $2x + 1$

(D) $\dfrac{2x + 1}{4}$

(E) $2\left(\dfrac{1}{4x + 1}\right)$

GO ON TO THE NEXT PAGE

22. If the triangle in Figure 3 is reflected across the *x*-axis, what will be the coordinates of the reflection of vertex *A*?

    (A) (−1, 1)
    (B) (1, 1)
    (C) (−1, −1)
    (D) (1, 0)
    (E) (0, −1)

USE THIS SPACE AS SCRATCH PAPER

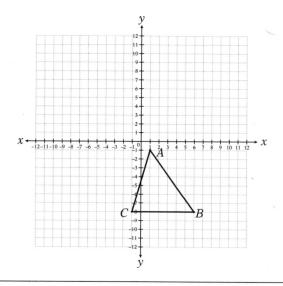

Figure 3

23. What is the measure of each exterior angle of a regular pentagon?

    (A) 90°
    (B) 60°
    (C) 120°
    (D) 108°
    (E) 72°

24. The triangle in Figure 4 has sides measuring 3, 4, and 5 units. What is the measure of θ?

    (A) 45°
    (B) 30°
    (C) 60°
    (D) 36.9°
    (E) 53.1°

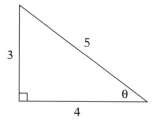

25. How many lines of symmetry does a rhombus have?

    (A) 0
    (B) 1
    (C) 2
    (D) 3
    (E) 4

Figure 4

26. sin 30° =

    (A) cos 60°
    (B) sin 60°
    (C) cos 30°
    (D) tan 60°
    (E) csc 30°

GO ON TO THE NEXT PAGE

27. $(\cos^2 \theta + \sin^2 \theta - 2)^3 =$

    (A) 1
    (B) −1
    (C) 0
    (D) 2
    (E) −8

28. If the equation of a circle is $x^2 + y^2 = 12$, then which of the following is a y-intercept?

    (A) 12
    (B) −12
    (C) −2$\sqrt{3}$
    (D) 0
    (E) Cannot be determined

29. If $f(x) = 5x + 3$ and $g(x) = \dfrac{x+1}{2}$, then what is $g(f(4))$?

    (A) 12
    (B) 11
    (C) 23
    (D) 15.5
    (E) 23.5

30. Figure 5 is a right hexagonal prism whose bases are regular polygons. Which of the following points lies in the plane determined by points E, K, and B?

    (A) H
    (B) A
    (C) G
    (D) C
    (E) D

31. If $f(x) = \dfrac{1}{x}$ and $-1 < x < 0$, then what is the range of the function?

    (A) All real numbers
    (B) $y > -1$
    (C) $y < -1$
    (D) $-1 < y < 0$
    (E) $y < 0$

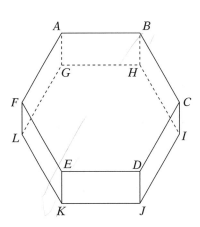

Figure 5

GO ON TO THE NEXT PAGE

32. Assuming both a and b are positive, if $ab = 16$ and $\dfrac{a}{b} = 4$, then what is the average of a and b?

    (A) 10
    (B) 6
    (C) 5
    (D) 4
    (E) 3

33. If $i = \sqrt{-1}$, then $(4 - i)(4 + i) =$

    (A) 17
    (B) 15
    (C) $16 + 8i$
    (D) $16 - i$
    (E) 16

34. What is the equation of the graph in Figure 6?

    (A) $f(x) = |x - 4|$
    (B) $f(x) = -|x - 4|$
    (C) $f(x) = |x + 4|$
    (D) $f(x) = -|x + 4|$
    (E) $f(x) = -|x| - 4$

35. What is the range of the function $f(x) = \dfrac{1}{2}\sin 2x$?

    (A) $-2 \le y \le 2$
    (B) $2 \le y \le 2$
    (C) $-1 \le y \le 1$
    (D) $-\dfrac{1}{2} \le y \le \dfrac{1}{2}$
    (E) $-\dfrac{1}{2} \le y \le 0$

36. If $f(x) = x^3 + 2x$, then $f(-2) + 2f(-1) =$

    (A) -6
    (B) 10
    (C) -15
    (D) 9
    (E) -18

USE THIS SPACE AS SCRATCH PAPER

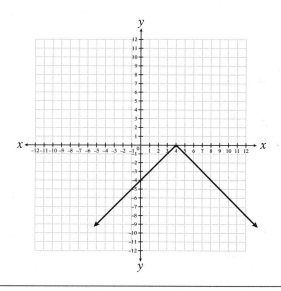

Figure 6

GO ON TO THE NEXT PAGE

37. In how many ways can the letters of the word GOLDEN be arranged using all of the letters?

    (A) 16
    (B) 24
    (C) 120
    (D) 720
    (E) 5,040

USE THIS SPACE AS SCRATCH PAPER

38. The operation ⌂ is defined as: $n \; ⌂ \; m = \dfrac{2n}{m}$. If n and m do not equal zero, then for all of the following values $n \; ⌂ \; m = m \; ⌂ \; n$ EXCEPT

    (A) $n = m$
    (B) $n = -m$
    (C) $m = -n$
    (D) $n = 1$ and $m = 1$
    (E) $n = 2$ and $m = \dfrac{1}{2}$

39. The top face of a rectangular prism has an area of 32 cm². The front face has an area of 16 cm² and the side face has an area of 8 cm². What is the volume of the prism?

    (A) 32 cm³
    (B) 64 cm³
    (C) 128 cm³
    (D) 256 cm³
    (E) 4,096 cm³

40. If $x - 4$, x, and $x + 4$ are the first three terms of an arithmetic sequence, then what is the fifth term of the sequence?

    (A) x
    (B) $x - 4$
    (C) $x + 8$
    (D) $x + 12$
    (E) 4

41. Claire can complete spring-cleaning in a house in 5 hours. Ruth can complete spring-cleaning in the same house in 7 hours. If Claire works for 1 hour alone and then Ruth joins her to finish the cleaning, what is the total time it takes to complete spring-cleaning?

    (A) 2 hours, 30 minutes
    (B) 2 hours, 20 minutes
    (C) 3 hours, 20 minutes
    (D) 3 hours
    (E) 2 hours, 33 minutes

GO ON TO THE NEXT PAGE

42. What is the area of the quadrilateral in Figure 7?

(A) 80
(B) 70
(C) 140
(D) 60
(E) 105

43. If $\dfrac{n}{x^2 - 36} = \dfrac{1}{x - 6} + \dfrac{1}{x + 6}$, then $n =$

(A) x
(B) $2x$
(C) $2(x + 6)$
(D) $2(x - 6)$
(E) 2

44. What is the lateral surface area of a right circular cone whose radius is 3 cm and whose slant height is 12 cm?

(A) 36 cm^2
(B) 18 cm^2
(C) $18\pi \text{ cm}^2$
(D) $36\pi \text{ cm}^2$
(E) $72\pi \text{ cm}^2$

45. If the measure of one angle of a rhombus is 120° and its perimeter is 16 cm, then what is the length of its longer diagonal?

(A) 4
(B) $2\sqrt{3}$
(C) $2\sqrt{2}$
(D) $4\sqrt{2}$
(E) $4\sqrt{3}$

46. a and b are positive. a is even and b is odd. Which of the following must also be odd?

(A) ab
(B) $\dfrac{a}{b}$
(C) $a + 2b$
(D) b^a
(E) $(ab)^a$

USE THIS SPACE AS SCRATCH PAPER

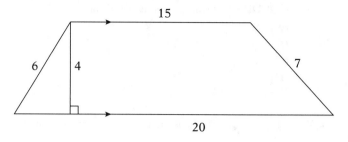

Figure 7

GO ON TO THE NEXT PAGE

47. In Figure 8, $\overline{RS} = \overline{RT} = \overline{TU}$. If $m\angle RTS = 50°$, then what is the measure of $\angle TRU$?
   (A) 25°
   (B) 50°
   (C) 10°
   (D) 80°
   (E) 40°

USE THIS SPACE AS SCRATCH PAPER

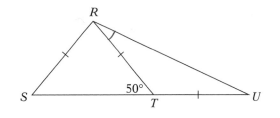

Figure 8

48. All of the following statements are true EXCEPT
   (A) All circles are similar.
   (B) All squares are similar.
   (C) All cubes are similar.
   (D) All spheres are similar.
   (E) All cones are similar.

49. Given the parallelogram ABCD in Figure 9, what is the measure of $\angle DCB$?
   (A) 34°
   (B) 44°
   (C) 102°
   (D) 30°
   (E) 40°

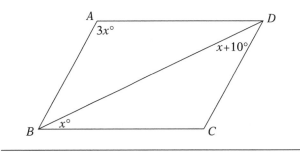

Figure 9

50. An equilateral triangle with sides of length 12 is inscribed in the circle shown in Figure 10. What is the area of the shaded region?
   (A) $36\sqrt{3}$
   (B) $144\pi - 36$
   (C) $108\pi - 36\sqrt{3}$
   (D) $192\pi - 144\sqrt{3}$
   (E) $48\pi - 36\sqrt{3}$

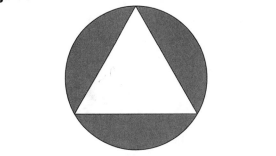

Figure 10

S T O P

IF YOU FINISH BEFORE TIME IS CALLED, GO BACK AND CHECK YOUR WORK.

ANSWER KEY

1. B	11. C	21. D	31. C	41. C
2. D	12. C	22. B	32. C	42. B
3. C	13. D	23. E	33. A	43. B
4. C	14. E	24. D	34. B	44. D
5. E	15. D	25. C	35. D	45. E
6. C	16. B	26. A	36. E	46. D
7. B	17. A	27. B	37. D	47. A
8. D	18. B	28. C	38. E	48. E
9. A	19. C	29. A	39. B	49. C
10. C	20. A	30. A	40. D	50. E

ANSWERS AND SOLUTIONS

1. **B** Since $d > 5$, the cost is \$4.50 for the first 5 days and \$2.50 for the remaining $d - 5$ days. The cost is $4.50 + 2.50(d - 5)$.

2. **D**

$$x^{-\frac{3}{2}} = \frac{1}{x^{\frac{3}{2}}} \text{ so } \frac{1}{2x^{\frac{-3}{2}}} = \frac{1}{\left(\dfrac{2}{x^{\frac{3}{2}}}\right)} = \frac{x^{\frac{3}{2}}}{2}$$

3. **C**

$$x - 3 > 9 - x^2$$
$$x - 3 > (3 - x)(3 + x)$$
$$x - 3 > -(x - 3)(x + 3)$$
$$x - 3 + (x - 3)(x + 3) > 0$$
$$(x - 3)[1 + (x + 3)] > 0$$
$$(x - 3)(x + 4) > 0$$
$$x < -4 \text{ or } x > 3$$

4. **C**

$$d = \sqrt{(x_2 + x_1)^2 + (y_2 - y_1)^2}$$
$$d = \sqrt{(5 - -3)^2 + (6 - 0)^2}$$
$$d = \sqrt{8^2 + 6^2} = \sqrt{100} = 10$$

5. **E**

Let $y = 0$ and solve for the x-intercept.
$$4x - 6(0) = -1$$
$$4x = -1$$
$$x = -\frac{1}{4}$$

6. **C**

$$4x^3 = -64$$
$$x^3 = -16$$
$$x = \sqrt[3]{-16} = -2\sqrt[3]{2}$$

7. **B**

$$\sqrt[4]{x^2} = 2$$
$$x^{\frac{1}{2}} = 2$$
$$x = 4$$

8. **D** The slope of the given line $2x + 6y = 18$ is $-\frac{1}{3}$. Perpendicular lines have slopes that are negative reciprocals of each other, so the slope of the line perpendicular to the given line is 3.

9. **A** Set up a system and solve using linear combinations. Start by multiplying the first equation by 3.

$$3x - 3y = 3(8)$$
$$+ \ 2x + 3y = 16$$
$$\overline{ 5x + 0y = 40}$$

$$x = 8$$

10. **C** Notice that the function $f(x) = \dfrac{x^2 - 16}{x - 4}$ is undefined when $x = 4$, since you cannot divide by zero. Both graphs look like the line $x - y = -4$, but $f(x)$ is undefined at $x = 4$. You can check your answer by graphing the two functions and checking the Table on your graphing calculator to find "Error" for the y-coordinate of $f(x)$ when $x = 4$.

11. **C**

$$(2^2 \times 2^3)^4 = (2^{2+3})^4$$

$$= (2^5)^4 = 2^{5(4)} = 2^{20}$$

12. **C** Parallel lines cut by a transversal form eight angles. The exterior angles on the same side of the transversal are supplementary, so 180° is the correct answer.

13. **D** 2^{10} is the greatest value. The other answers simplify to 2^8, 2^7, 2^8, and $(256 + 16)$, respectively.

14. **E**

$$\tan\theta = \frac{\text{opposite}}{\text{adjacent}} = \frac{13}{a}$$

$$a = \frac{13}{\tan 48°} \approx 11.7$$

15. **D** Since ℓ_2 is perpendicular to ℓ_1 and has a positive y-intercept, its x-intercept must be negative. ℓ_1 has a positive x-intercept, so the x-intercept of ℓ_1 must be greater than the x-intercept of ℓ_2.

16. **B** Since more than half of the teachers have salaries greater than or equal to $50,000, the median (middle value) salary must also be above $50,000. You do not know enough information to determine the mean and mode.

17. **A**

Substitute $x = \dfrac{1}{2}$ into the equation to get

$$2\left(\frac{1}{2}\right)^2 + 15\left(\frac{1}{2}\right) + k = 0$$

$$\frac{1}{2} + \frac{15}{2} + k = 0$$

$$8 + k = 0$$

$$k = -8$$

18. **B** $x^4 - 16$ is the difference of perfect squares. It can be factored as $(x^2 - 4)(x^2 + 4)$, but $x^2 - 4$ is also the difference of perfect squares and can be further factored to

$$(x - 2)(x + 2)(x^2 + 4)$$

19. **C**

$$\frac{8}{(8 + 3)} = \frac{10}{(10 + x)}$$

$$8(10 + x) = 110$$

$$80 + 8x = 110$$

$$8x = 30$$

$$x = 3.75$$

20. **A** Let $x =$ the measure of the angle. Then its complement measures $90 - x$ and its supplement measures $180 - x$.

$$180 - x = 4(90 - x)$$

$$180 - x = 360 - 4x$$

$$3x = 180$$

$$x = 60°$$

Remember that x equals the measure of the original angle, so its complement is $90 - 60 = 30°$.

21. **D** Interchange the x and y values in the function $f(x) = \dfrac{4x-1}{2}$, and solve for y.

$$y = \frac{4x-1}{2}$$

$$x = \frac{4y-1}{2}$$

$$2x = 4y - 1$$

$$\frac{2x+1}{4} = f(x)^{-1}$$

Check your answer by graphing $f(x) = 2x - \dfrac{1}{2}$ and $f(x)^{-1} = \dfrac{1}{2}x + \dfrac{1}{4}$ to see that the inverse function is the original function reflected across the line $y = x$.

22. **B** The triangle is reflected above the x-axis, so the x- and y-coordinates of the reflection of point A will be positive. $(1, 1)$ is the correct answer.

23. **E** The sum of the exterior angles of any polygon is $360°$, so each exterior angle of a *regular* pentagon must measure

$$\frac{360}{5} = 72°$$

24. **D** One way to solve for θ is to use the arctangent function to solve for the angle whose tangent is $\dfrac{3}{4}$.

$$\tan^{-1}\left(\frac{3}{4}\right) = \theta$$

$$\theta = 36.9°$$

25. **C** The line containing each diagonal of a rhombus is a line of symmetry, so a rhombus has 2 lines of symmetry.

26. **A**

$$\sin 30° = \cos (90° - 30°)$$

$$\sin 30° = \cos 60°$$

27. **B** Remember $\cos^2 \theta + \sin^2 \theta = 1$. Substituting 1 into the expression results in

$$(1 - 2)^3 = (-1)^3 = -1$$

28. **C** This is a circle centered at the origin with a radius of $\sqrt{12}$ or $2\sqrt{3}$ units. The y-intercepts are the points $\left(0, 2\sqrt{3}\right)$ and $\left(0, -2\sqrt{3}\right)$.

29. **A**

$$f(4) = 5(4) + 3 = 23$$

$$g(23) = \frac{23+1}{2} = \frac{24}{2} = 12$$

30. **A** The plane determined by the three vertices E, K, and B must contain the edges $\overline{EK}$ and $\overline{BH}$. Vertex H is, therefore, the correct answer.

31. **C** The range of $f(x) = \dfrac{1}{x}$ is all real numbers except $y = 0$. The domain of the function is restricted, however, so the range is the set of all y values that result when x is between -1 and 0, exclusive. Check the graph on your graphing calculator to verify that $y < -1$ is the correct answer.

32. **C** Since $\dfrac{a}{b} = 4$, $a = 4b$. Substitute $4b$ for a in the first equation to get

$$4b(b) = 16$$

$$b^2 = 4$$

$$b = 2 \text{ (Remember } b \text{ must be positive)}$$

$2a = 16$, so $a = 8$. The average of 2 and 8 is $\dfrac{2+8}{2} = 5$.

33. **A** Use the FOIL method to multiply the binomials:

$$(4 - i)(4 + i) = 16 + 4i - 4i - i^2$$

Since $i = \sqrt{-1}, i^2 = \left(\sqrt{-1}\right)^2 = -1$. Substituting -1 into the product above results in

$$16 - (-1) = 17$$

34. **B** This is the graph of $f(x) = |x|$ reflected over the x-axis and shifted 4 units to the right, so $f(x) = -|x - 4|$ is the correct answer. You can check this by graphing the function on your calculator.

35. **D** The graph of the function $f(x) = \dfrac{1}{2}\sin 2x$ is the graph of $y = \sin 2x$ "shrunk" by a factor of $\dfrac{1}{2}$. To check

the range, graph $y = \dfrac{1}{2}\sin 2x$ on your calculator and check the y values under Table.

36. **E**

$$f(-2) + 2f(-1)$$
$$= (-2)^3 + 2(-2) + 2[(-1)^3 + 2(-1)]$$
$$= -8 - 4 + 2(-1 - 2)$$
$$= -12 + 2(-3) = -18$$

37. **D** Find the number of permutations of six letters taken six at a time.

$$6! = 6 \times 5 \times 4 \times 3 \times 2 \times 1 = 720$$

38. **E** If $n \,\text{⌂}\, m = m \,\text{⌂}\, n$, then:

$$\frac{2n}{m} = \frac{2m}{n}$$
$$2n^2 = 2m^2$$
$$n^2 = m^2$$

Answers A through D are all true statements. Answer E is not true since $\dfrac{2(2)}{\left(\dfrac{1}{2}\right)} \neq \dfrac{2\left(\dfrac{1}{2}\right)}{2}$.

39. **B** The volume of the prism is found using $V = \ell wh$. Using the three given areas, you know

$$\ell w = 32$$
$$wh = 8$$
$$h\ell = 16$$

One way to solve for the volume is to solve for h in the second and third equations above and set those values equal to each other.

$$h = \frac{8}{w} = \frac{16}{\ell}$$

$$8\ell = 16w \text{ so } \ell = 2w$$

Substituting $2w$ for ℓ in the first equation results in

$$2w(w) = 32$$
$$2w^2 = 32$$
$$w^2 = 16$$
$$w = 4$$

If $w = 4$, then $8 = h(4)$, so $h = 2$. $\ell(4) = 32$, so $\ell = 8$.

$$V = \ell wh = 8(4)(2) = 64 \text{ cm}^3$$

40. **D** Since $x - 4$, x, and $x + 4$ are the first three terms of the sequence, the common difference between terms is 4. The fourth term of the sequence is

$$x + 4 + 4 = x + 8$$

The fifth term of the sequence must be

$$x + 8 + 4 = x + 12$$

41. **C** Let $t =$ the number of hours Claire and Ruth work together.

$$\frac{t+1}{5} + \frac{t}{7} = 1$$
$$7(t + 1) + 5t = 35$$
$$12t = 28$$
$$t = 2.33$$

Since the problem asks for the total time, add the 1 hour that Claire worked alone to get 3.33 hours, or 3 hours and 20 minutes.

42. **B** Recognize that the quadrilateral is a trapezoid. Its area is given by the formula:

$$A = \frac{1}{2}(b_1 + b_2)h$$
$$A = \frac{1}{2}(15 + 20)4 = 35(2) = 70$$

43. **B** Multiply both sides of the equation by the LCD, $(x + 6)(x - 6)$, to get

$$n = (x + 6) + (x - 6)$$
$$n = 2x$$

44. **D** The formula for the lateral surface area of a cone is given in the Reference Information.

$$\text{Lateral Area} = \frac{1}{2}c\ell$$

$$\text{Lateral Area} = \frac{1}{2}(2\pi r)\ell = \frac{1}{2}(2\pi)(3)(12)$$

$$= 36\pi \text{ cm}^2$$

45. **E** One way to solve for the length of the diagonal is to use special right triangles. The longer diagonal splits the rhombus into two congruent triangles with angles measuring 30°, 30°, and 120°. From one of the 120° angles, draw an altitude creating two 30°-60°-90° triangles. The side opposite the 90° angle measures 4 (16/4), so the side opposite the 60° angle measures $2\sqrt{3}$. This represents half of the diagonal's length. The entire length of the diagonal is

$$2\left(2\sqrt{3}\right) = 4\sqrt{3} \text{ cm}$$

46. **D** An odd number raised to an even power equals an odd number. Take $3^2 = 9$, for example. b^a is the correct answer.

47. **A** $\angle RTU$ is a linear pair with $\angle RTS$, so it must measure 130°. Since ΔRTU is isosceles, its base angles are congruent. $m\angle TRU = m\angle TUR$.

$$m\angle TRU = \frac{180 - 130}{2} = 25°$$

48. **E** Since Answer E does not specify a type of cone (i.e., a right circular cone or an oblique cone), it is not true. A right circular cone is obviously not similar in shape to an oblique cone.

49. **C** $m\angle ABD = x + 10°$, since $\angle ABD$ and $\angle BDC$ are alternate interior angles. Consecutive angles of a parallelogram are supplementary, so:

$$x + x + 10 + 3x = 180°$$

$$5x = 170$$

$$x = 34°$$

The question asks for the measure of $\angle DCB$. Opposite angles of a parallelogram are congruent, so you know

$$m\angle DBC = 3x = 3(34) = 102°$$

50. **E** Since the triangle is equilateral its area is simply $A = s^2\dfrac{\sqrt{3}}{4} = 12^2\dfrac{\sqrt{3}}{4} = 36\sqrt{3}$.

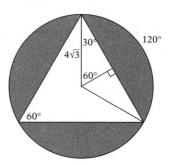

You need to find the length of the radius in order to determine the area of the circle. Draw the two radii that intercept one of the 120° arcs of the circle to make an isosceles triangle. Then draw the altitude from the 120° central angle. Two 30°-60°-90° triangles are created as shown.

The side opposite the 90° angle measures $\dfrac{12}{\sqrt{3}}$, or $4\sqrt{3}$. This is the radius of the circle, so the circle's area is $A = \pi r^2 = \pi\left(4\sqrt{3}\right)^2 = 48\pi$.

The area of the shaded region equals the area of the circle minus the area of the triangle:

$$48\pi - 36\sqrt{3}$$

Diagnose Your Strengths and Weaknesses

Check the number of each question answered correctly and "X" the number of each question answered incorrectly.

Algebra	1	2	3	6	7	9	11	13	17	18	41	43	Total Number Correct
12 questions													

Plane Geometry	12	19	20	23	25	42	45	47	49	50	Total Number Correct
10 questions											

Solid Geometry	30	39	44	48	Total Number Correct
4 questions					

Coordinate Geometry	4	5	8	15	22	28	Total Number Correct
6 questions							

Trigonometry	14	24	26	27	35	Total Number Correct
5 questions						

Functions	10	21	29	31	34	36	Total Number Correct
6 questions							

Data Analysis, Statistics, and Probability	16	32	37	Total Number Correct
3 questions				

Number and Operations	33	38	40	46	Total Number Correct
4 questions					

Number of correct answers $-\frac{1}{4}$ **(Number of incorrect answers) = Your raw score**

_____ $-\frac{1}{4}$ (_____) = _____

Compare your raw score with the approximate SAT Subject test score below:

	Raw Score	SAT Subject test Approximate Score
Excellent	46–50	750–800
Very Good	41–45	700–750
Good	36–40	640–700
Above Average	29–35	590–640
Average	22–28	510–590
Below Average	< 22	<510

PRACTICE TEST 3

Treat this practice test as the actual test and complete it in one 60-minute sitting. Use the following answer sheet to fill in your multiple-choice answers. Once you have completed the practice test:

1. Check your answers using the Answer Key.
2. Review the Answer Explanations.
3. Fill in the "Diagnose Your Strengths and Weaknesses" sheet and determine areas that require further preparation.

PRACTICE TEST 3
MATH LEVEL 1

Tear out this answer sheet and use it to complete the practice test.

Determine the BEST answer for each question. Then fill in the appropriate oval using a No. 2 pencil.

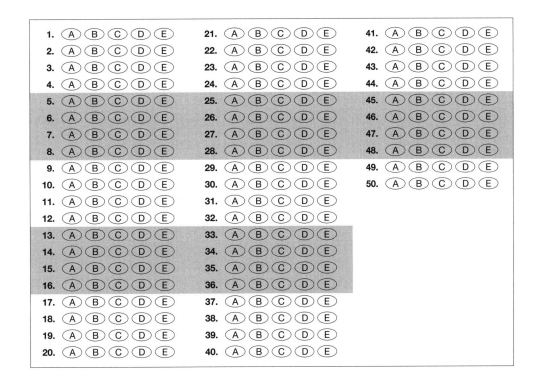

PRACTICE TEST 3

Time: 60 Minutes

<u>Directions:</u> Select the BEST answer for each of the 50 multiple-choice questions. If the exact solution is not one of the five choices, select the answer that is the best approximation. Then fill in the appropriate oval on the answer sheet.

<u>Notes:</u>

(1) A calculator will be needed to answer some of the questions on the test. Scientific, programmable, and graphing calculators are permitted. It is up to you to determine when and when not to use your calculator.

(2) All angles on the Level 1 test are measured in degrees, not radians. Make sure your calculator is set to degree mode.

(3) Figures are drawn as accurately as possible and are intended to help solve some of the test problems. If a figure is not drawn to scale, this will be stated in the problem. All figures lie in a plane unless the problem indicates otherwise.

(4) Unless otherwise stated, the domain of a function f is assumed to be the set of real numbers x for which the value of the function, $f(x)$, is a real number.

(5) Reference information that may be useful in answering some of the test questions can be found below.

Reference Information	
Right circular cone with radius r and height h:	Volume $= \dfrac{1}{3}\pi r^2 h$
Right circular cone with circumference of base c and slant height ℓ:	Lateral Area $= \dfrac{1}{2}c\ell$
Sphere with radius r:	Volume $= \dfrac{4}{3}\pi r^3$ Surface Area $= 4\pi r^2$
Pyramid with base area B and height h:	Volume $= \dfrac{1}{3}Bh$

GO ON TO THE NEXT PAGE

1. If a car travels 300 miles in 6 hours, then assuming the car travels at the same rate, how long will it take to travel 360 miles?

   (A) 5 hours
   (B) 6 hours
   (C) 7 hours
   (D) 7 hours, 12 minutes
   (E) 7 hours, 20 minutes

2. A number n is decreased by 4. The square root of the result equals 0.8. $n =$

   (A) 23.04
   (B) 0.8
   (C) 0.64
   (D) 4.64
   (E) −3.36

3. If $f(x) = x^4 - 2x^3 + 6x - 1$, then $f(-2) =$

   (A) −13
   (B) 19
   (C) 32
   (D) 11
   (E) 43

4. What is the midpoint of the segment with endpoints $A(-3, -8)$ and $B(4, 6)$?

   (A) $\left(\dfrac{1}{2}, -1\right)$

   (B) $\left(-1, \dfrac{1}{2}\right)$

   (C) $\left(-\dfrac{1}{2}, 1\right)$

   (D) $(-7, -14)$

   (E) $\left(-\dfrac{7}{2}, -7\right)$

5. What is $\dfrac{1}{2}$ percent of 6?

   (A) 3
   (B) 0.06
   (C) 0.03
   (D) 12
   (E) 0.003

USE THIS SPACE AS SCRATCH PAPER

GO ON TO THE NEXT PAGE

6. What are the x-intercept(s) of the graph of $f(x) = x^2 - 9$?

   (A) $(3, 0)$
   (B) $(0, 3)$
   (C) $(0, -9)$
   (D) $(-3, 0)$
   (E) $(\pm 3, 0)$

USE THIS SPACE AS SCRATCH PAPER

7. All of the following are equivalent to the equation of the line containing points $(0, 1)$ and $(4, 3)$ EXCEPT

   (A) $y = \dfrac{1}{2}x + 1$

   (B) $x - 2y = -2$

   (C) $(y - 3) = \dfrac{1}{2}(x - 4)$

   (D) $2x - y + 1 = 0$

   (E) $(y - 1) = \dfrac{1}{2}x$

8. What are all the values of x for which $x^2 + 5x - 14 \le 0$?

   (A) $x \le -7$ or $x \ge 2$
   (B) $-7 \le x \le 2$
   (C) $x \ge 2$
   (D) $x \ge -7$
   (E) $x \le 2$

9. If $f(x) = x^3$ and f^{-1} is the inverse function of f, then $f^{-1}(27) =$

   (A) 27^3
   (B) 3
   (C) -3
   (D) 9
   (E) 5.2

10. What is the slope of the line containing the points $(6, 0)$ and $(6, 7)$?

   (A) 7
   (B) 0
   (C) Undefined
   (D) $\dfrac{1}{6}$
   (E) -7

11. The triangle in Figure 1 has sides measuring 6, 8, and 10 units. What is the measure of θ?

    (A) 53.1°
    (B) 36.9°
    (C) 60°
    (D) 30°
    (E) 45°

12. How many total diagonals can be drawn from all of the vertices of a 15-gon?

    (A) 13
    (B) 12
    (C) 180
    (D) 90
    (E) 77

13. $\dfrac{2 - \sqrt{3}}{2 + \sqrt{3}} =$

    (A) 0
    (B) −1
    (C) $\dfrac{1}{7 + 4\sqrt{3}}$
    (D) $7 - 4\sqrt{3}$
    (E) $1 - 4\sqrt{3}$

14. $(a^2 - 1)(a^2 - 4) =$
    (A) $(a - 1)(a + 1)(a - 2)(a + 2)$
    (B) $a^2 + 4$
    (C) $a^4 + 5a^2 + 4$
    (D) $a^4 - 5a^2 - 4$
    (E) $(a - 1)(a - 4)$

15. In Figure 2, $\ell_1 \parallel \ell_2$. What is the value of x?
    (A) 140°
    (B) 70°
    (C) 110°
    (D) 40°
    (E) 35°

USE THIS SPACE AS SCRATCH PAPER

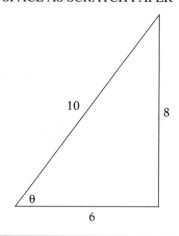

Figure 1

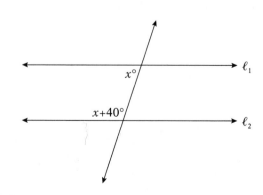

Figure 2

GO ON TO THE NEXT PAGE

16. If $\triangle ABC$ is congruent to $\triangle JKL$, then all of the following parts are congruent by CPCTC EXCEPT

    (A) $\overline{AB} \cong \overline{JK}$
    (B) $\overline{CA} \cong \overline{JL}$
    (C) $\angle B \cong \angle K$
    (D) $\overline{CB} \cong \overline{LJ}$
    (E) $\angle C \cong \angle L$

17. What is the measure of y in Figure 3?

    (A) 18°
    (B) 72°
    (C) 90°
    (D) 108°
    (E) 162°

18. If the sides of a cube are doubled, then its volume is increased by what factor?

    (A) 2
    (B) 3
    (C) 4
    (D) 8
    (E) 16

19. In Figure 4, the length of $\overline{XZ}$ is 16 and $\overline{XY}$ is one-third the length of $\overline{YZ}$. What is the length of $\overline{XY}$?

    (A) 3
    (B) 4
    (C) 5.3
    (D) 12
    (E) 21.3

20. What is the length of the altitude of $\triangle ABC$ in Figure 5 given that the measure of $\angle ABC$ is 35°?

    (A) 5.6
    (B) 10
    (C) 4.6
    (D) 6
    (E) 6.6

USE THIS SPACE AS SCRATCH PAPER

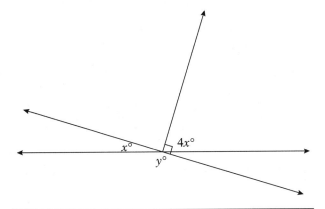

Figure 3

Figure 4

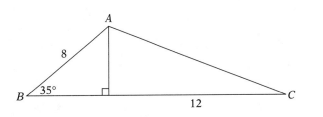

Figure 5

GO ON TO THE NEXT PAGE

21. All of the following statements are true regarding the graph of $y = x^2$ EXCEPT

    (A) It is concave up.
    (B) Its vertex is the origin.
    (C) Its directrix is the line $y = -\dfrac{1}{4}$.
    (D) It does not represent a function.
    (E) It is symmetric with respect to the y-axis.

22. What is the domain of the function $f(x) = \sqrt{x^2 - 10}$?

    (A) $x \geq 0$
    (B) $x \leq -\sqrt{10}$ or $x \geq \sqrt{10}$
    (C) $-\sqrt{10} \quad x \leq \sqrt{10}$
    (D) $-10 \leq x \leq 10$
    (E) $x \geq \sqrt{10}$

23. Which of the following shapes has exactly four lines of symmetry?

    (A) Square
    (B) Rhombus
    (C) Parallelogram
    (D) Rectangle
    (E) Circle

24. Sarah wants to purchase a new car. At the car dealership, there are 4 different models to choose from in her price range. For each model, there are 5 different colors (black, silver, green, navy, and red) and 2 different engine types (4-cylinder or 6-cylinder). How many combinations of model-color-engine type are there?

    (A) 11
    (B) 20
    (C) 40
    (D) 8
    (E) 10

25. If $\log_n 18 - \log_n x = \log_n 6$, then $x =$

    (A) 3
    (B) 0.48
    (C) 12
    (D) 6
    (E) 108

GO ON TO THE NEXT PAGE

26. If the sum of two numbers is 40, then what is their greatest possible product?

    (A) 391
    (B) 396
    (C) 400
    (D) 399
    (E) 420

27. If $i = \sqrt{-1}$, then $\dfrac{5 - i}{5 + i} =$

    (A) -1
    (B) $\dfrac{13}{12} - \dfrac{5}{12}i$
    (C) $\dfrac{12}{13} - \dfrac{5}{13}i$
    (D) $24 - 10i$
    (E) $\dfrac{3}{2}$

28. Mark received a 92 percent and a 78 percent on the first two math tests. What grade must he receive on the third test to have an average of 84 percent?

    (A) 80%
    (B) 82%
    (C) 84%
    (D) 85%
    (E) 86%

29. All of the following triplets could be the lengths of the sides of a right triangle EXCEPT

    (A) 6, 8, 10
    (B) 15, 20, 25
    (C) 7, 24, 25
    (D) $\sqrt{3}, \sqrt{4}, \sqrt{5}$
    (E) $1, 2, \sqrt{5}$

30. A cone-shaped cup has a height of 10 units and a radius of 3 units. The cup is filled with water and the height of the water is 6 units. What is radius of the surface of the water?

    (A) 1.5 units
    (B) 1.8 units
    (C) 2 units
    (D) 3 units
    (E) 5 units

GO ON TO THE NEXT PAGE

31. How many degrees does the hour hand of a clock rotate in 20 minutes?

    (A) 30°
    (B) 10°
    (C) 6°
    (D) 15°
    (E) 7.5°

32. $(6\sin x)(3\sin x) - (9\cos x)(-2\cos x) =$

    (A) 1
    (B) −18
    (C) 18
    (D) −1
    (E) $18\sin^2 x - 18\cos^2 x$

33. Figure 6 is the graph of which of the following?

    (A) $y \geq |x + 6|$
    (B) $y \leq |x + 6|$
    (C) $y \geq |x - 6|$
    (D) $y < |x - 6|$
    (E) $y = |x - 6|$

34. What is the minimum value of the function $f(x) = x^4 + 2x^2 + 1$?

    (A) 0
    (B) 1
    (C) −1
    (D) 2
    (E) 4

35. In $\triangle ABC$ in Figure 7, $m\angle CAB = 60°$ and $\overline{AB} = 4\sqrt{3}$. What is the length of $\overline{BC}$?

    (A) $2\sqrt{3}$
    (B) $8\sqrt{3}$
    (C) 24
    (D) 12
    (E) 8

USE THIS SPACE AS SCRATCH PAPER

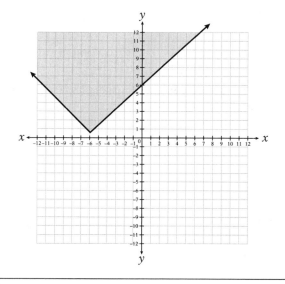

Figure 6

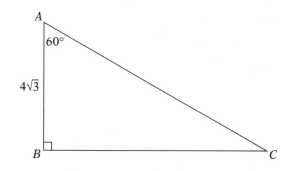

Figure 7

GO ON TO THE NEXT PAGE

36. If $f(x) = x + 1$ and $g(x) = x^2 - 1$, then what is $g(f(x))$?

    (A) $x^2 + 1$
    (B) $x^2 - 1$
    (C) $x^2 + 2x - 1$
    (D) $x^2 + 2x + 1$
    (E) $x^2 + 2x$

USE THIS SPACE AS SCRATCH PAPER

37. In rectangle $ABCD$, $\overline{AB} = 3$ cm and $\overline{AD} = 3\sqrt{3}$. If a square has the same area as the area of $ABCD$, what is the length of a side of the square?

    (A) 3
    (B) $3\sqrt{3}$
    (C) 5.2
    (D) 3.9
    (E) 7.8

38. Solve $(x - 3)^{\frac{3}{5}} = 8$.

    (A) 32
    (B) 35
    (C) 19
    (D) 67
    (E) 29

39. Assuming each dimension must be an integer, how many different rectangular prisms with a volume of 18 cm^3 are there?

    (A) 2
    (B) 3
    (C) 4
    (D) 5
    (E) 6

40. What is the range of the function $f(x) = 6^x$?

    (A) All real numbers
    (B) $y \geq 1$
    (C) $y \geq 0$
    (D) $y > 0$
    (E) All real numbers except $y = 0$

41. How many points may be contained in the intersection of two distinct circles?

    I. 0 points
    II. 1 point
    III. 2 points
    IV. 3 points

    (A) III only
    (B) II or III only
    (C) III or IV only
    (D) I, II, or III only
    (E) I, II, III, or IV

GO ON TO THE NEXT PAGE

42. How many different chords can be drawn from 8 distinct points on a circle?

    (A) 48
    (B) 7
    (C) 8
    (D) 16
    (E) 28

43. Assuming $a > 1$, which of the following expressions represents the greatest value?

    (A) $\dfrac{a+1}{a+1}$

    (B) $\dfrac{a}{a+1}$

    (C) $\dfrac{a}{a-1}$

    (D) $\dfrac{a-1}{a-2}$

    (E) $\dfrac{a+1}{a-1}$

44. If $4n + 1$, $6n$, and $7n + 2$ are the first three terms of an arithmetic sequence, what is the value of n?

    (A) $\dfrac{3}{2}$

    (B) 2
    (C) 3
    (D) 1
    (E) 6

45. All of the following are equivalent to the expression $(4x - 8)(x + 1)$ EXCEPT

    (A) $4(x - 2)(x + 1)$
    (B) $-4(2 - x)(x + 1)$
    (C) $4(x^2 - x - 2)$
    (D) $(1 + x)(8 - 4x)$
    (E) $4x^2 - 4x - 8$

46. $\sqrt{4 + 4x^2} + \sqrt{9x^2 + 9} =$

    (A) $\sqrt{13x^2 + 13}$

    (B) $5x + 5$

    (C) $5\sqrt{x^2 + 1}$

    (D) $\sqrt{13(x^2 + 1)}$

    (E) $6x + 6$

GO ON TO THE NEXT PAGE

47. A ball is dropped from a height of 8 feet. If it always rebounds $\frac{2}{3}$ the distance it has fallen, how high will it reach after it hits the ground for the third time?

    (A) 5.33
    (B) 3.56
    (C) 2.37
    (D) 1.58
    (E) 2.73

48. The solution set of $8x^2 - 16x - 24 = 0$ is which of the following?

    (A) $\{-1, 3\}$
    (B) $\{-3, 1\}$
    (C) $\{-1, 3, 8\}$
    (D) $\{-1, -3\}$
    (E) $\{1, 3\}$

49. If $x^2 - 5x + 1 = (x - a)^2 + c$, then what is the value of c?

    (A) $-\frac{29}{4}$

    (B) $-\frac{21}{4}$

    (C) $-\frac{5}{2}$

    (D) $-\frac{25}{4}$

    (E) 1

50. Solve $3x - 5\sqrt{x} - 2 = 0$

    (A) $\left\{\frac{1}{9}, 4\right\}$

    (B) $\left\{\frac{1}{9}\right\}$

    (C) $\{4\}$

    (D) $\left\{-\frac{1}{9}, -4\right\}$

    (E) $\{-4\}$

S T O P

IF YOU FINISH BEFORE TIME IS CALLED, GO BACK AND CHECK YOUR WORK.

ANSWER KEY

1. D	11. A	21. D	31. B	41. D
2. D	12. D	22. B	32. C	42. E
3. B	13. D	23. A	33. A	43. E
4. A	14. A	24. C	34. B	44. C
5. C	15. B	25. A	35. D	45. D
6. E	16. D	26. C	36. E	46. C
7. D	17. E	27. C	37. D	47. C
8. B	18. D	28. B	38. B	48. A
9. B	19. B	29. D	39. C	49. B
10. C	20. C	30. B	40. D	50. C

ANSWERS AND SOLUTIONS

1. **D**

$$\frac{300}{6} = \frac{360}{t}$$

$$t = \frac{6(360)}{300} = 7.2 \text{ hours}$$

7.2 hours is equivalent to 7 hours and 12 minutes.

2. **D**

$$\sqrt{n - 4} = 0.8$$

$$n - 4 = 0.64$$

$$n = 4.64$$

3. **B**

$$f(-2) = (-2)^4 - 2(-2)^3 + 6(-2) - 1$$

$$= 16 + 16 - 12 - 1$$

$$= 19$$

4. **A**

The midpoint is given by $\left(\dfrac{x_1 + x_2}{2}, \dfrac{y_1 + y_2}{2} \right)$

The x-coordinate is $\left(\dfrac{-3 + 4}{2} \right) = \dfrac{1}{2}$.

The y-coordinate is $\dfrac{(-8 + 6)}{2} = -1$.

5. **C**

$$a = \frac{1}{2}\% \text{ of } 6$$

$$a = 0.005(6)$$

$$a = 0.03$$

6. **E** Set $y = 0$ and solve for x.

$$0 = x^2 - 9$$

$$9 = x^2$$

$$x = \pm 3$$

The x-intercepts are the two points $(3, 0)$ and $(-3, 0)$.

7. **D** The slope of the line containing $(0, 1)$ and $(4, 3)$ equals $\dfrac{2}{4}$ or $\dfrac{1}{2}$. Answer D cannot be correct because the slope of the line is 2.

8. **B**

$$x^2 + 5x - 14 \le 0$$

$$(x + 7)(x - 2) \le 0$$

The critical points of the graph are $x = -7$ and $x = 2$. Test the inequality when $x = 0$ to see that $0^2 + 5(0) - 14 \le 0$ is a true statement. The interval between -7 and 2, inclusive, satisfies the inequality.

9. **B** The inverse function of $f(x) = x^3$ is $f^{-1} = \sqrt[3]{x}$.

$$f^{-1} = \sqrt[3]{27} = 3$$

10. **C**

$$\text{Slope} = \frac{y_2 - y_1}{x_2 - x_1}$$

$$m = \frac{7 - 0}{6 - 6} = \frac{7}{0} = \text{undefined}$$

11. **A**

$$\sin \theta = \frac{8}{10}, \text{ so}$$

$$\theta = \sin^{-1}(0.8) = 53.1°$$

12. **D** Recall that $\dfrac{n(n-3)}{2}$ is the total number of diagonals in a polygon, assuming n = the number of sides. (The number of diagonals that can be drawn from one vertex is $n - 3$.)

$$\frac{n(n-3)}{2} = \frac{15(12)}{2} = 90$$

13. **D**

$$\frac{2 - \sqrt{3}}{2 + \sqrt{3}} = \frac{2 - \sqrt{3}}{2 + \sqrt{3}} \times \frac{2 - \sqrt{3}}{2 - \sqrt{3}}$$

$$= \frac{4 - 4\sqrt{3} + 3}{4 - 3} = 7 - 4\sqrt{3}$$

14. **A** Recognize that both binomials are the difference of perfect squares which can be factored as:

$$(a - 1)(a + 1)(a - 2)(a + 2)$$

15. **B**

$$x + x + 40 = 180°$$

$$2x = 140$$

$$x = 70°$$

16. **D** $\overline{CB}$ is congruent to $\overline{LK}$, not $\overline{LJ}$. Answer D is not a true statement.

17. **E** The smaller angle adjacent to the angle measuring $4x$ is a vertical angle to the angle measuring x. Therefore, it must also measure $x°$.

$$4x + x = 90$$

$$5x = 90$$

$$x = 18°$$

$$y = 180 - 18 = 162°$$

18. **D** If the original cube has sides of length e, its volume is e^3. Doubling the sides of the cube results in a volume of $(2e)^3 = 8e^3$. The volume is increased by a factor of 2^3 or 8.

19. **B**

Let $YZ = x$.

$$\frac{1}{3}x + x = 16$$

$$\frac{4}{3}x = 16$$

$$x = \frac{16(3)}{4} = 12$$

$$XY = \frac{1}{3}(YZ) = \frac{1}{3}(12) = 4$$

20. **C**

$$\sin 35° = \frac{h}{8}$$

$$h = 8(\sin 35°) \approx 4.6$$

21. **D** Parabolas in the form $y = x^2$ represent a function. You can check this by graphing the equation on your calculator and seeing that the graph passes the vertical line test. Parabolas in the form $x = y^2$ are not functions, however. D is the correct answer.

22. **B**

$$x^2 - 10 \geq 0$$

$$= x^2 \geq 10$$

$-\sqrt{10}$ and $\sqrt{10}$ are the critical points. Test $x = 0$ to see that the interval between $-\sqrt{10}$ and $\sqrt{10}$ does not satisfy the equation. The correct answer is $x \leq -\sqrt{10}$ or $x \geq \sqrt{10}$.

23. **A** A square has exactly 4 lines of symmetry: the lines containing each diagonal and the lines connecting the midpoints of opposite sides. (Since a square is a special parallelogram, *some*, but not all, parallelograms have 4 lines of symmetry.)

24. **C** Using the Fundamental Counting Principle, there are $4 \times 5 \times 2 = 40$ possible combinations.

25. **A**

$$\log_n 18 - \log_n x = \log_n 6$$

$$\frac{18}{x} = 6$$

$$x = 3$$

26. **C** Let x = one number and $40 - x$ = the second number. The product of the two numbers is given by the function:

$$P(x) = x(40 - x)$$
$$P(x) = 40x - x^2$$

The maximum value occurs when

$$x = -\frac{b}{2a} = -\frac{40}{2(-1)} = 20$$

When $x = 20$, the maximum product of the two numbers is:

$$P(x) = 20(40 - 20) = 20(20) = 400$$

27. **C** Multiply the numerator and the denominator by $5 - i$, the conjugate of $5 + i$. (Recall that $i^2 = -1$.)

$$\frac{5 - i}{5 + i} \times \frac{5 - i}{5 - i}$$

$$= \frac{(5 - i)(5 - i)}{(5 + i)(5 - i)}$$

$$= \frac{25 - 10i + i^2}{25 - i^2}$$

$$= \frac{24 - 10i}{26} = \frac{12}{13} - \frac{5}{13}i$$

28. **B** Let t = Mark's grade on the third test.

$$\frac{92 + 78 + t}{3} = 84$$

$$170 + t = 3(84)$$

$$t = 252 - 170 = 82$$

29. **D** Substitute the lengths of the sides of the triangle into the Pythagorean Theorem to see if they satisfy the equation.

$$\sqrt{3}^2 + \sqrt{4}^2 = \sqrt{5}^2$$

$$3 + 4 \neq 5$$

It is impossible to have a right triangle with sides of lengths $\sqrt{3} + \sqrt{4}$ and $\sqrt{5}$.

30. **B** Filling the cone-shaped cup with water creates a cone similar to the cup itself. The radii and heights of the two cones are proportional. Let r = the radius of the surface of the water.

$$\frac{6}{10} = \frac{r}{3}$$

$$18 = 10r$$

$$1.8 = r$$

31. **B** Between two consecutive numbers on a clock, there are $\frac{360}{12}$ or 30°. In 20 minutes, the hour hand moves

$$\frac{20}{60}(30) = 10°$$

32. **C**

$$(6\sin x)(3\sin x) - (9\cos x)(-2\cos x)$$

$$= 18\sin^2 x + 18\cos^2 x$$

$$= 18(\sin^2 x + \cos^2 x)$$

$$= 18(1) = 18$$

33. **A** The graph represents the absolute value of an expression since it is "V-shaped." It is shifted 6 units to the left of the origin because of the $(x + 6)$ term. Since the graph is shaded above the "V-shaped" lines and the lines are solid (not dashed), it represents a "greater than or equal to" expression. $y \geq |x + 6|$ is the only possible answer. You can check this by graphing the expression using the Inequal application on your TI graphing calculator.

34. **B** The minimum value of the function is the y-coordinate of its vertex. Graph the function $f(x) = x^4 + 2x^2 + 1$ on your graphing calculator to find its vertex $(0, 1)$. The minimum value is 1.

35. **D** $\triangle ABC$ is a 30°-60°-90° right triangle. Since the side opposite the 30° angle measures $4\sqrt{3}$, $\overline{BC}$ (the side opposite the 60°) must measure

$$4\sqrt{3}\left(\sqrt{3}\right) = 12$$

36. **E**

$$g(f(x)) = g(x + 1) = (x + 1)^2 - 1$$

$$= x^2 + 2x + 1 - 1$$

$$= x^2 + 2x$$

37. **D** The area of the rectangle is $3\left(3\sqrt{3}\right) = 9\sqrt{3} = 15.59$ cm². One side of the square must be equal to the square root of 15.59.

$$\sqrt{15.59} \approx 3.9 \text{ cm}$$

38. **B**

$$(x-3)^{\frac{3}{5}} = 8$$

$$\left[(x-3)^{\frac{3}{5}}\right]^{\frac{5}{3}} = 8^{\frac{5}{3}}$$

$$(x-3) = (2^3)^{\frac{5}{3}}$$

$$(x-3) = 2^5 = 32$$

$$x = 32 + 3 = 35$$

39. **C** The volume of a rectangular prism is given by the formula $V = \ell \times w \times h$, so you need to find three integers whose product is 18. There are four possibilities:

$1 \times 1 \times 18$

$1 \times 2 \times 9$

$1 \times 3 \times 6$

$2 \times 3 \times 3$

40. **D** Notice that as x increases without bound, the value of $f(x) = 6^x$ gets larger. As x decreases without bound, the value of the function approaches zero. 6^x will never equal zero and will never be negative, however, so $y > 0$ is the correct answer.

41. **D** Tangent circles intersect in one point. Of course, if distinct circles did not intersect, their intersection would contain zero points, and two non-tangent, intersecting circles intersect in two points. I, II, and III are possible answers.

42. **E** 7 different chords can be drawn from the first point. 6 additional chords can be drawn from the second point, since the chords must be distinct and one has already been drawn. 5 additional chords can be drawn from the third point, since you cannot count the 2 already drawn. Continue this pattern to get

$$7 + 6 + 5 + 4 + 3 + 2 + 1 = 28 \text{ chords}$$

43. **E** Answer A equals 1 and Answer B is less than 1, so both can be eliminated. Since C and E have the same denominator and $a < a + 1$, C will always be less than E. It can also be eliminated as a possible answer choice. Substitute a few values of a into answers D and E to compare the expressions.

If $a = 7$, $\dfrac{6}{5} < \dfrac{8}{6}$

If $a = 10$, $\dfrac{9}{8} < \dfrac{11}{9}$

Answer E will always result in a greater value.

44. **C** Since the expressions represent the terms of an arithmetic sequence, there must be a common difference between consecutive terms.

$$6n - (4n + 1) = 7n + 2 - 6n$$

$$2n - 1 = n + 2$$

$$n = 3$$

45. **D** The expression $-(1 + x)(8 - 4x)$ is equivalent to the given expression, but $(1 + x)(8 - 4x)$ is not. By the Commutative Property of Addition, $1 + x$ is equivalent to $x + 1$. $8 - 4x$ is not equivalent to $4x - 8$, however.

46. **C**

$$\sqrt{4 + 4x^2} + \sqrt{9x^2 + 9}$$

$$= \sqrt{4(1 + x^2)} + \sqrt{9(x^2 + 1)}$$

$$= 2\sqrt{1 + x^2} + 3\sqrt{x^2 + 1}$$

$$= 5\sqrt{1 + x^2}$$

47. **C** Recognize that the heights of the bouncing ball form a geometric sequence with a common ratio of $\dfrac{2}{3}$ and an initial term of 8. After hitting the ground for the first time, the ball will reach a height of $(8)\left(\dfrac{2}{3}\right) = 5.33$. After the second bounce, the ball will reach a height of $(8)\left(\dfrac{2}{3}\right)^2 = 3.56$. After the third bounce, the ball will reach a height of $(8)\left(\dfrac{2}{3}\right)^3 = 2.37$ feet.

48. **A**

$$8x^2 - 16x - 24 = 0$$

$$8(x^2 - 2x - 3) = 0$$

$$8(x - 3)(x + 1) = 0$$

$$x = 3 \text{ or } x = -1$$

49. **B** Complete the square to get a perfect binomial squared plus a constant.

$$x^2 - 5x + 1$$

$$= \left[x^2 + 5x + \left(\frac{5}{2} \right)^2 \right] - \left(\frac{5}{2} \right)^2 + 1$$

$$= \left(x - \frac{5}{2} \right)^2 - \frac{25}{4} + \frac{4}{4}$$

$$= \left(x - \frac{5}{2} \right)^2 - \frac{21}{4}, \text{ so } c = -\frac{21}{4}$$

50. **C** Isolate the radical expression and square both sides to solve for x.

$$3x - 5\sqrt{x} - 2 = 0$$

$$3x - 2 = 5\sqrt{x}$$

$$(3x - 2)^2 = \left(\sqrt{5x} \right)^2$$

$$9x^2 - 12x + 4 = 25x$$

$$9x^2 - 37x + 4 = 0$$

$$(9x - 1)(x - 4) = 0$$

$$x = \frac{1}{9} \text{ or } x = 4$$

Remember to check for extraneous roots by substituting both solutions into the original equation. $\frac{1}{9}$ is an extraneous root since $3\left(\frac{1}{9} \right) - 5\sqrt{\frac{1}{9}} - 2 \neq 0$. The only solution is $x = 4$.

Diagnose Your Strengths and Weaknesses

Check the number of each question answered correctly and "X" the number of each question answered incorrectly.

Algebra	1	2	5	8	13	14	26	38	45	46	48	49	50	Total Number Correct
13 questions														

Plane Geometry	12	15	16	17	18	23	29	31	37	41	Total Number Correct
10 questions											

Solid Geometry	18	30	39	Total Number Correct
3 questions				

Coordinate Geometry	4	6	7	10	21	33	Total Number Correct
6 questions							

Trigonometry	11	20	32	35	Total Number Correct
4 questions					

Functions	3	9	22	34	36	40	Total Number Correct
6 questions							

Data Analysis, Statistics, and Probability	24	28	42	Total Number Correct
3 questions				

Number and Operations	25	27	43	44	47	Total Number Correct
5 questions						

Number of correct answers $- \frac{1}{4}$ **(Number of incorrect answers) = Your raw score**

$$\rule{3cm}{0.4pt} - \frac{1}{4} (\rule{3cm}{0.4pt}) = \rule{2cm}{0.4pt}$$

Compare your raw score with the approximate SAT Subject test score below:

	Raw Score	**SAT Subject test Approximate Score**
Excellent	46–50	750–800
Very Good	41–45	700–750
Good	36–40	640–700
Above Average	29–35	590–640
Average	22–28	510–590
Below Average	< 22	<510

PRACTICE TEST 4

Treat this practice test as the actual test and complete it in one 60-minute sitting. Use the following answer sheet to fill in your multiple-choice answers. Once you have completed the practice test:

1. Check your answers using the Answer Key.
2. Review the Answer Explanations.
3. Fill in the "Diagnose Your Strengths and Weaknesses" sheet and determine areas that require further preparation.

PRACTICE TEST 4

MATH LEVEL 1

ANSWER SHEET

Tear out this answer sheet and use it to complete the practice test.

Determine the BEST answer for each question. Then fill in the appropriate oval using a No. 2 pencil.

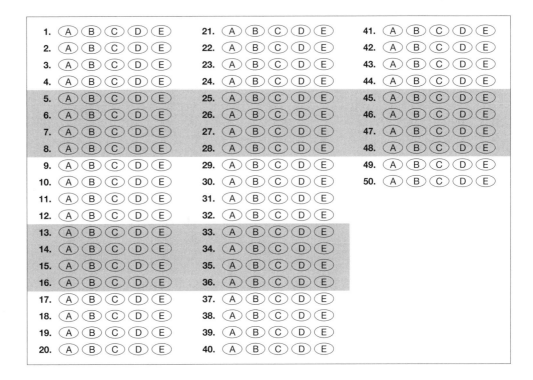

PRACTICE TEST 4

Time: 60 Minutes

<u>Directions:</u> Select the BEST answer for each of the 50 multiple-choice questions. If the exact solution is not one of the five choices, select the answer that is the best approximation. Then fill in the appropriate oval on the answer sheet.

<u>NOTES:</u>

(1) A calculator will be needed to answer some of the questions on the test. Scientific, programmable, and graphing calculators are permitted. It is up to you to determine when and when not to use your calculator.

(2) All angles on the Level 1 test are measured in degrees, not radians. Make sure your calculator is set to degree mode.

(3) Figures are drawn as accurately as possible and are intended to help solve some of the test problems. If a figure is not drawn to scale, this will be stated in the problem. All figures lie in a plane unless the problem indicates otherwise.

(4) Unless otherwise stated, the domain of a function f is assumed to be the set of real numbers x for which the value of the function, $f(x)$, is a real number.

(5) Reference information that may be useful in answering some of the test questions can be found below.

Reference Information	
Right circular cone with radius r and height h:	Volume $= \dfrac{1}{3}\pi r^2 h$
Right circular cone with circumference of base c and slant height ℓ:	Lateral Area $= \dfrac{1}{2}c\ell$
Sphere with radius r:	Volume $= \dfrac{4}{3}\pi r^3$ Surface Area $= 4\pi r^2$
Pyramid with base area B and height h:	Volume $= \dfrac{1}{3}Bh$

GO ON TO THE NEXT PAGE

1. If $3x = 7$, then $9x =$

   (A) $\dfrac{7}{3}$

   (B) 18

   (C) 14

   (D) 21

   (E) 63

USE THIS SPACE AS SCRATCH PAPER

2. If $\dfrac{3}{10} = \dfrac{5}{x}$, then $x =$

   (A) $\dfrac{50}{3}$

   (B) $\dfrac{3}{50}$

   (C) 16

   (D) 12

   (E) 17

3. $9\sin^2 x + 9\cos^2 x =$

   (A) 1

   (B) -1

   (C) 9

   (D) -9

   (E) 0

4. If the supplement of twice an angle is 124°, then what is the measure of the angle?

   (A) 60°

   (B) 30°

   (C) 56°

   (D) 28°

   (E) 27°

5. Two times a number k is decreased by 1. If the cube root of that result is -2, then $k =$

   (A) -7

   (B) -3.5

   (C) -8

   (D) -3

   (E) -4.5

6. All of the following triplets could be the lengths of the sides of a triangle EXCEPT

   (A) 3, 4, 5

   (B) 3, 3, 5

   (C) 1, 1, 2

   (D) 6, 8, 10

   (E) 7, 5, 11

GO ON TO THE NEXT PAGE

7. Valerie drives 10 miles due east, then drives 20 miles due north, and finally drives 5 miles due west. Which of the following represents the straight-line distance Valerie is from her starting point?

   (A) 24 miles
   (B) 22.4 miles
   (C) 25 miles
   (D) 35 miles
   (E) 20.6 miles

8. The measures of the angles of a quadrilateral are x, $2x + 7$, $3x$, and $5x + 1$. What is the measure of the largest angle?

   (A) 33°
   (B) 32°
   (C) 161°
   (D) 166°
   (E) 168°

9. How many sides does a regular polygon have if each interior angle measures 140°?

   (A) 6
   (B) 7
   (C) 8
   (D) 9
   (E) 10

10. What is the solution to the system below?

$$\begin{cases} 2x + y = \dfrac{5}{2} \\ x - 2y = 5 \end{cases}$$

   (A) $\left(2, \dfrac{3}{2}\right)$

   (B) $\left(2, -\dfrac{3}{2}\right)$

   (C) $\left(0, -\dfrac{5}{2}\right)$

   (D) $\left(\dfrac{10}{3}, -\dfrac{5}{6}\right)$

   (E) $\left(0, \dfrac{5}{2}\right)$

USE THIS SPACE AS SCRATCH PAPER

GO ON TO THE NEXT PAGE

11. Which of the following is NOT an irrational number?

    (A) π
    (B) $\sqrt{2}$
    (C) e
    (D) $1.666\ldots$
    (E) $\dfrac{\sqrt{3}}{2}$

12. What is the distance between the points with coordinates $(-2, 6)$ and $(2, -3)$?

    (A) 9.85
    (B) 97
    (C) 65
    (D) 8.06
    (E) 3

13. Which of the following best describes the figure with vertices $P(-2, 3)$, $Q(3, 3)$, $R(3, -1)$, and $S(-2, -1)$?

    (A) Square
    (B) Rectangle
    (C) Parallelogram
    (D) Trapezoid
    (E) Rhombus

14. Which of the following are solutions to the equation $30x^2 + 49x - 11 = 0$?

    (A) $\left\{-\dfrac{1}{5}, \dfrac{11}{6}\right\}$
    (B) $\left\{-\dfrac{1}{30}, -11\right\}$
    (C) $\left\{\dfrac{1}{5}, -\dfrac{11}{6}\right\}$
    (D) $\left\{\dfrac{1}{30}, 11\right\}$
    (E) $\left\{-\dfrac{11}{15}, -\dfrac{1}{2}\right\}$

15. The points $(4, -2)$ and (x, y) are symmetric to each other with respect to the origin. $(x, y) =$

    (A) $(-2, 4)$
    (B) $(2, -4)$
    (C) $(4, 2)$
    (D) $(-4, -2)$
    (E) $(-4, 2)$

GO ON TO THE NEXT PAGE

16. Each of the following is equivalent to $4\sqrt{2}$ EXCEPT

(A) $2\sqrt{2} + 2\sqrt{2}$

(B) $\sqrt{32}$

(C) $\sqrt{8}(\sqrt{4})$

(D) $\dfrac{\sqrt{64}}{\sqrt{2}}$

(E) $\sqrt{20} + \sqrt{12}$

17. In $\triangle ABC$ in Figure 1, $\overline{AB} = 4$ and $\overline{AC} = 4$. What is the length of $\overline{AC}$?

(A) 4

(B) $4\sqrt{2}$

(C) $4\sqrt{3}$

(D) 8

(E) 5

18. A local newspaper company prints 520 pages of the newspaper every 30 minutes. How many pages will it print in 5 hours?

(A) 2,600 pages

(B) 86.7 pages

(C) 5,200 pages

(D) 10,400 pages

(E) 1,300 pages

19. When n is divided by 3, the remainder is 1, and when m is divided by 3, the remainder is 2. What is the remainder when the product nm is divided by 3?

(A) 0

(B) 1

(C) 2

(D) 3

(E) Cannot be determined

20. If a is positive and $\log_{3a} 36 = 2$, then $a =$

(A) 2

(B) 3

(C) 6

(D) $2\sqrt{3}$

(E) 9

USE THIS SPACE AS SCRATCH PAPER

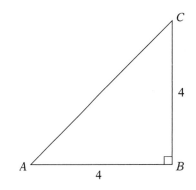

Figure 1

GO ON TO THE NEXT PAGE

21. What is the radius of the circle represented by the equation $x^2 - 2x + y^2 + 6y + 6 = 0$?

    (A) 2
    (B) 4
    (C) 1
    (D) 3
    (E) 16

22. What is the perimeter of ΔDEF in Figure 2?

    (A) 48
    (B) 6
    (C) 8
    (D) 12
    (E) 24

23. If $f(x) = x^2 + 3x$, then $f(3x) =$

    (A) $3(x^2 + 3x)$
    (B) $9(x + 1)$
    (C) $9x^2 + 9x$
    (D) $3x^2 + 9x$
    (E) $9x^2 + 6x$

24. If the graph of $\dfrac{x^2}{a} + \dfrac{y^2}{b} = 1$ contains the point $(0, 1)$, then which of the following must be a true statement?

    (A) $a = b$
    (B) $b = 0$
    (C) $b = 1$
    (D) $b = -1$
    (E) $a = 1$

25. If $f(x) = x^2 + 5$ and $g(x) = -\sqrt{x}$, then $f(g(7)) =$

    (A) 7.6
    (B) -2
    (C) 54
    (D) 9
    (E) 12

26. If 20 percent of a given number is 11, then what is 55 percent of the same number?

    (A) 55
    (B) 30.25
    (C) 100
    (D) 36
    (E) 27.5

USE THIS SPACE AS SCRATCH PAPER

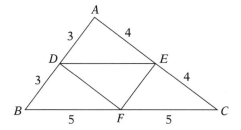

Figure 2

GO ON TO THE NEXT PAGE

27. All of the following are properties of a parallelogram EXCEPT

   (A) The diagonals are perpendicular.
   (B) Opposite sides are congruent.
   (C) Consecutive angles are supplementary.
   (D) A diagonal forms two congruent triangles.
   (E) The diagonals bisect each other.

28. Standing 20 feet away from a flagpole, the angle of elevation of the top of the pole is 42°. Assuming the flagpole is perpendicular to the ground, what is its height?

   (A) 18
   (B) 22
   (C) 13
   (D) 15
   (E) 16

29. Which equation describes the graph in Figure 3?

   (A) $y = (x + 2)^2$
   (B) $x^2 + y^2 = 4$
   (C) $|x| = 4$
   (D) $x^2 = 4$
   (E) $y = \dfrac{2}{x}$

30. What is the volume of the right triangular prism in Figure 4?

   (A) 650 cm³
   (B) 600 cm³
   (C) 300 cm³
   (D) 325 cm³
   (E) 780 cm³

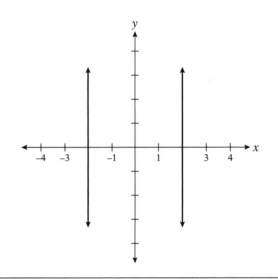

Figure 3

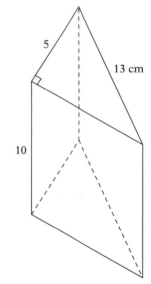

Figure 4

GO ON TO THE NEXT PAGE

31. What is the maximum value of $f(x) = 4 - (x + 1)^2$?

    (A) −1
    (B) 4
    (C) 1
    (D) −4
    (E) −5

32. In circle R in Figure 5, the measure of arc UT is 100°. What is the measure of $\angle STU$?

    (A) 50°
    (B) 40°
    (C) 100°
    (D) 30°
    (E) 45°

33. A rectangular prism has a length of 15 cm, a width of 9 cm, and a height of 6 cm. If each dimension is divided by 3, what is the ratio of the volume of the original prism to the second prism?

    (A) 1:9
    (B) 3:1
    (C) 9:1
    (D) 27:1
    (E) 81:1

34. If $f(x) = x^2 + 3$ for $-1 \le x \le 3$, then what is the range of f?

    (A) $y \ge 0$
    (B) $y \ge 3$
    (C) $-1 \le y \le 3$
    (D) $4 \le y \le 12$
    (E) $3 \le y \le 12$

35. What is the domain of the function $f(x) = \dfrac{x}{x + 6}$?

    (A) All real numbers.
    (B) All real numbers except 0.
    (C) All real numbers except 6.
    (D) All real numbers except −6.
    (E) All real numbers greater than or equal to −6.

36. If three numbers x, y, and z are added in pairs, their sums are 3, 9, and 28. What is the smallest of the three numbers?

    (A) 3
    (B) 17
    (C) −3
    (D) −8
    (E) 9

USE THIS SPACE AS SCRATCH PAPER

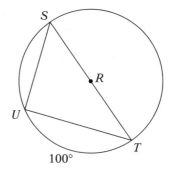

Figure 5

GO ON TO THE NEXT PAGE

37. Given the three points $A(1, 2)$, $B(6, 2)$, and $C(6, 5)$, what is the tangent of $\angle CAB$?

   (A) $\dfrac{3}{5}$

   (B) $\dfrac{5}{3}$

   (C) $\dfrac{3}{4}$

   (D) $\dfrac{3\sqrt{34}}{34}$

   (E) $\dfrac{1}{2}$

38. In Figure 6, $\overline{VW}$ and $\overline{XY}$ are parallel. The measure of $\angle ZXY$ is 75° and the measure of $\angle ZYX$ is 25°. What is the measure of $\angle VZY$?

   (A) 75°
   (B) 80°
   (C) 155°
   (D) 165°
   (E) 105°

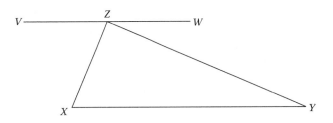

Figure 6

39. In Figure 7, $\overline{AB}$ is congruent to $\overline{DC}$, $\overline{DB} = 10$ units, and $m\angle DBC = 40°$. What is the perimeter of quadrilateral $ABCD$?

   (A) 40
   (B) 28.2
   (C) 20
   (D) 26
   (E) 21.6

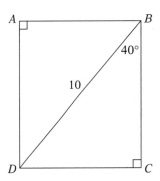

Figure 7

40. What real values of a and b satisfy the equation $a + b + 9i = 6 + (2a - b)i$?

   (A) $a = 5, b = -1$
   (B) $a = 5, b = 1$
   (C) $a = 6, b = 0$
   (D) $a = 4, b = 2$
   (E) $a = 1, b = 5$

GO ON TO THE NEXT PAGE

41. What is the length of the edge of a cube having the same total surface area as a rectangular prism measuring 3 cm by 4 cm by 8 cm?

    (A) 22.7 cm
    (B) 4.8 cm
    (C) 136 cm
    (D) 5.8 cm
    (E) 11.7 cm

42. What are the x-intercepts of the graph $f(x) = -25 - 5x^2$?

    (A) $\pm\sqrt{5}$
    (B) ±5
    (C) 0
    (D) -25
    (E) None

43. The number of tails showing when a pair of coins was tossed 10 times was $\{0, 1, 2, 2, 1, 1, 0, 2, 0, 1\}$. What is the mean of the data?

    (A) 0
    (B) 0.5
    (C) 1
    (D) 1.5
    (E) 2

44. Christine's average score on the first three math tests of the term is 89 percent. If she earns an 81 percent on the fourth test, what will her new average be?

    (A) 87%
    (B) 85%
    (C) 86.8%
    (D) 88%
    (E) 85.5%

45. The diagonals of a rhombus measure 24 and 10 inches. What is the measure of the larger angle of the rhombus?

    (A) 45.2°
    (B) 150°
    (C) 145°
    (D) 120°
    (E) 134.8°

USE THIS SPACE AS SCRATCH PAPER

GO ON TO THE NEXT PAGE

46. Eighteen students took an 8-question quiz. The graph in Figure 8 shows the number of students who earned each possible score from 0 to 8. What is the median for the quiz scores?

    (A) 5.3
    (B) 5
    (C) 4
    (D) 6
    (E) 5.5

USE THIS SPACE AS SCRATCH PAPER

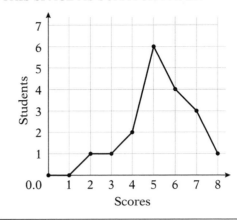

Figure 8

47. If $f(x) = 3x + 1$ and $g(x) = x^2 - 2x + 1$, then $(f + g)(2) =$

    (A) 7
    (B) 1
    (C) 8
    (D) 6
    (E) 15

48. $(2x - 3)^3 =$

    (A) $8x^3 - 27$
    (B) $8x^3 - 36x^2 + 54x - 27$
    (C) $(2x - 3)(4x^2 + 12x + 9)$
    (D) $8x^3 - 18x^2 + 54x - 27$
    (E) $2x^3 - 36x^2 - 54x - 27$

49. If (x, y) is a point on the graph of a function, then which of the following must be a point on the graph of the inverse of the function?

    (A) (y, x)
    (B) $(-x, -y)$
    (C) $(-y, -x)$
    (D) $(x, -y)$
    (E) $(-x, y)$

50. If the length of a rectangle is 7 feet more than its width and if its area is 18 square feet, then what are the dimensions of the rectangle?

    (A) -9×-2 feet
    (B) 1×18 feet
    (C) 3×6 feet
    (D) 2×9 feet
    (E) 1×8 feet

S T O P

IF YOU FINISH BEFORE TIME IS CALLED, GO BACK AND CHECK YOUR WORK.

ANSWER KEY

1. D	11. D	21. A	31. B	41. B
2. A	12. A	22. D	32. B	42. E
3. C	13. B	23. C	33. D	43. C
4. D	14. C	24. C	34. E	44. A
5. B	15. E	25. E	35. D	45. E
6. C	16. E	26. B	36. D	46. B
7. E	17. B	27. A	37. A	47. C
8. C	18. C	28. A	38. C	48. B
9. D	19. C	29. D	39. B	49. A
10. B	20. A	30. C	40. B	50. D

ANSWERS AND SOLUTIONS

1. **D** Tripling both sides of the equation $3x = 7$ results in $9x = 3(7) = 21$.

2. **A**
$$\frac{3}{10} = \frac{5}{x}$$
$$3x = 50$$
$$x = \frac{50}{3}$$

3. **C**
$$9\sin^2 x + 9\cos^2 x$$
$$= 9(\sin^2 x + \cos^2 x)$$
$$= 9(1) = 9$$

4. **D** Let x = the measure of the angle. The supplement of twice the angle is $180 - 2x$.
$$180 - 2x = 124$$
$$-2x = -56$$
$$x = 28°$$

5. **B**
$$\sqrt[3]{2k - 1} = -2$$
$$2k - 1 = (-2)^3 = -8$$
$$2k = -7$$
$$k = -\frac{7}{2} = -3.5$$

6. **C** The Triangle Inequality Theorem states that the sum of the lengths of two sides of a triangle must be greater than the length of the third side. It is impossible to have a triangle with sides measuring 1, 1, and 2 units, since $1 + 1$ is not greater than 2.

7. **E** Use the Pythagorean Theorem to solve for the length of the hypotenuse of the right triangle below.

$$5^2 + 20^2 = d^2$$

$$\sqrt{425} = d$$

$$d \approx 20.6 \text{ miles}$$

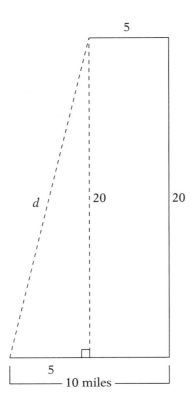

8. **C**

$$x + 2x + 7 + 3x + 5x + 1 = 360$$

$$11x + 8 = 360$$

$$11x = 352$$

$$x = 32$$

The largest angle measures $5(32) + 1 = 161°$.

9. **D**

Let n = the number of sides of the polygon.

$$\frac{180(n-2)}{n} = 140$$

$$180(n-2) = 140n$$

$$180n - 360 = 140n$$

$$40n = 360$$

$$n = 9$$

10. **B** Multiply the first equation by a factor of 2 to eliminate y and then solve for x.

$$4x + 2y = 5$$
$$+ \quad x - 2y = 5$$
$$\overline{5x + 0y = 10}$$

$$x = 2$$

Substituting $x = 2$ into the second equation results in:

$$2 - 2y = 5$$

$$y = -\frac{3}{2}$$

11. **D** Irrational numbers are nonterminating and nonrepeating. 1.666 . . . is not irrational, since it is a repeating decimal.

12. **A**

$$d = \sqrt{(-2-2)^2 + (6 - -3)^2}$$

$$d = \sqrt{(-4)^2 + (9)^2}$$

$$d = \sqrt{16 + 81}$$

$$d = \sqrt{97} \approx 9.85$$

13. **B** $PQ = SR = 5$ units. $PS = QR = 4$ units. Since opposite sides are congruent and consecutive sides are perpendicular, the figure is a rectangle.

14. **C**

$$30x^2 + 49x - 11 = 0$$

$$(5x - 1)(6x + 11) = 0$$

$$x = \frac{1}{5} \text{ or } x = -\frac{11}{6}$$

15. **E** Reflecting the point $(4, -2)$ about the origin results in the point $(-4, 2)$. In other words, the origin is the midpoint of the segment with endpoints $(4, -2)$ and $(-4, 2)$.

16. **E**

$\sqrt{20} + \sqrt{12} \neq \sqrt{32}$, so it is not equivalent to $4\sqrt{2}$. $\sqrt{20} + \sqrt{12} = 2\sqrt{5} + 2\sqrt{3}$.

17. **B** Recognize that $\triangle ABC$ is a 45°-45°-90° right triangle. If each leg measures 4 units, the hypotenuse is a factor of $\sqrt{2}$ larger than 4. $4\sqrt{2}$ is the correct answer.

18. **C** Let p = the number of pages printed in 5 hours. Set up a proportion to solve for p, remembering to use consistent units for time (either minutes or hours). Let's change 30 minutes to 0.5 hours.

$$\frac{520}{0.5} = \frac{p}{5}$$

$$5(520) = 0.5p$$

$$10(520) = p$$

$$p = 5{,}200 \text{ pages}$$

19. **C**

Let $n = 3x + 1$ and $m = 3x + 2$.

$$nm = (3x + 1)(3x + 2)$$

$$nm = 9x^2 + 9x + 2$$

Both $9x^2$ and $9x$ are divisible by 3, so the constant 2 is the remainder. Try substituting values for n and m to see what happens to their product. If $n = 4$ and $m = 5$, $nm = 20$. $20 \div 3 = 6$ remainder 2.

20. **A**

Since $\log_{3a} 36 = 2$, $(3a)^2 = 36$.

$$9a^2 = 36$$

$$a^2 = 4$$

$a = 2$ ($a \neq -2$ because the problem states a is positive.)

21. **A** Write the equation of the circle in standard form by completing the square for x and y.

$$x^2 - 2x + y^2 + 6y + 6 = 0$$

$$(x^2 - 2x) + (y^2 + 6y) = -6$$

$$(x^2 - 2x + 1) + (y^2 + 6y + 9) = -6 + 1 + 9$$

$$(x - 1)^2 + (y + 3)^2 = 4$$

The center of the circle is $(1, -3)$, and its radius has a length of $\sqrt{4} = 2$ units.

22. **D** The three sides of $\triangle DEF$ are the midsegments of $\triangle ABC$. Each midsegment connects the midpoint of two sides of $\triangle ABC$ and is half the length of the third side. The perimeter of $\triangle DEF$ is

$$3 + 4 + 5 = 12 \text{ units}$$

23. **C**

Given $f(x) = x^2 + 3x$,

$$f(3x) = (3x)^2 + 3(3x)$$

$$f(3x) = 9x^2 + 9x$$

24. **C** The equation $\dfrac{x^2}{a} = \dfrac{y^2}{b} = 1$ represents an ellipse with center $(0, 0)$. Since the graph contains the point $(0, 1)$,

$$\frac{0^2}{a} + \frac{1^2}{b} = 1$$

$$\frac{1}{b} = 1$$

$$b = 1$$

Answers A and E *may* also be true, but the question asks which statements *must* be true. Answer B can be immediately eliminated, since you cannot divide by zero.

25. **E**

Apply the inside function, $g(7)$, first.

$$g(7) = -\sqrt{7}$$

$$f(g(7)) = \left(-\sqrt{7}\right)^2 + 5 = 7 + 5 = 12$$

26. **B**

Let x = the given number.

$$0.20x = 11$$

$$x = 55$$

$$0.55(55) = 30.25$$

27. **A** The diagonals of a rhombus (and, therefore, a square) are perpendicular. The diagonals of a parallelogram are not, so A is not a true statement.

28. **A**

Let h = the height of the flagpole.

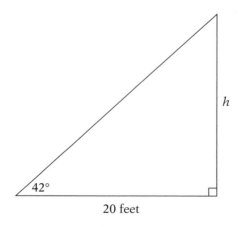

$$\tan 42° = \frac{h}{20}$$

$$h = 20(\tan 42°) \approx 18 \text{ feet}$$

29. **D** The graph shows two vertical lines: one at $x = 2$ and one at $x = -2$. The equation $x^2 = 4$ is true when $x = 2$ or $x = -2$, so the graph describes the equation in Answer D.

30. **C** Volume is given by the formula $V = Bh$, where B is the area of the base. The area of the base of the right triangular prism is

$$B = \frac{1}{2}(12)5 = 30 \text{ cm}^2$$

The volume of the prism is then

$$V = Bh = 30(10) = 300 \text{ cm}^3$$

31. **B** The maximum value of the function is the y-coordinate of the parabola's vertex. For the function $f(x) = 4 - (x + 1)^2$, the vertex is $(-1, 4)$. (You can check this by graphing the parabola on your graphing calculator.) The maximum value is, therefore, 4.

An alternate way of solving for the maximum is to find the y value when $x = -\dfrac{b}{2a}$. In this case,

$$x = -\frac{(-2)}{2(-1)} = -1, \text{ so } y = 4 - (-1 + 1)^2 = 4.$$

32. **B** $m\angle SUT = 90°$, since the angle intercepts a semicircle. An inscribed angle measures half of its intercepted arc, so $m\angle UST = \dfrac{1}{2}(100) = 50°$.

In $\triangle UST$, one angle measures 90° and one measures 50°. The remaining angle, $\angle STU$, must measure $180 - (90 + 50) = 40°$.

33. **D** The scale factor of the two similar prisms is 3:1. The ratio of their volumes is, therefore, $3^3 : 1^3$ or 27 :1.

34. **E** The graph of $f(x) = x^2 + 3$ is a parabola with vertex $(0, 3)$ and concave up. Since the domain is specified, the curve has a beginning and an ending point.

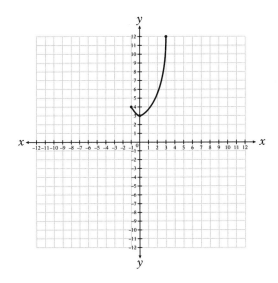

When $x = -1$, $y = 4$, and when $x = 3$, $y = 12$. The range is the set of all possible y values, so don't forget to include the vertex whose y value is less than 4. The range is $3 \le y \le 12$.

35. **D**

The function $f(x) = \dfrac{x}{x + 6}$ is undefined when the denominator is zero.

$$x + 6 = 0$$
$$x = -6$$

The function is defined for all real numbers except $x = -6$.

36. **D**

$$x + y = 3$$
$$x + z = 9$$
$$y + z = 28$$

Solving the first equation for y results in $y = 3 - x$.

$$(3 - x) + z = 28, \text{ so } -x + z = 25$$

Now set up a system using the two equations in x and z.

$$-x + z = 25$$
$$+\ x + z = 9$$
$$\overline{2z = 34}$$
$$z = 17$$

Since $y + z = 28$, $y = 28 - 17 = 11$. Since $x + z = 9$, $x = 9 - 17 = -8$. The smallest of the three numbers is -8.

37. **A**

Graphing the points *A*, *B*, and *C* results in a right triangle.

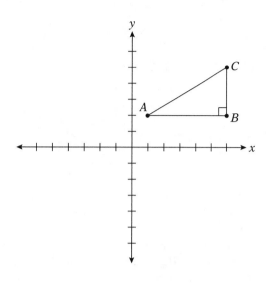

The tangent of ∠CAB is

$$\tan \angle CAB = \frac{\text{opposite}}{\text{adjacent}} = \frac{CB}{AB}$$

$$\tan \angle CAB = \frac{3}{5}$$

38. **C**

∠VZX and ∠ZXY are alternate interior angles and are, therefore, congruent. $m\angle VZX = 75°$. Since $m\angle ZYX = 25°$ and $m\angle VZX = 75°$, the remaining angle in ΔZYX must measure $180 - (75 + 25) = 80°$.

$$m\angle VZY = 75 + 80 = 155°$$

39. **B**

Let $x = DC$ and $y = BC$.

$$\sin 40° = \frac{x}{10} \qquad \cos 40° = \frac{y}{10}$$
$$x = 6.428 \qquad\qquad y = 7.660$$

Since $AB = DC$, *DB* divides the quadrilateral into two congruent triangles. *AD* must equal *BC*. The perimeter of the quadrilateral is therefore

$$2(6.428) + 2(7.660) = 28.2 \text{ units}$$

40. **B**

Since $a + b + 9i = 6 + (2a - b)i$, $a + b = 6$ and $2a - b = 9$. Set up a system and use the linear combination method to solve for *a* and *b*.

$$a + b = 6$$
$$\underline{+\ 2a - b = 9}$$
$$3a + 0b = 15$$

$$a = 5$$

$$5 + b = 6, \text{ so } b = 1$$

41. **B**

The surface area of the prism is

$$SA = 2(3)(4) + 2(3)(8) + 2(4)(8) = 136 \text{ cm}^2$$

The surface area of the cube is given by the formula $SA = 6e^2$, where e = the length of an edge of the cube.

$$136 = 6e^2$$

$$22.67 = e^2$$

$$e = 4.8 \text{ cm}$$

42. **E**

Let $y = 0$ and solve for *x*.

$$f(x) = -25 - 5x^2$$

$$0 = -25 - 5x^2$$

$$25 = -5x^2$$

$$-5 = x^2$$

No real solution for *x*.

43. **C** The mean is the sum of the data divided by the number of terms.

$$\frac{0 + 1 + 2 + 2 + 1 + 1 + 0 + 2 + 0 + 1}{10} = \frac{10}{10} = 1$$

44. **A**

Let s = the sum of the scores on Christine's first three tests.

$$\frac{s}{3} = 89$$

$$s = 267$$

Christine's new average is $\dfrac{267 + 81}{4} = 87\%$.

45. **E** Recall that the diagonals of a rhombus are perpendicular, bisect each other, and bisect the vertex angles of the rhombus. Let x and y equal the measures of the angles as shown below.

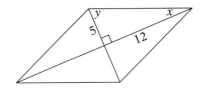

$$\tan x = \frac{5}{12}$$

$$x = \tan^{-1}\frac{5}{12} = 22.6°$$

$$\tan y = \frac{12}{5}$$

$$y = \tan^{-1}\frac{12}{5} = 67.4°$$

One angle of the rhombus measures $2(22.6) \approx 45.2°$, while the other angle measures $2(67.4) \approx 134.8°$. Since the problem asks for the greater of the two angles, $134.8°$ is the correct answer.

46. **B** The graph shows the set of scores as:

{2, 3, 4, 4, 5, 5, 5, 5, 5, 5, 6, 6, 6, 6, 7, 7, 7, 8}. Since the scores are in order from lowest to highest, simply count over to the middle value to determine the median. The median is the average of the ninth and tenth terms. In this example, both the ninth and tenth terms are 5, so the median is 5.

47. **C**

$$(f + g)(2) = f(2) + g(2)$$

$$= 3(2) + 1 + (2)^2 - 2(2) + 1$$

$$= 7 + 1 = 8$$

48. **B** The binomial expansion of $(x + y)^3$

$$= 1x^3 + 3x^2y + 3xy^2 + y^3.$$

Substitute $x = 2x$ and $y = -3$ to get:

$$1(2x)^3 + 3(2x)^2(-3) + 3(2x)(-3)^2 + (-3)^3$$

$$= 8x^3 - 36x^2 + 54x - 27$$

Of course, you could multiply $(2x - 3)(2x - 3)(2x - 3)$ and get the same product, but remembering the Binomial Theorem will save time.

49. **A** The graph of the inverse of a function is the graph of the function reflected over the line $y = x$. If (x, y) is a point on f, then (y, x), the reflection of the point over the line $y = x$, is on the graph of f^{-1}.

50. **D**

Let w = the width of the rectangle. Its length is then $w + 7$.

Area $= w(w + 7) = 18$

$$w^2 + 7w - 18 = 0$$

$$(w + 9)(w - 2) = 18$$

$$w = -9 \text{ or } w = 2$$

The solution -9 is a root, however, since the width of the rectangle cannot be negative. The dimensions of the rectangle are $2 \times (2 + 7)$ or 2×9 feet.

Diagnose Your Strengths and Weaknesses

Check the number of each question answered correctly and "X" the number of each question answered incorrectly.

Algebra	1	5	10	11	12	14	16	18	19	26	36	48	50	Total Number Correct
13 questions														

Plane Geometry	4	6	7	8	9	17	22	27	32	38	Total Number Correct
10 questions											

Solid Geometry	30	33	41	Total Number Correct
3 questions				

Coordinate Geometry	13	15	21	24	29	34	42	Total Number Correct
7 questions								

Trigonometry	3	28	37	39	45	Total Number Correct
5 questions						

Functions	23	25	31	35	47	49	Total Number Correct
6 questions							

Data Analysis, Statistics, and Probability	43	44	46	Total Number Correct
3 questions				

Number and Operations	2	20	40	Total Number Correct
3 questions				

Number of correct answers $- \frac{1}{4}$ **(Number of incorrect answers) = Your raw score**

_____ $- \frac{1}{4}$ (_____) = _____

Compare your raw score with the approximate SAT Subject test score below:

	Raw Score	**SAT Subject test Approximate Score**
Excellent	46–50	750–800
Very Good	41–45	700–750
Good	36–40	640–700
Above Average	29–35	590–640
Average	22–28	510–590
Below Average	< 22	<510

PRACTICE TEST 5

Treat this practice test as the actual test and complete it in one 60-minute sitting. Use the following answer sheet to fill in your multiple-choice answers. Once you have completed the practice test:

1. Check your answers using the Answer Key.
2. Review the Answer Explanations.
3. Fill in the "Diagnose Your Strengths and Weaknesses" sheet and determine areas that require further preparation.

PRACTICE TEST 5

MATH LEVEL 1

ANSWER SHEET

Tear out this answer sheet and use it to complete the practice test.

Determine the BEST answer for each question. Then fill in the appropriate oval using a No. 2 pencil.

1. Ⓐ Ⓑ Ⓒ Ⓓ Ⓔ	21. Ⓐ Ⓑ Ⓒ Ⓓ Ⓔ	41. Ⓐ Ⓑ Ⓒ Ⓓ Ⓔ
2. Ⓐ Ⓑ Ⓒ Ⓓ Ⓔ	22. Ⓐ Ⓑ Ⓒ Ⓓ Ⓔ	42. Ⓐ Ⓑ Ⓒ Ⓓ Ⓔ
3. Ⓐ Ⓑ Ⓒ Ⓓ Ⓔ	23. Ⓐ Ⓑ Ⓒ Ⓓ Ⓔ	43. Ⓐ Ⓑ Ⓒ Ⓓ Ⓔ
4. Ⓐ Ⓑ Ⓒ Ⓓ Ⓔ	24. Ⓐ Ⓑ Ⓒ Ⓓ Ⓔ	44. Ⓐ Ⓑ Ⓒ Ⓓ Ⓔ
5. Ⓐ Ⓑ Ⓒ Ⓓ Ⓔ	25. Ⓐ Ⓑ Ⓒ Ⓓ Ⓔ	45. Ⓐ Ⓑ Ⓒ Ⓓ Ⓔ
6. Ⓐ Ⓑ Ⓒ Ⓓ Ⓔ	26. Ⓐ Ⓑ Ⓒ Ⓓ Ⓔ	46. Ⓐ Ⓑ Ⓒ Ⓓ Ⓔ
7. Ⓐ Ⓑ Ⓒ Ⓓ Ⓔ	27. Ⓐ Ⓑ Ⓒ Ⓓ Ⓔ	47. Ⓐ Ⓑ Ⓒ Ⓓ Ⓔ
8. Ⓐ Ⓑ Ⓒ Ⓓ Ⓔ	28. Ⓐ Ⓑ Ⓒ Ⓓ Ⓔ	48. Ⓐ Ⓑ Ⓒ Ⓓ Ⓔ
9. Ⓐ Ⓑ Ⓒ Ⓓ Ⓔ	29. Ⓐ Ⓑ Ⓒ Ⓓ Ⓔ	49. Ⓐ Ⓑ Ⓒ Ⓓ Ⓔ
10. Ⓐ Ⓑ Ⓒ Ⓓ Ⓔ	30. Ⓐ Ⓑ Ⓒ Ⓓ Ⓔ	50. Ⓐ Ⓑ Ⓒ Ⓓ Ⓔ
11. Ⓐ Ⓑ Ⓒ Ⓓ Ⓔ	31. Ⓐ Ⓑ Ⓒ Ⓓ Ⓔ	
12. Ⓐ Ⓑ Ⓒ Ⓓ Ⓔ	32. Ⓐ Ⓑ Ⓒ Ⓓ Ⓔ	
13. Ⓐ Ⓑ Ⓒ Ⓓ Ⓔ	33. Ⓐ Ⓑ Ⓒ Ⓓ Ⓔ	
14. Ⓐ Ⓑ Ⓒ Ⓓ Ⓔ	34. Ⓐ Ⓑ Ⓒ Ⓓ Ⓔ	
15. Ⓐ Ⓑ Ⓒ Ⓓ Ⓔ	35. Ⓐ Ⓑ Ⓒ Ⓓ Ⓔ	
16. Ⓐ Ⓑ Ⓒ Ⓓ Ⓔ	36. Ⓐ Ⓑ Ⓒ Ⓓ Ⓔ	
17. Ⓐ Ⓑ Ⓒ Ⓓ Ⓔ	37. Ⓐ Ⓑ Ⓒ Ⓓ Ⓔ	
18. Ⓐ Ⓑ Ⓒ Ⓓ Ⓔ	38. Ⓐ Ⓑ Ⓒ Ⓓ Ⓔ	
19. Ⓐ Ⓑ Ⓒ Ⓓ Ⓔ	39. Ⓐ Ⓑ Ⓒ Ⓓ Ⓔ	
20. Ⓐ Ⓑ Ⓒ Ⓓ Ⓔ	40. Ⓐ Ⓑ Ⓒ Ⓓ Ⓔ	

PRACTICE TEST 5

Time: 60 Minutes

<u>Directions:</u> Select the BEST answer for each of the 50 multiple-choice questions. If the exact solution is not one of the five choices, select the answer that is the best approximation. Then fill in the appropriate oval on the answer sheet.

<u>NOTES:</u>

(1) A calculator will be needed to answer some of the questions on the test. Scientific, programmable, and graphing calculators are permitted. It is up to you to determine when and when not to use your calculator.

(2) All angles on the Level 1 test are measured in degrees, not radians. Make sure your calculator is set to degree mode.

(3) Figures are drawn as accurately as possible and are intended to help solve some of the test problems. If a figure is not drawn to scale, this will be stated in the problem. All figures lie in a plane unless the problem indicates otherwise.

(4) Unless otherwise stated, the domain of a function f is assumed to be the set of real numbers x for which the value of the function, $f(x)$, is a real number.

(5) Reference information that may be useful in answering some of the test questions can be found below.

Reference Information	
Right circular cone with radius r and height h:	Volume $= \dfrac{1}{3}\pi r^2 h$
Right circular cone with circumference of base c and slant height ℓ:	Lateral Area $= \dfrac{1}{2}c\ell$
Sphere with radius r:	Volume $= \dfrac{4}{3}\pi r^3$ Surface Area $= 4\pi r^2$
Pyramid with base area B and height h:	Volume $= \dfrac{1}{3}Bh$

GO ON TO THE NEXT PAGE

1. If $a = b^3$ and $b = 4k$, then what is the value of a when $k = -\dfrac{1}{2}$?

   (A) 8
   (B) −8
   (C) 4
   (D) 2
   (E) −2

2. If $\dfrac{3}{8} = \dfrac{1}{4x - 1}$, then $x =$

   (A) $\dfrac{3}{4}$

   (B) $\dfrac{9}{4}$

   (C) 11

   (D) $\dfrac{11}{12}$

   (E) $\dfrac{5}{12}$

3. If $4 - 3(5 - x) = 2(x + 5) - 1$, then $x =$

   (A) −2
   (B) 20
   (C) −15
   (D) 4
   (E) 21

4. $\dfrac{1}{2}$ percent of 50 percent of 1,000 is

   (A) $\dfrac{5}{2}$

   (B) 5
   (C) 0.25
   (D) 25
   (E) 250

5. What is the least positive integer divisible by 2, 6, and 27?

   (A) 108
   (B) 54
   (C) 18
   (D) 324
   (E) 162

USE THIS SPACE AS SCRATCH PAPER

GO ON TO THE NEXT PAGE

6. If the area of a square is 100 cm², then its perimeter is

   (A) 10 cm
   (B) 20 cm
   (C) 40 cm
   (D) 200 cm
   (E) 100 cm

7. The sides of pentagon *ABCDE* in Figure 1 are extended. What is the sum of the measures of the five marked angles?

   (A) 180°
   (B) 270°
   (C) 360°
   (D) 540°
   (E) 720°

USE THIS SPACE AS SCRATCH PAPER

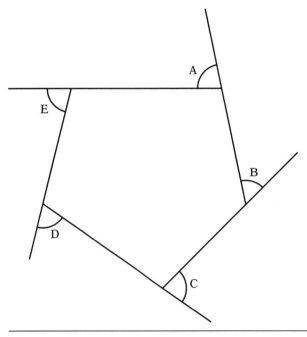

Figure 1

8. What is the *y*-intercept of the line $y - 1 = -\frac{1}{2}(x + 8)$?

   (A) 8
   (B) −4
   (C) −5
   (D) −3
   (E) $-\frac{1}{2}$

9. If $4x - y = 6z + w$, then what does the expression $12 - 4x + y$ equal in terms of *z* and *w*?

   (A) $12 - w$
   (B) $12 - 6z$
   (C) $12 + 6z + w$
   (D) $12 - 6z + w$
   (E) $12 - 6z - w$

10. For all *x* except $x = 9$, $\dfrac{3x^2 - 28x + 9}{9 - x} =$

    (A) $-2x + 28$
    (B) $3x - 1$
    (C) $-3x + 1$
    (D) $3x + 3$
    (E) $3x^2 - 28$

GO ON TO THE NEXT PAGE

11. In Figure 2, if the length of $\overline{DF} = 4x + 2$ and the length of $\overline{EF}$ is $\frac{3}{4}x + 1$, what is the length of $\overline{DE}$?

   (A) $\frac{13}{4}x + 3$

   (B) $\frac{13}{4}x + 1$

   (C) $x + 1$

   (D) $\frac{19}{4}x + 3$

   (E) $3x + 1$

12. What are three consecutive even integers whose sum is 48?

   (A) 12, 14, 16
   (B) 16, 18, 20
   (C) 13, 15, 17
   (D) 15, 16, 17
   (E) 14, 16, 18

13. $\left\| -4 \right| - \left| (-2)^3 \right\| =$

   (A) 4
   (B) −4
   (C) 8
   (D) 0
   (E) 2

14. If $x + y = -1$ and $x - y = 6$, then $\frac{x}{y} =$

   (A) $\frac{5}{2}$

   (B) $-\frac{7}{2}$

   (C) $-\frac{5}{7}$

   (D) $-\frac{7}{9}$

   (E) $-\frac{7}{5}$

15. If $f(x) = \frac{16}{x^5}$ and $x \neq 0$, then $f(-2) =$

   (A) $-\frac{1}{2}$

   (B) $\frac{1}{2}$

   (C) $\frac{1}{4}$

   (D) 1
   (E) −1

USE THIS SPACE AS SCRATCH PAPER

Figure 2

GO ON TO THE NEXT PAGE

16. How many diagonals can be drawn from one vertex of a 20-gon?

    (A) 15
    (B) 16
    (C) 17
    (D) 18
    (E) 170

17. Which of the following lines is perpendicular to the line $y = -3x + 1$?

    (A) $y = -3x + 4$
    (B) $y = 3x$
    (C) $y = \dfrac{1}{3}x + 1$
    (D) $y = -\dfrac{1}{3}x - 1$
    (E) $y = -3x - 1$

18. If the point $(-1, 2)$ is on a graph that is symmetric with respect to the y-axis, then which of the following points must also be on the graph?

    (A) $(1, 2)$
    (B) $(-1, -2)$
    (C) $(1, -2)$
    (D) $(-2, 1)$
    (E) $(2, -1)$

19. $-9\cos^2 \theta - 9\sin^2 \theta =$

    (A) 0
    (B) 1
    (C) −1
    (D) 9
    (E) −9

20. The midpoint of $\overline{AB}$ is $(5, -6)$ and the coordinates of endpoint A are $(-1, 2)$. What are the coordinates of B?

    (A) $(-7, 10)$
    (B) $(11, -14)$
    (C) $(2, -2)$
    (D) $(-2, 2)$
    (E) $(-1, 4)$

21. What is the volume of the rectangular pyramid in Figure 3?

    (A) $\dfrac{3n^2}{2}$
    (B) $\dfrac{3n^3}{4}$
    (C) $\dfrac{3n^3}{2}$
    (D) $\dfrac{n^3}{2}$
    (E) n^3

USE THIS SPACE AS SCRATCH PAPER

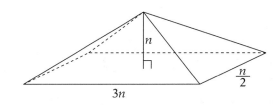

Figure 3

GO ON TO THE NEXT PAGE

22. $2x^3 + 9x^2 + 3x - 4$ divided by $(x + 1) =$

    (A) $2x^2 + 11x + 14$
    (B) $(2x - 1)(x - 4)$
    (C) $2x^2 + 7x + 10$
    (D) $2x^2 + 7x - 4$
    (E) $2x^3 + 7x^2 - 4x$

23. In the triangle shown in Figure 4, what is the value of c?

    (A) $\sqrt{3}$
    (B) $3\sqrt{3}$
    (C) $6\sqrt{3}$
    (D) $9\sqrt{3}$
    (E) $9\sqrt{2}$

24. Which one of the following is a counterexample to the statement "If two angles are supplementary, then they are right angles?"

    (A) If two angles are complementary, then they are not right angles.
    (B) If two angles are right angles, then they are supplementary.
    (C) If two angles are not supplementary, then they are not right angles.
    (D) If two angles are supplementary, then one could measure 100° and one could measure 80°.
    (E) If two angles are not right angles, then they are not supplementary.

25. What is the domain of the function $f(x) = \sqrt{36 - x^2}$

    (A) $x \le -6$ or $x \ge 6$
    (B) $x \ge \pm 6$
    (C) $x \ne \pm 6$
    (D) $x \le 6$
    (E) $-6 \le x \le 6$

26. What is the maximum value of the function $f(x) = \dfrac{1}{x}$ over the interval $\dfrac{1}{2} \le x \le \dfrac{3}{2}$?

    (A) $\dfrac{1}{2}$
    (B) $\dfrac{3}{2}$
    (C) 2
    (D) $\dfrac{2}{3}$
    (E) Infinity

USE THIS SPACE AS SCRATCH PAPER

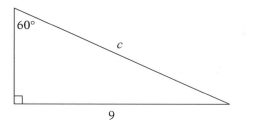

Figure 4

GO ON TO THE NEXT PAGE

27. If $a = \dfrac{n+1}{n^4}$ and $b = \dfrac{1-n}{n^4}$, then, for $n \neq 0$, $a - b =$

 (A) $\dfrac{2}{n^4}$

 (B) $\dfrac{2}{n^3}$

 (C) 0

 (D) $2n$

 (E) $\dfrac{2n-2}{n^4}$

28. What is the volume of a sphere whose surface area is 100π square units?

 (A) $\dfrac{100}{3}\pi$ cubic units or units^3

 (B) $\dfrac{500}{3}\pi$ units^3

 (C) 160π units^3

 (D) $\dfrac{375}{4}\pi$ units^3

 (E) 520 units^3

29. What is the circumference of a circle whose area is 64π cm^2?

 (A) 16

 (B) 8π

 (C) 8

 (D) 128π

 (E) 16π

30. Which of the following is the solution of $|2x - 4| < 1$?

 (A) $\dfrac{3}{2} < x < \dfrac{5}{2}$

 (B) $x < \dfrac{5}{2}$

 (C) $x < \dfrac{3}{2}$ or $x > \dfrac{5}{2}$

 (D) $x > 0$

 (E) $x \leq \dfrac{3}{2}$ or $x \geq \dfrac{5}{2}$

31. Which of the following is the equation of a circle with center $(-1, 7)$ and a radius of length 3?

 (A) $(x + 1)^2 - (y + 7)^2 = 9$

 (B) $(x + 1)^2 + (y - 7)^2 = 3$

 (C) $(x - 1)^2 + (y + 7)^2 = 3$

 (D) $(x + 1)^2 + (y - 7)^2 = 9$

 (E) $(x - 1)^2 + (y + 7)^2 = 9$

GO ON TO THE NEXT PAGE

32. An equation of the line parallel to $8x - 2y = 5$ and containing the point $(-2, 2)$ is

    (A) $y - 2 = 4(x - 2)$

    (B) $y = 4x + \dfrac{5}{2}$

    (C) $y = 4x - \dfrac{5}{2}$

    (D) $y + 2 = 4(x - 2)$

    (E) $y = 4x + 10$

33. If the letters of the word PROBLEMS are written on cards and put in a hat, what is the probability of randomly drawing either "E" or "S"?

    (A) $\dfrac{1}{8}$

    (B) $\dfrac{1}{56}$

    (C) $\dfrac{1}{4}$

    (D) $\dfrac{1}{64}$

    (E) $\dfrac{1}{16}$

34. If $\tan 10° = \cot \theta$, then $\theta =$

    (A) $10°$

    (B) $80°$

    (C) $70°$

    (D) $-10°$

    (E) $90°$

35. In circle O in Figure 5, $\overline{OE} = 3$, $\overline{OF} = 2$, and $\overline{OG} = 4$. Which of the following lists the three chords in order from longest to shortest?

    (A) OG, OE, OF

    (B) DF, CG, BE

    (C) BC, AB, DC

    (D) DC, AB, BC

    (E) DC, BC, AB

36. If $\cos (45 + 2x)° = \sin (3x)°$, then $x =$

    (A) $18°$

    (B) $27°$

    (C) $45°$

    (D) $22.5°$

    (E) $9°$

USE THIS SPACE AS SCRATCH PAPER

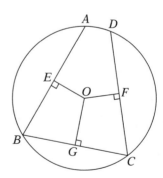

Figure 5

GO ON TO THE NEXT PAGE

37. If $2^3\left(2^{3n}\right)(2) = \dfrac{1}{4}$, then $n =$

  (A) $-\dfrac{5}{3}$

  (B) -2

  (C) $-\dfrac{2}{9}$

  (D) $-\dfrac{2}{3}$

  (E) $-\dfrac{1}{3}$

38. If $f(x) = \dfrac{3}{2}x + \sqrt{x}$, then $f\left(f(4)\right) =$

  (A) $12 + 2\sqrt{2}$

  (B) 20

  (C) $14\sqrt{2}$

  (D) 8

  (E) 16

39. The operation ♠ is defined for all real numbers a and b as $a ♠ b = b^{2a}$. If $n ♠ 5 = 125$, then $n =$

  (A) 1

  (B) 2

  (C) 3

  (D) $\dfrac{3}{2}$

  (E) $\dfrac{1}{2}$

40. How many common tangents can be drawn to the two circles in Figure 6?

  (A) 0

  (B) 1

  (C) 2

  (D) 3

  (E) 4

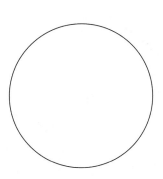
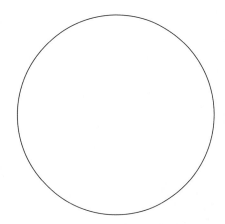

Figure 6

GO ON TO THE NEXT PAGE

41. The boys' basketball team scored an average of 54 points per game in their first 5 games of the season. The girls' basketball team scored an average of 59 points per game in their first 6 games. What was the average of points scored in all 11 games?

    (A) 56.5
    (B) 56.7
    (C) 56.0
    (D) 57.1
    (E) 62.4

42. The rectangle in Figure 7 is rotated about side $\overline{WZ}$. What is the volume of the resulting solid?

    (A) 432
    (B) 108π
    (C) 432π
    (D) 72π
    (E) 330

43. If $i = \sqrt{-1}$, then all of the following expressions are equivalent EXCEPT

    (A) i^4
    (B) $(i^4)^4$
    (C) i^8
    (D) i^{20}
    (E) $i^4 + i^4$

44. For $x \neq -1$ and $x \neq \dfrac{1}{3}$, if $f(x) = 1 - 3x$ and $g(x) = 3x^2 + 2x - 1$, then $\left(\dfrac{f}{g}\right)(x) =$

    (A) $\dfrac{1}{3}x^2 - \dfrac{3}{2}x$
    (B) $\dfrac{-1}{x+1}$
    (C) $\dfrac{1}{x+1}$
    (D) $\dfrac{-1}{x-1}$
    (E) $3x^2 + 5x - 2$

45. If $\sin x = \dfrac{7}{25}$, then $\tan x =$

    (A) $\dfrac{7}{20}$
    (B) $\dfrac{24}{25}$
    (C) $\dfrac{7}{24}$
    (D) $\dfrac{24}{7}$
    (E) $\dfrac{8}{24}$

USE THIS SPACE AS SCRATCH PAPER

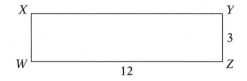

Figure 7

GO ON TO THE NEXT PAGE

46. Kate needs to complete 5 more courses—calculus, English, French, computer science, and history—in order to graduate from high school. She plans to schedule the courses during the first 5 periods of the school day, and all 5 courses are offered during each of the 5 periods. How many different schedules are possible?

    (A) 25
    (B) 24
    (C) 240
    (D) 120
    (E) 60

47. If the pattern of the terms $3\sqrt{3}$, 27, $81\sqrt{3}$, ... continues, which of the following would be the sixth term of the sequence?

    (A) $\left(3\sqrt{3}\right)^6$

    (B) $\left(\sqrt{3}\right)^6$

    (C) 3^6

    (D) $\left(3\sqrt{3}\right)^5$

    (E) 3^7

48. The quotient from dividing the sum of the measures of the interior angles of a regular polygon by the number of its sides is 157.5°. How many sides does the polygon have?

    (A) 14
    (B) 15
    (C) 16
    (D) 17
    (E) 18

49. What is the value of k if
$$\frac{1}{(x-2)(x+4)} = \frac{h}{(x-2)} + \frac{k}{(x+4)}?$$

    (A) 2
    (B) −4
    (C) $-\dfrac{1}{6}$
    (D) $\dfrac{1}{6}$
    (E) −2

50. What is the perimeter of the regular hexagon shown in Figure 8 if the apothem, *XO*, measures $2\sqrt{3}$ units?

    (A) 12
    (B) $12\sqrt{3}$
    (C) 24
    (D) $24\sqrt{3}$
    (E) 36

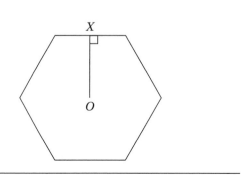

Figure 8

S T O P

IF YOU FINISH BEFORE TIME IS CALLED, GO BACK AND CHECK YOUR WORK.

ANSWER KEY

1. B	11. B	21. D	31. D	41. B
2. D	12. E	22. D	32. E	42. B
3. B	13. A	23. C	33. C	43. E
4. A	14. C	24. D	34. B	44. B
5. B	15. A	25. E	35. D	45. C
6. C	16. C	26. C	36. E	46. D
7. C	17. C	27. B	37. B	47. A
8. D	18. A	28. B	38. A	48. C
9. E	19. E	29. E	39. D	49. C
10. C	20. B	30. A	40. E	50. C

ANSWERS AND SOLUTIONS

1. **B** When $k = -\dfrac{1}{2}$, $b = 4\left(-\dfrac{1}{2}\right) = -2$.

   $a = (-2)^3 = -8$

2. **D**

   $$\frac{3}{8} = \frac{1}{4x - 1}$$
   $$3(4x - 1) = 8$$
   $$12x - 3 = 8$$
   $$12x = 11$$
   $$x = \frac{11}{12}$$

3. **B**

   $$4 - 3(5 - x) = 2(x + 5) - 1$$
   $$4 - 15 + 3x = 2x + 10 - 1$$
   $$3x - 11 = 2x + 9$$
   $$x = 9 + 11 = 20$$

4. **A**

   $$\frac{1}{2}\% \text{ of } 50\% \text{ of } 1{,}000 = \frac{\frac{1}{2}}{100}\left(\frac{50}{100}\right)(1{,}000)$$
   $$= \frac{\frac{1}{2}}{100}(500)$$
   $$= \frac{1}{2}(5)$$
   $$= \frac{5}{2}$$

5. **B** Take the prime factorization of each of the three numbers.

   2 is prime.

   $6 = 2(3)$

   $27 = 3^3$

   The least integer divisible by all three numbers equals $2(3^3) = 2(27) = 54$.

6. **C** The area of a square is given by the formula $A = s^2$ where $s =$ the length of its side.

$$100 = s^2$$
$$s = 10$$

The square's perimeter is $4(10) = 40$ cm.

7. **C** The five marked angles are the five exterior angles of pentagon $ABCDE$. The sum of the exterior angles of any polygon is $360°$, so C is the correct answer.

8. **D** Rewrite the equation of the line in slope-intercept form, $y = mx + b$ where b is the y-intercept.

$$y - 1 = -\frac{1}{2}(x + 8)$$
$$y - 1 = -\frac{1}{2}x - 4$$
$$y = -\frac{1}{2}x - 3$$

The y-intercept is -3.

9. **E**

$$12 - 4x + y = 12 - (4x - y)$$
$$= 12 - (6z + w)$$
$$= 12 - 6z - w$$

10. **C**

$$\frac{3x^2 - 28x + 9}{9 - x}$$
$$= \frac{(3x - 1)(x - 9)}{-(x - 9)}$$
$$= -(3x - 1) = -3x + 1$$

11. **B**

$$DE = DF - EF$$
$$DE = 4x + 2 - \left(\frac{3}{4}x + 1\right)$$
$$DE = \frac{13}{4}x + 1$$

12. **E** Let $x =$ the first even integer, $x + 2 =$ the second even integer, and $x + 4 =$ the third.

$$x + x + 2 + x + 4 = 48$$
$$3x + 6 = 48$$
$$3x = 42$$
$$x = 14$$

If 14 is the first even integer, 16 and 18 are the other two.

13. **A**

$|-4| = 4$ and $|(-2)^3| = |-8| = 8$, so the given expression becomes

$$\big| |-4| - |(-2)^3| \big| = \big| 4 - 8 \big| = \big| -4 \big| = 4$$

14. **C** Set up a system and use the linear combination method to solve for x.

$$\begin{array}{r} x + y = -1 \\ +\ x - y = 6 \\ \hline 2x\qquad = 5 \end{array}$$

$$x = \frac{5}{2}$$

Since $x + y = -1$, $\frac{5}{2} + y = -1$, so $y = -\frac{7}{2}$.

$$\frac{x}{y} = \frac{\frac{5}{2}}{-\frac{7}{2}} = -\frac{5}{7}$$

15. **A**

Since $f(x) = \frac{16}{x^5}$,

$$f(-2) = \frac{16}{(-2)^5} = \frac{16}{(-32)} = -\frac{1}{2}$$

16. **C** $n - 3$ diagonals can be drawn from *one* vertex of any polygon, assuming $n =$ the number of sides of the polygon. $20 - 3 = 17$ diagonals.

17. **C** Perpendicular lines have slopes that are negative reciprocals. The slope of the given lines is $m = -3$. The negative reciprocal of -3 is $\frac{1}{3}$, and Answer C is the only answer in which $m = \frac{1}{3}$.

18. **A** If (a, b) is a point on a graph symmetric with respect to the y-axis, then $(-a, b)$ is also on the graph. $(1, 2)$ is the reflection of the point $(-1, 2)$ over the y-axis.

19. **E**

$$-9\cos^2 \theta - 9\sin^2 \theta$$

$$= -9(\cos^2 \theta + \sin^2 \theta)$$

$$= -9(1) = -9$$

20. **B** Let point B have coordinates (x, y). Since you know the coordinates of the midpoint, use the midpoint formula to solve for x and y.

$$\frac{-1 + x}{2} = 5 \qquad \frac{2 + y}{2} = -6$$

$$-1 + x = 10 \qquad 2 + y = -12$$

$$x = 11 \qquad y = -14$$

21. **D**

$V = \frac{1}{3}Bh$ where B is the area of the base and h is the height.

$$V = \frac{1}{3}(3n)\left(\frac{n}{2}\right)(n)$$

$$= \frac{n^3}{2}$$

22. **D** $2x^3 + 9x^2 + 3x - 4$ divided by $(x + 1)$ can be simplified using either long division or synthetic division.

$$-1 \begin{array}{|cccc} 2 & 9 & 3 & -4 \\ & 2 & 7 & -4 & 0 \end{array}$$

The remainder is zero. -4 is the constant term. 7 is the coefficient of the first-degree term, and 2 is the coefficient of the second-degree term. The quotient is

$$2x^2 + 7x - 4$$

23. **C** The triangle is a 30°-60°-90° special right triangle. Since the side opposite the 60° angle measures 9, the side opposite the 30° angle measures:

$$\frac{9}{\sqrt{3}} = \frac{9\sqrt{3}}{3} = 3\sqrt{3}$$

The side opposite the 90° angle, c, is, therefore, $2\left(3\sqrt{3}\right)$ or $6\sqrt{3}$ units.

24. **D** A counterexample is an example that proves a statement to be false. Answer D shows one example where angles are supplementary but are not right angles, since one measures 100° and the other measures 80°.

25. **E** The radicand must be greater than or equal to zero, so

$$36 - x^2 \geq 0$$

$$-x^2 \geq -36$$

$$x^2 \leq 36$$

$$-6 \leq x \leq 6$$

26. **C** The graph of the function $f(x) = \frac{1}{x}$ has asymptotes of the y- and x-axes. As x approaches zero, the value of the function approaches infinity. Since the domain is restricted to the interval $\frac{1}{2} \leq x \leq \frac{3}{2}$, the maximum value of the function occurs when $x = \frac{1}{2}$.

$$f(x) = \frac{1}{\frac{1}{2}} = 2$$

27. **B**

$$a - b = \frac{n + 1}{n^4} - \frac{1 - n}{n^4}$$

$$= \frac{(n + 1 - 1 + n)}{n^4}$$

$$= \frac{2n}{n^4}$$

$$= \frac{2}{n^3}$$

28. **B** The formula for the surface area of a sphere is $SA = 4\pi r^2$.

$$100\pi = 4\pi r^2$$

$$25 = r^2$$

$$5 = r$$

The volume is, therefore, $\frac{4}{3}\pi r^3 = \frac{4}{3}\pi(5)^3 = \frac{4}{3}\pi(125)$

$$= \frac{500}{3}\pi.$$

29. **E**

$$A = \pi r^2$$

$$64\pi = \pi r^2$$

$$r = 8$$

The circumference of a circle is given by the formula $C = 2\pi r$, so $C = 2\pi(8) = 16\pi$.

30. **A**

$$|2x - 4| < 1$$

$$= -1 < 2x - 4 < 1$$

$$= 3 < 2x < 5$$

$$= \frac{3}{2} < x < \frac{5}{2}$$

31. **D** The general equation of a circle is

$(x - h)^2 + (y - k)^2 = r^2$ where (h, k) is the center and r is the length of the radius. The equation of a circle with center $(-1, 7)$ and a radius of length 3 is

$$(x - -1)^2 + (y - 7)^2 = 3^2$$

$$(x + 1)^2 + (y - 7)^2 = 9$$

32. **E** Write the equation of the line $8x - 2y = 5$ in slope-intercept form to determine its slope.

$$-2y = -8x + 5$$

$$y = 4x - \frac{5}{2}$$

$$m = 4$$

The equation of the line parallel to it and passing through the point $(-2, 2)$ is

$$y - 2 = 4(x - -2)$$

$$y - 2 = 4x + 8$$

$$y = 4x + 10$$

33. **C** Drawing either "E" or "S" are mutually exclusive events. The probability of drawing an "E" is $\frac{1}{8}$ and the probability of drawing "S" is $\frac{1}{8}$. The probability of drawing either "E" or "S" is

$$\frac{1}{8} + \frac{1}{8} = \frac{2}{8} = \frac{1}{4}$$

34. **B**

$$\tan 10° = \cot (90 - 10)°$$

$$\tan 10° = \cot 80°$$

$$\theta = 80°$$

35. **D** Recall that a chord is a segment that connects two points on a circle. The longer the chord, the closer it is to the center of the circle. The lengths of $\overline{OE}$, $\overline{OF}$, and $\overline{OG}$ are the distance the three chords are from the center O, since the segments are the perpendiculars from point O to each chord. $\overline{OF}$ is the smallest length, so $\overline{DC}$ is the longest chord. $\overline{OE}$ is the middle length, so $\overline{AB}$ is the next to longest chord. $\overline{OG}$ is the largest length, so $\overline{BC}$ is the shortest chord.

36. **E** Since $\cos x = \sin (90 - x)$, you know

$$\cos (45 + 2x) = \sin [90 - (45 + 2x)]$$

$$90 - (45 + 2x) = 3x$$

$$45 - 2x = 3x$$

$$45 = 5x$$

$$x = 9°$$

37. **B**

$$2^3(2^{3n})(2) = \frac{1}{4}$$

$$2^{3 + 3n + 1} = 2^{-2}$$

$$3n + 4 = -2$$

$$3n = -6$$

$$n = -2$$

38. **A**

Since $f(x) = \frac{3}{2}x + \sqrt{x}$,

$$f(4) = \frac{3}{2}(4) + \sqrt{4} = 6 + 2 = 8$$

$$f(f(4)) = f(8) = \frac{3}{2}(8) + \sqrt{8} = 12 + 2\sqrt{2}$$

39. **D** Since $n \spadesuit 5 = 125$, $5^{2n} = 125$.

$5^3 = 125$, so $2n$ must equal 3.

$$2n = 3$$

$$n = \frac{3}{2}$$

40. **E** Four common tangents can be drawn as shown:

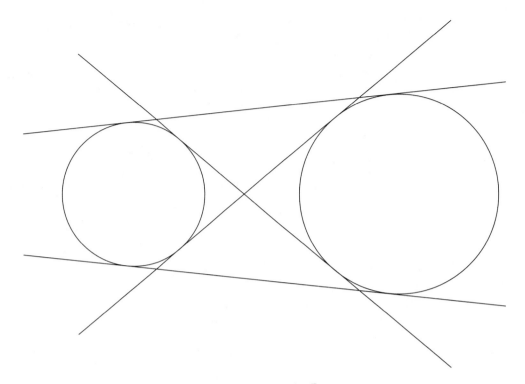

41. **B** Since the boys' team scored a total of 5(54) or 270 points in their first 5 games and the girls' team scored a total of 6(59) or 354 points in their first 6 games, the average for all 11 games is

$$\frac{270 + 354}{11} = 56.7 \text{ points}$$

42. **B** Rotating the rectangle creates a cylinder of radius 3 and height 12. The volume of the cylinder is

$$V = \pi r^2 h = \pi(3^2)(12) = 108\pi$$

43. **E** $i = \sqrt{-1}$, $i^2 = -1$, $i^3 = -i$, and $i^4 = 1$. If i is raised to an exponent that is a multiple of 4, the expression simplifies to 1. All of the expressions simplify to 1, except Answer E.

$i^4 = 1$

$(i^4)^4 = i^{16} = 1$

$i^8 = 1$

$i^{20} = 1$

$i^4 + i^4 = 1 + 1 = 2$

44. **B**

$$\left(\frac{f}{g}\right)(x) = \frac{f(x)}{g(x)}$$

$$= \frac{1 - 3x}{3x^2 + 2x - 1}$$

$$= \frac{-(3x - 1)}{(x + 1)(3x - 1)}$$

$$= \frac{-1}{x + 1}$$

45. C Think of a right triangle with a hypotenuse of length 25 and a leg of length 7. The sine of one of the acute angles of the triangle would, therefore, be $\frac{7}{25}$.

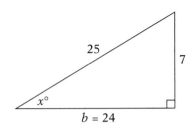

Use the Pythagorean Theorem to find the length of the other leg.

$$7^2 + b^2 = 25^2$$

$$b = 24$$

$$\tan x = \frac{\text{opposite}}{\text{adjacent}} = \frac{7}{24}$$

46. D Kate chooses one course out of the five for her first-period class. She chooses one course out of the remaining four for her second period class. Then, she chooses one out of the remaining three for her third period class and one out of the remaining two for her fourth period class.

$$5 \times 4 \times 3 \times 2 \times 1 = 120$$

47. A The given sequence is a geometric sequence whose nth term is $\left(3\sqrt{3}\right)^n$.

$$\left(3\sqrt{3}\right)^1 = 3\sqrt{3}$$

$$\left(3\sqrt{3}\right)^2 = 9(3) = 27$$

$$\left(3\sqrt{3}\right)^3 = 3^3\left(\sqrt{3}\right)^3 = 27\left(3\sqrt{3}\right) = 81\sqrt{3}$$

The sixth term is, therefore, $\left(3\sqrt{3}\right)^6$.

48. C The sum of the interior angles of a polygon is given by the expression $180(n - 2)$ where n = the number of sides of the polygon.

$$\frac{180(n - 2)}{n} = 157.5$$

$$180n - 360 = 157.5n$$

$$22.5n = 360$$

$$n = 16 \text{ sides}$$

49. C Start by multiplying both sides by the LCD:

$$\frac{1}{(x - 2)(x + 4)} = \frac{h}{x - 2} + \frac{k}{x + 4}$$

$$1 = h(x + 4) + k(x - 2)$$

How to solve for k may not be immediately obvious. One way to solve for k is to substitute -4 for x, so the h term cancels out.

$$1 = h(-4 + 4) + k(-4 - 2)$$

$$1 = k(-6)$$

$$k = -\frac{1}{6}$$

50. C Each angle of a regular hexagon measures 120°. Using XO as one leg, sketch a 30°-60°-90° right triangle as shown:

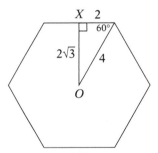

The side opposite the 30° angle measures 2 units. The regular hexagon can be broken into 12 right triangles that are congruent to the one shown in the diagram. The perimeter of the hexagon is, therefore, 12(2) or 24 units.

Diagnose Your Strengths and Weaknesses

Check the number of each question answered correctly and "X" the number of each question answered incorrectly.

Algebra	1	2	3	4	5	10	12	13	14	22	27	30	37	49	Total Number Correct
14 questions															

Plane Geometry	6	7	11	16	23	24	29	35	40	48	50	Total Number Correct
11 questions												

Solid Geometry	21	28	42	Total Number Correct
3 questions				

Coordinate Geometry	8	17	18	20	31	32	Total Number Correct
6 questions							

Trigonometry	19	34	36	45	Total Number Correct
4 questions					

Functions	15	25	26	38	44	Total Number Correct
5 questions						

Data Analysis, Statistics, and Probability	33	41	46	Total Number Correct
3 questions				

Number and Operations	9	39	43	47	Total Number Correct
4 questions					

Number of correct answers $-\frac{1}{4}$ **(Number of incorrect answers) = Your raw score**

_____ $-\frac{1}{4}$ (_____) = _____

Compare your raw score with the approximate SAT Subject test score below:

	Raw Score	SAT Subject test Approximate Score
Excellent	46–50	750–800
Very Good	41–45	700–750
Good	36–40	640–700
Above Average	29–35	590–640
Average	22–28	510–590
Below Average	< 22	< 510

PRACTICE TEST 6

Treat this practice test as the actual test and complete it in one 60-minute sitting. Use the following answer sheet to fill in your multiple-choice answers. Once you have completed the practice test:

1. Check your answers using the Answer Key.
2. Review the Answer Explanations.
3. Fill in the "Diagnose Your Strengths and Weaknesses" sheet and determine areas that require further preparation.

PRACTICE TEST 6

MATH LEVEL 1

ANSWER SHEET

Tear out this answer sheet and use it to complete the practice test.

Determine the BEST answer for each question. Then fill in the appropriate oval using a No. 2 pencil.

1. Ⓐ Ⓑ Ⓒ Ⓓ Ⓔ	21. Ⓐ Ⓑ Ⓒ Ⓓ Ⓔ	41. Ⓐ Ⓑ Ⓒ Ⓓ Ⓔ
2. Ⓐ Ⓑ Ⓒ Ⓓ Ⓔ	22. Ⓐ Ⓑ Ⓒ Ⓓ Ⓔ	42. Ⓐ Ⓑ Ⓒ Ⓓ Ⓔ
3. Ⓐ Ⓑ Ⓒ Ⓓ Ⓔ	23. Ⓐ Ⓑ Ⓒ Ⓓ Ⓔ	43. Ⓐ Ⓑ Ⓒ Ⓓ Ⓔ
4. Ⓐ Ⓑ Ⓒ Ⓓ Ⓔ	24. Ⓐ Ⓑ Ⓒ Ⓓ Ⓔ	44. Ⓐ Ⓑ Ⓒ Ⓓ Ⓔ
5. Ⓐ Ⓑ Ⓒ Ⓓ Ⓔ	25. Ⓐ Ⓑ Ⓒ Ⓓ Ⓔ	45. Ⓐ Ⓑ Ⓒ Ⓓ Ⓔ
6. Ⓐ Ⓑ Ⓒ Ⓓ Ⓔ	26. Ⓐ Ⓑ Ⓒ Ⓓ Ⓔ	46. Ⓐ Ⓑ Ⓒ Ⓓ Ⓔ
7. Ⓐ Ⓑ Ⓒ Ⓓ Ⓔ	27. Ⓐ Ⓑ Ⓒ Ⓓ Ⓔ	47. Ⓐ Ⓑ Ⓒ Ⓓ Ⓔ
8. Ⓐ Ⓑ Ⓒ Ⓓ Ⓔ	28. Ⓐ Ⓑ Ⓒ Ⓓ Ⓔ	48. Ⓐ Ⓑ Ⓒ Ⓓ Ⓔ
9. Ⓐ Ⓑ Ⓒ Ⓓ Ⓔ	29. Ⓐ Ⓑ Ⓒ Ⓓ Ⓔ	49. Ⓐ Ⓑ Ⓒ Ⓓ Ⓔ
10. Ⓐ Ⓑ Ⓒ Ⓓ Ⓔ	30. Ⓐ Ⓑ Ⓒ Ⓓ Ⓔ	50. Ⓐ Ⓑ Ⓒ Ⓓ Ⓔ
11. Ⓐ Ⓑ Ⓒ Ⓓ Ⓔ	31. Ⓐ Ⓑ Ⓒ Ⓓ Ⓔ	
12. Ⓐ Ⓑ Ⓒ Ⓓ Ⓔ	32. Ⓐ Ⓑ Ⓒ Ⓓ Ⓔ	
13. Ⓐ Ⓑ Ⓒ Ⓓ Ⓔ	33. Ⓐ Ⓑ Ⓒ Ⓓ Ⓔ	
14. Ⓐ Ⓑ Ⓒ Ⓓ Ⓔ	34. Ⓐ Ⓑ Ⓒ Ⓓ Ⓔ	
15. Ⓐ Ⓑ Ⓒ Ⓓ Ⓔ	35. Ⓐ Ⓑ Ⓒ Ⓓ Ⓔ	
16. Ⓐ Ⓑ Ⓒ Ⓓ Ⓔ	36. Ⓐ Ⓑ Ⓒ Ⓓ Ⓔ	
17. Ⓐ Ⓑ Ⓒ Ⓓ Ⓔ	37. Ⓐ Ⓑ Ⓒ Ⓓ Ⓔ	
18. Ⓐ Ⓑ Ⓒ Ⓓ Ⓔ	38. Ⓐ Ⓑ Ⓒ Ⓓ Ⓔ	
19. Ⓐ Ⓑ Ⓒ Ⓓ Ⓔ	39. Ⓐ Ⓑ Ⓒ Ⓓ Ⓔ	
20. Ⓐ Ⓑ Ⓒ Ⓓ Ⓔ	40. Ⓐ Ⓑ Ⓒ Ⓓ Ⓔ	

PRACTICE TEST 6
Time: 60 Minutes

NOTES:

(1) A calculator will be needed to answer some of the questions on the test. Scientific, programmable, and graphing calculators are permitted. It is up to you to determine when and when not to use your calculator.

(2) All angles on the Level 1 test are measured in degrees, not radians. Make sure your calculator is set to degree mode.

(3) Figures are drawn as accurately as possible and are intended to help solve some of the test problems. If a figure is not drawn to scale, this will be stated in the problem. All figures lie in a plane unless the problem indicates otherwise.

(4) Unless otherwise stated, the domain of a function f is assumed to be the set of real numbers x for which the value of the function, $f(x)$, is a real number.

(5) Reference information that may be useful in answering some of the test questions can be found below.

Reference Information	
Right circular cone with radius r and height h:	Volume $= \frac{1}{3}\pi r^2 h$
Right circular cone with circumference of base c and slant height ℓ:	Lateral Area $= \frac{1}{2}c\ell$
Sphere with radius r:	Volume $= \frac{4}{3}\pi r^3$ Surface Area $= 4\pi r^2$
Pyramid with base area B and height h:	Volume $= \frac{1}{3}Bh$

1. If $\dfrac{7^2 - x}{7 + x} = 6$, then $x =$

   (A) $\dfrac{6}{7}$

   (B) 1

   (C) $\dfrac{7}{5}$

   (D) -1

   (E) $\dfrac{7}{6}$

2. If $\dfrac{2}{4x^2 + 1} = \dfrac{2}{5}$, then $x =$

   (A) 4

   (B) 1

   (C) ± 1

   (D) $\pm\sqrt{\dfrac{6}{4}}$

   (E) $\pm\sqrt{\dfrac{6}{2}}$

3. Which of the following equations has the same solution(s) as $|x - 5| = 2$?

   (A) $\dfrac{x}{2} = \dfrac{3}{2}$

   (B) $3x = 21$

   (C) $x^2 - 10x + 21 = 0$

   (D) $x^2 - 4x - 21 = 0$

   (E) $x^2 = 49$

4. $x^3 + 8x^2 - 1$ subtracted from $5x^3 - x^2 + 2x + 1$ equals which of the following?

   (A) $4x^3 - 8x^2 + 2x - 2$

   (B) $-4x^3 + 9x^2 - 2x - 2$

   (C) $4x^3 + 7x^2 + 2x$

   (D) $4x^3 - 9x^2 + 2x$

   (E) $4x^3 - 9x^2 + 2x + 2$

5. A cell phone company charges $30 a month for a phone plan plus an additional 40 cents for each minute over the allotted 300 minutes that come with the plan. Assuming the phone is used for m minutes and $m > 300$, which of the following is an expression for the monthly cost?

   (A) $30 + 0.40m$

   (B) $30 + 0.40(m - 300)$

   (C) $30 + 0.40(m + 300)$

   (D) $30 + 40(m - 300)$

   (E) $30.40m$

GO ON TO THE NEXT PAGE

USE THIS SPACE AS SCRATCH PAPER

6. If $\sqrt[3]{8 - 7x} = -3$, then $x =$

   (A) $-\dfrac{19}{7}$

   (B) 5

   (C) $\dfrac{19}{7}$

   (D) -5

   (E) $-\dfrac{1}{7}$

7. If two similar octagons have a scale factor of 3:5, then the ratio of their areas is

   (A) 3:5

   (B) $\sqrt{3} : \sqrt{5}$

   (C) 9:25

   (D) 27:125

   (E) 6:10

8. What is the ratio of the circumference of a circle to its area?

   (A) 2:r

   (B) r:2

   (C) 1:r

   (D) 2r:1

   (E) 2:r^2

9. Kelli has taken a job with a starting salary of \$35,000. If she receives annual raises of \$2,800, what will her salary be during her fourth year on the job?

   (A) \$11,900

   (B) \$37,800

   (C) \$40,600

   (D) \$43,400

   (E) \$46,200

10. If $x = \sqrt[3]{y}$ and $y = 2n$, then what is the value of x when $n = -4$?

    (A) 2

    (B) -2

    (C) 8

    (D) -8

    (E) $2\sqrt{2}$

GO ON TO THE NEXT PAGE

11. In $\triangle ABC$, $AB = 4$ and $BC = 7$. If the length of the third side is an integer, then what is the greatest possible value for AC?

    (A) 8
    (B) 14
    (C) 11
    (D) 10
    (E) 12

12. If the measure of each exterior angle of a regular polygon is 20°, how many sides does the polygon have?

    (A) 18
    (B) 9
    (C) 27
    (D) 22
    (E) 36

13. The ratio of the measures of the angles of a quadrilateral is 1:2:4:5. What is the measure of the largest angle?

    (A) 30°
    (B) 150°
    (C) 154°
    (D) 120°
    (E) 144°

14. If $-2x + y = -17$ and $x + y = 16$, then $x - y =$

    (A) 5
    (B) 11
    (C) 6
    (D) 4
    (E) 10

15. Which of the following is the graph of $2x - y \geq -1$?

    (A)

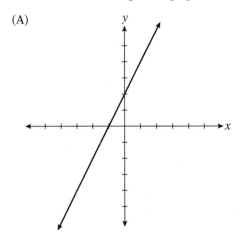

GO ON TO THE NEXT PAGE

(B)

(C)

(D)

(E)

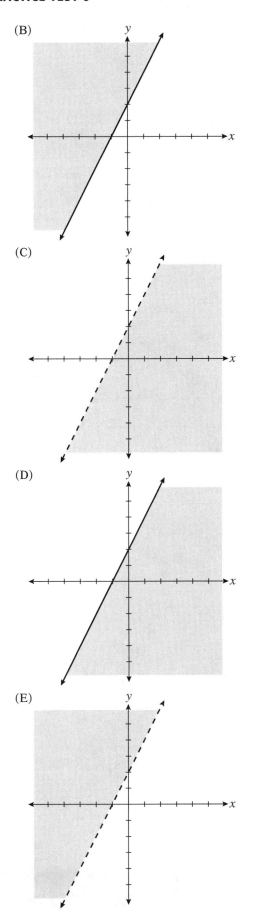

GO ON TO THE NEXT PAGE

16. If the point $(-2, a)$ is on the graph of the equation $y = x^2 - 7$, then $a =$

    (A) 4
    (B) 3
    (C) $\pm\sqrt{5}$
    (D) -11
    (E) -3

17. $(x + y + 5)(x + y - 5) =$

    (A) $(x + y)^2 - 25$
    (B) $(x + y)^2 + 10(x + y) + 25$
    (C) $(x + y)^2 + 10(x + y)$
    (D) $x^2 + y^2 - 5^2$
    (E) $x^2 + 2xy + y^2 + 5^2$

18. In Figure 1, $\dfrac{ST}{TR} = \dfrac{11}{14}$. $\sin \theta =$

    (A) $\dfrac{11}{317}$
    (B) 0.618
    (C) 0.786
    (D) 0.222
    (E) 0.733

19. If points $(0, 0)$, $(3, 7)$, and $(11, 0)$ are the vertices of an isosceles trapezoid, then which of the following points is the remaining vertex?

    (A) $(8, -7)$
    (B) $(14, 7)$
    (C) $(7, 8)$
    (D) $(3, -7)$
    (E) $(8, 7)$

20. A point Q is in the second quadrant at a distance of $\sqrt{41}$ from the origin. Which of the following could be the coordinates of Q?

    (A) $(-1, 41)$
    (B) $(-4, 5)$
    (C) $\left(-8, \sqrt{23}\right)$
    (D) $(5, -4)$
    (E) $(-6, 5)$

21. If $\sqrt[5]{\sqrt{x}} = 2$, then $x =$

    (A) 20
    (B) 1,024
    (C) 64
    (D) 128
    (E) 512

USE THIS SPACE AS SCRATCH PAPER

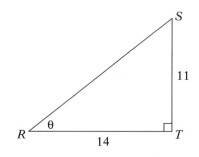

Figure 1

GO ON TO THE NEXT PAGE

22. What is the area of the triangle in Figure 2?

    (A) $64\sqrt{3}$

    (B) $64\sqrt{2}$

    (C) $32\sqrt{3}$

    (D) 64

    (E) 32

23. If $4^x = 36^3 \div 9^3$, then $x =$

    (A) 2

    (B) 3

    (C) 4

    (D) 5

    (E) 16

24. For $x \neq 0$, if $3^{-2} - 6^{-2} = x^{-2}$, then $x =$

    (A) $3\sqrt{3}$

    (B) $2\sqrt{3}$

    (C) ± 12

    (D) $\pm 2\sqrt{3}$

    (E) ± 6

25. Which of the following is the equation of a line that will never intersect the line $5x - 9y = -1$?

    (A) $-5x - 9y = -1$

    (B) $y = x + \dfrac{1}{9}$

    (C) $y = \dfrac{5}{9}x - 2$

    (D) $5x + 9y = 0$

    (E) $y = \dfrac{9}{5}x + 1$

26. If 2 percent of a 12-gallon solution is sodium, how many gallons of pure sodium must be added to make a new solution that is 6 percent sodium?

    (A) 1.79

    (B) 1.02

    (C) 8

    (D) 5

    (E) 0.51

27. The product of the roots of a quadratic equation is −5 and their sum is −4. Which of the following could be the quadratic equation?

    (A) $x^2 - 4x + 5 = 0$

    (B) $x^2 - 4x - 5 = 0$

    (C) $x^2 + 4x - 5 = 0$

    (D) $x^2 + 5x - 4 = 0$

    (E) $x^2 - 5x - 4 = 0$

USE THIS SPACE AS SCRATCH PAPER

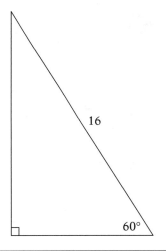

Figure 2

GO ON TO THE NEXT PAGE

28. If $f(x) = x^2 + 4$ and $g(x) = 1 - x^3$, then $f(g(-1)) =$

    (A) 6
    (B) 5
    (C) 16
    (D) 4
    (E) 8

29. $(1 + \sin \theta)(1 - \sin \theta) =$

    (A) $1 - \sin \theta$
    (B) $\cos^2 \theta$
    (C) $1 - 2\sin \theta + \sin^2 \theta$
    (D) $\cos \theta$
    (E) 1

30. If $25x^2 - 20x + k = 0$ has $\dfrac{2}{5}$ as a double root, $k =$

    (A) 4
    (B) $\dfrac{4}{25}$
    (C) 5
    (D) −5
    (E) 1

31. If a is an even integer and b is an odd integer, then which of the following must be odd?

    (A) ab
    (B) a^b
    (C) $a + b + 1$
    (D) $2b + 1$
    (E) $a - 2b$

32. Which of the following equations has roots of 4 and $-\dfrac{1}{2}$?

    (A) $2x^3 + x^2 - 32x - 16 = 0$
    (B) $2x^2 + 7x - 4 = 0$
    (C) $2x^2 - 9x - 4 = 0$
    (D) $2x^2 - 7x - 4 = 0$
    (E) $4(2x + 1) = 0$

33. What is the area of the quadrilateral in Figure 3?

    (A) $2\sqrt{2}$ units^2
    (B) $8\sqrt{2}$ units^2
    (C) $\dfrac{16}{2}$ units^2
    (D) 16 units^2
    (E) 8 units^2

USE THIS SPACE AS SCRATCH PAPER

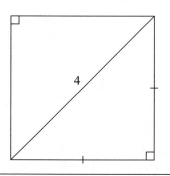

Figure 3

GO ON TO THE NEXT PAGE

34. The volume of a cube is *V*. If the sides of the cube are cut if half, the volume of the resulting solid is

    (A) 2*V*

    (B) $\dfrac{1}{2}V$

    (C) $\dfrac{1}{4}V$

    (D) $\dfrac{1}{8}V$

    (E) $\dfrac{1}{16}V$

35. *y* = *f*(*x*) is graphed in Figure 4. Which of the following is the graph of *y* = |*f*(*x*)|?

    (A)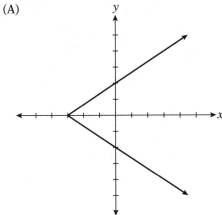

    (B)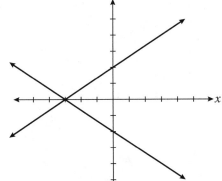

    (C)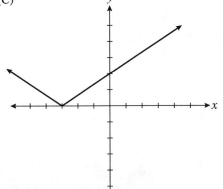

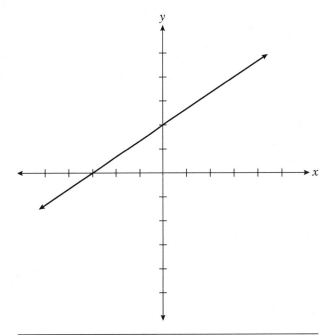

Figure 4

GO ON TO THE NEXT PAGE

(D)

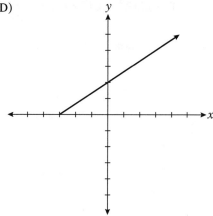

(E)

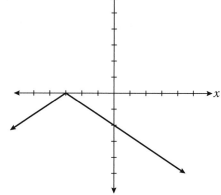

36. In Figure 5, which of the following must be true?

   I. $\cot x = \dfrac{3}{4}$

   II. $\cos x = \sin y$

   III. $\tan x = \tan y$

   (A) I only
   (B) II only
   (C) II and III only
   (D) I and II only
   (E) I, II, and III

37. What is the lateral area of the right circular cone shown in Figure 6?

   (A) 50π
   (B) 75π
   (C) $\dfrac{125\sqrt{3}}{3}\pi$
   (D) $25\sqrt{3}\pi$
   (E) 100π

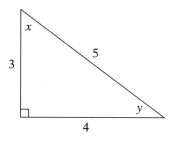

Figure 5

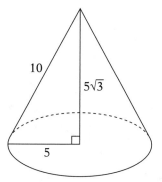

Figure 6

GO ON TO THE NEXT PAGE

38. If $f(x) = -4(x + 2)^2 - 1$ for $-4 \le x \le 0$, then which of the following is the range of f?

    (A) $y \le -1$
    (B) $-4 \le y \le 0$
    (C) $y \le 0$
    (D) $-17 \le y \le -1$
    (E) $y \le -17$

39. If $f(x) = \sqrt{x}$ and $f(g(x)) = 2\sqrt{x}$, then $g(x) =$

    (A) $4x$
    (B) $2x$
    (C) $2x^2$
    (D) $\dfrac{x}{2}$
    (E) x^3

40. If $i = \sqrt{-1}$, then $(6 - i)(6 + i) =$

    (A) 35
    (B) $36 - i$
    (C) 37
    (D) $35 + 12i$
    (E) 36

41. What is the volume of the right triangular prism in Figure 7?

    (A) $200 \ \text{cm}^3$
    (B) $100\sqrt{2} \ \text{cm}^3$
    (C) $100 \ \text{cm}^3$
    (D) $\dfrac{100}{3} \ \text{cm}^3$
    (E) $\dfrac{100\sqrt{2}}{3} \ \text{cm}^3$

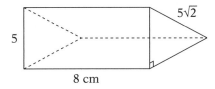

Figure 7

42. $\tan \theta (\sin \theta) + \cos \theta =$

    (A) $2\cos \theta$
    (B) $\cos \theta + \sec \theta$
    (C) $\csc \theta$
    (D) $\sec \theta$
    (E) 1

43. The French Club consists of 10 members and is holding officer elections to select a president, secretary, and treasurer for the club. A member can only be selected for one position. How many possibilities are there for selecting the three officers?

    (A) 30
    (B) 27
    (C) 72
    (D) 720
    (E) 90

GO ON TO THE NEXT PAGE

44. Which of the following is symmetric with respect to the origin?

    (A) $y = x^2 - 1$
    (B) $y = x^3 - 2x$
    (C) $y^2 = x + 8$
    (D) $y = -|x + 1|$
    (E) $y = (x + 3)^2$

45. In parallelogram *JKLM* shown in Figure 8, $\overline{JK} = 18$, $\overline{KL} = 12$, and $m\angle JKL = 120°$. What is the area of *JKLM*?

    (A) $108\sqrt{3}$
    (B) $72\sqrt{3}$
    (C) $54\sqrt{3}$
    (D) $36\sqrt{3}$
    (E) $90\sqrt{3}$

46. Thirteen students receive the following grades on a math test:

    60, 78, 90, 67, 88, 92, 81, 100, 95, 83, 83, 86, 74

    What is the interquartile range of the test scores?

    (A) 14
    (B) 83
    (C) 15
    (D) 16
    (E) 40

47. $p \square q$ is defined as $\dfrac{p^q}{pq}$ for all positive real numbers. Which of the following is equivalent to $\dfrac{p}{2}$?

    (A) $p \square 1$
    (B) $p \square p$
    (C) $p \square \dfrac{1}{2}$
    (D) $1 \square q$
    (E) $p \square 2$

USE THIS SPACE AS SCRATCH PAPER

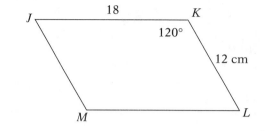

Figure 8

GO ON TO THE NEXT PAGE

USE THIS SPACE AS SCRATCH PAPER

48. Matt and Alysia are going to get their driver's licenses. The probability that Matt passes his driving test is $\frac{9}{10}$. The probability that Alysia passes her driving test is $\frac{7}{9}$. Assuming that their result is not dependent on how the other does, what is the probability that Matt passes and Alysia fails?

(A) $\frac{101}{90}$

(B) $\frac{1}{5}$

(C) $\frac{7}{10}$

(D) $\frac{11}{90}$

(E) $\frac{27}{100}$

49. The circle shown in Figure 9 has an area of 36π cm². What is the area of the shaded segment?

(A) 9π cm²
(B) $9\pi - 36$ cm²
(C) 18 cm²
(D) $9\pi - 18$ cm²
(E) $18\pi - 18$ cm²

50. If $f(n) = 9^{-n}$, then $f\left(-\frac{1}{4}\right) =$

(A) $9^{-\frac{1}{4}}$
(B) 3
(C) $\sqrt{3}$
(D) $\frac{1}{9}$
(E) 9

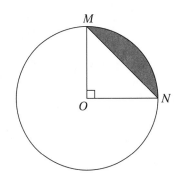

Figure 9

S T O P

IF YOU FINISH BEFORE TIME IS CALLED, GO BACK AND CHECK YOUR WORK.

ANSWER KEY

1. B	11. D	21. B	31. D	41. C
2. C	12. A	22. C	32. D	42. D
3. C	13. B	23. B	33. E	43. D
4. E	14. C	24. D	34. D	44. B
5. B	15. D	25. C	35. C	45. A
6. B	16. E	26. E	36. D	46. C
7. C	17. A	27. C	37. A	47. E
8. A	18. B	28. E	38. D	48. B
9. D	19. E	29. B	39. A	49. D
10. B	20. B	30. A	40. C	50. C

ANSWERS AND SOLUTIONS

1. **B**

$$\frac{7^2 - x}{7 + x} = 6$$

$$7^2 - x = 6(7 + x)$$

$$49 - x = 42 + 6x$$

$$7 = 7x$$

$$x = 1$$

2. **C**

$$\frac{2}{4x^2 + 1} = \frac{2}{5}$$

$$2(4x^2 + 1) = 5(2)$$

$$4x^2 + 1 = 5$$

$$4x^2 = 4$$

$$x^2 = 1$$

$$x = \pm 1$$

3. **C**

$$|x - 5| = 2$$

$$x - 5 = 2 \quad \text{or} \quad x - 5 = -2$$

$$x = 7 \qquad\qquad x = 3$$

The equation in Answer C, $x^2 - 10x + 21 = 0$, can be factored as:

$$(x - 7)(x - 3) = 0$$

Its solutions are also $x = 3$ or $x = 7$.

4. **E**

$$5x^3 - x^2 + 2x + 1 - (x^3 + 8x^2 - 1)$$

$$= 5x^3 - x^2 + 2x + 1 - x^3 - 8x^2 + 1$$

$$= 4x^3 - 9x^2 + 2x + 2$$

5. **B** Since $30 is the initial cost and $0.40 is charged for $(m - 300)$ additional minutes, the correct expression is:

$$30 + 0.40(m - 300)$$

6. **B**

$$\sqrt[3]{(8 - 7x)} = -3$$

$$\left[\sqrt[3]{(8 - 7x)}\right]^3 = (-3)^3$$

$$8 - 7x = -27$$

$$-7x = -35$$

$$x = 5$$

7. **C** The scale factor of the similar octagons is 3:5, so their areas must be in the ratio of $3^2:5^2$.

$3^2:5^2$ equals 9:25

8. **A** $C = 2\pi r$ and $A = \pi r^2$, so the ratio of the circumference to area is

$$\frac{2\pi r}{2\pi r^2} = \frac{2}{r} \text{ or } 2:r$$

9. **D** Kelli receives the following salaries during the indicated years:

Year 1: 35,000

Year 2: 35,000 + 2,800 = \$37,800

Year 3: 35,000 + 2(2,800) = \$40,600

Year 4: 35,000 + 3(2,800) = \$43,400

10. **B**

When $n = -4$, $y = 2(-4) = -8$.

$x = \sqrt[3]{-8} = -2$

11. **D** The Triangle Inequality Theorem states that the sum of any two sides of a triangle must be greater than the third side.

$4 + 7 > AC$

$11 > AC$

10 is the greatest integer less than 11.

12. **A** The sum of the exterior angles of any polygon is 360°. If each exterior angle measures 20°, the polygon has

$$\frac{360}{20} = 18 \text{ sides}$$

13. **B** Since the angles are in the ratio 1:2:4:5, let x, $2x$, $4x$, and $5x$ represent the four angle measures.

$x + 2x + 4x + 5x = 360$

$12x = 360$

$x = 30$

The largest angle measures 5(30) or 150°.

14. **C** Multiply the second equation by 2 to get a coefficient of 2 for the x term: $2x + 2y = 32$. Then, solve the system using the linear combination method.

$$\begin{array}{r} -2x + y = -7 \\ + 2x + 2y = 32 \\ \hline 3y = 15 \end{array}$$

$y = 5$

If $y = 5$, $x + 5 = 16$, so $x = 11$.

$x - y = 11 - 5 = 6$

15. **D** Graph the line first. The line is solid, not dashed, since the inequality has a "greater than or equal to" sign.

$2x - y \geq -1$

$2x + 1 \geq y$

Test a point, (0, 0) for example, to determine whether to shade above or below the line. The origin satisfies the inequality since $2(0) + 1 \geq 0$, so shade below the line. Answer D is the appropriate graph.

16. **E** Substitute $x = -2$ into the equation, and solve for the corresponding y value.

$y = x^2 - 7$

$y = (-2)^2 - 7$

$y = 4 - 7 = -3$

17. **A**

$(x + y + 5)(x + y - 5)$

$= [(x + y) + 5][(x + y) - 5]$

$= (x + y)^2 - 25$

18. **B**

$$\tan\theta - \frac{ST}{TR} = \frac{11}{14}$$

$$\tan^{-1}\left(\frac{11}{14}\right) = 38.157$$

$\theta = 38.157°$

$\sin 38.157° = 0.618$

You can also solve this problem by using the Pythagorean Theorem to determine the length of the hypotenuse of ΔSTR. $SR = \sqrt{317}$, so sin

$$\theta = \frac{11}{\sqrt{317}} = 0.618.$$

19. **E** The vertex (8, 7) results in an isosceles trapezoid as shown:

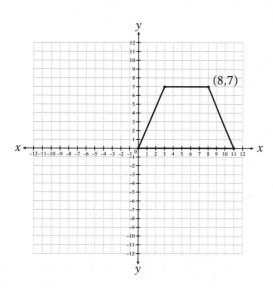

20. **B** (–4, 5) is the only given point that is both in the second quadrant and at a distance of $\sqrt{41}$ from the origin.

$$\sqrt{(-4-0)^2 + (5-0)^2}$$
$$= \sqrt{4^2 + 5^2}$$
$$= \sqrt{16 + 25}$$
$$= \sqrt{41}$$

21. **B**

$$\sqrt[5]{\sqrt{x}} = 2$$
$$\sqrt{x} = 2^5$$
$$x = \left(2^5\right)^2$$
$$x = 2^{10} = 1{,}024$$

22. **C** Since the triangle is a 30°-60°-90° right triangle, its legs measure 8 and $8\sqrt{3}$ units. Its area is

$$A = \frac{1}{2}bh = \frac{1}{2}(8)\left(8\sqrt{3}\right)$$
$$= \frac{1}{2}\left(64\sqrt{3}\right) = 32\sqrt{3}$$

23. **B**

$$4^x = 36^3 \div 9^3$$
$$4^x = (36 \div 9)^3$$
$$4^x = 4^3$$
$$x = 3$$

24. **D**

$$3^{-2} - 6^{-2} = x^{-2}$$
$$\frac{1}{3^2} - \frac{1}{6^2} = \frac{1}{x^2}$$
$$\frac{1}{9} - \frac{1}{36} = \frac{1}{x^2}$$

Multiply both sides of the equation by the LCD, $36x^2$.

$$4x^2 - x^2 = 36$$
$$3x^2 = 36$$
$$x^2 = 12$$
$$x = \pm\sqrt{12} = \pm 2\sqrt{3}$$

25. **C** In order for two lines to never intersect, they must be parallel. Parallel lines have the same slope, so determine which of the given lines has the same slope as $5x - 9y = -1$.

$$5x - 9y = -1$$
$$-9y = -5x - 1$$
$$y = \frac{5}{9}x + \frac{1}{9}$$

The given line has a slope of $\frac{5}{9}$. Since the equation in Answer C is in slope-intercept form, you can quickly determine that its slope is also $\frac{5}{9}$. The line $y = \frac{5}{9}x - 2$ will, therefore, never intersect the line $5x - 9y = -1$.

26. **E** Let x = the number of gallons of sodium added.

$$2\%(12) + 100\%(x) = 6\%(12 + x)$$
$$2(12) + 100(x) = 6(12 + x)$$
$$24 + 100x = 72 + 6x$$
$$94x = 48$$
$$x = \frac{48}{94} = 0.51 \text{ gallons}$$

27. **C** Recall that a quadratic equation can be thought of as:

$a[x^2 - (\text{sum of the roots})x + (\text{product of the roots})] = 0$. Substitute the sum = -4 and the product = -5 to get:

$a(x^2 - -4x + -5) = 0$

$a(x^2 + 4x - 5) = 0$

When $a = 1$, the result is the equation given in Answer C: $x^2 + 4x - 5 = 0$.

28. **E**

$g(-1) = 1 - (-1)^3 = 1 - -1 = 2$

$f(g(-1)) = f(2) = (2)^2 + 4 = 8$

29. **B** Recall that $\sin^2 \theta + \cos^2 \theta = 1$, so $\cos^2 \theta = 1 - \sin^2 \theta$.

$(1 + \sin \theta)(1 - \sin \theta)$

$= 1 - \sin \theta + \sin \theta - \sin^2 \theta$

$= 1 - \sin^2 \theta$

$= \cos^2 \theta$

30. **A** Since $\frac{2}{5}$ is a double root, $\left(x - \frac{2}{5}\right)$ is a factor of the quadratic equation two times.

$\left(x - \frac{2}{5}\right)\left(x - \frac{2}{5}\right) = 0$

$(5x - 2)(5x - 2) = 0$

$25x^2 - 20x + 4 = 0$

$k = 4$

31. **D** Since b is odd, multiplying b by 2 will always result in an even number. Adding 1 to an even product will always result in an odd number, so Answer D is the correct choice. If you're not sure about number theory, try substituting values for a and b. Let $a = 4$ and $b = 3$.

$ab = 4(3) = 12$

$a^b = 4^3 = 64$

$a + b + 1 = 4 + 3 + 1 = 8$

$2b + 1 = 2(3) + 1 = 7$

$a - 2b = 4 - 2(3) = 4 - 6 = -2$

7 is the only odd result.

32. **D** An equation with roots of 4 and $-\frac{1}{2}$ has factors $x - 4$ and $x + \frac{1}{2}$.

$(x - 4)\left(x + \frac{1}{2}\right) = 0$

$(x - 4)(2x + 1) = 0$

$2x^2 + x - 8x - 4 = 0$

$2x^2 - 7x - 4 = 0$

33. **E** The diagonal divides the square into 2 congruent right triangles. Since the triangles are isosceles right triangles and the hypotenuse measures 4 units, each leg measures

$\frac{4}{\sqrt{2}} = 2\sqrt{\frac{4}{2}} = 2\sqrt{2}$ units

The area of the square units

$A = bh = 2\sqrt{2}\left(2\sqrt{2}\right) = 4(2) = 8$ square units.

34. **D** The scale factor of the cubes is 2:1, so their volumes are in the ratio $2^3:1^3$. The new volume is $\frac{1}{2^3}$ or $\frac{1}{8} V$ the volume of the original cube.

35. **C** Absolute value results in a number greater than or equal to zero. Since $y = |f(x)|$, y must be positive. The portion of the graph of $f(x)$ below the x-axis should be reflected over the x-axis, resulting in the graph given in Answer C.

36. **D**

The first statement is true because

$\cot x = \dfrac{\text{adjacent}}{\text{opposite}} = \dfrac{3}{4}$

The second statement is also true, since

$\cos x = \dfrac{3}{5}$ and $\sin y = \dfrac{3}{5}$

The third statement is not true, since

$\tan x = \dfrac{4}{3}$ and $\tan y = \dfrac{3}{4}$

Answer D is the correct choice.

37. **A** The lateral area of a cone equals $\frac{1}{2}c\ell$, where c = the circumference of the base and ℓ = the slant height.

For the given cone:

$$L = \frac{1}{2}c\ell = \frac{1}{2}(2\pi)(5)(10)$$

$$= \frac{1}{2}(100\pi) = 50\pi$$

38. **D** The graph of $f(x) = -4(x + 2)^2 - 1$ is a parabola concave down with vertex at $(-2, -1)$.

When $x = -4$, $f(-4) = -4(-4 + 2)^2 - 1 = -17$.

When $x = 0$, $f(0) = -4(0 + 2)^2 - 1 = -17$.

The range spans from the least value of y, -17, to the greatest, -1, which occurs at the vertex.

An alternate way to determine the range is to graph the function on your graphing calculator and check the Table values for y when $-4 \le x \le 0$.

39. **A** Since you know the composition of f and g results in $2\sqrt{x}$, you need to determine what input value of f will result in $2\sqrt{x}$.

$$\sqrt{4x} = 2\sqrt{x}$$

Therefore, $g(x) = 4x$. Test your answer by checking the composition.

$$g(x) = 4x, \text{ so } f(g(x)) = f(4x) = \sqrt{4x} = 2\sqrt{x}$$

40. **C**

Since $i = \sqrt{-1}$, $i^2 = \sqrt{-1}\left(\sqrt{-1}\right) = -1$.

$(6 - i)(6 + i)$

$= 36 + 6i - 6i - i^2$

$= 36 - i^2$

$= 36 - (-1) = 37$

41. **C** $V = BH$ where B = the area of the base. In this case, the base is a right triangle. Since one leg measures 5 cm and the hypotenuse measures $5\sqrt{2}$ cm, the triangle is an isosceles right triangle. The other leg must also measure 5 cm.

The area of the triangle is

$$A = \frac{1}{2}bh = \frac{1}{2}(5)(5) = \frac{25}{2}.$$

The volume of the solid is, therefore,

$$V = BH = \frac{25}{2}(8) = 100 \text{ cm}^3$$

42. **D**

$$\tan\theta(\sin\theta) + \cos\theta$$

$$= \frac{\sin\theta}{\cos\theta}(\sin\theta) + \cos\theta$$

$$= \frac{\sin^2\theta}{\cos\theta} + \frac{\cos^2\theta}{\cos\theta}$$

$$= \frac{\sin^2\theta + \cos^2\theta}{\cos\theta}$$

$$= \frac{1}{\cos\theta} = \sec\theta$$

43. **D** There are 10 possible people that could serve as president. Once the president is chosen, there are 9 possible people that could serve as secretary, and once that person is chosen, there are 8 remaining people that could serve as treasurer. The total number of ways of selecting the three officers is

$$10 \times 9 \times 8 = 720$$

44. **B** If the graph is symmetric with respect to the origin, the points (x, y) and $(-x, -y)$ satisfy the equation. Replace x with $-x$ and y with $-y$ to determine if the resulting equation is equivalent to the given one.

For the equation in Answer B:

$-y = (-x)^3 - 2(-x)$

$-y = -x^3 + 2x$

$y = x^3 - 2x$

The resulting equation is equivalent to the original, $y = x^3 - 2x$, so the graph is symmetric with respect to the origin.

45. A Consecutive angles in a parallelogram are supplementary so $m\angle KLM = 180 - 120 = 60°$. Sketch a $30° = -60°-90°$ right triangle to determine the height of the parallelogram.

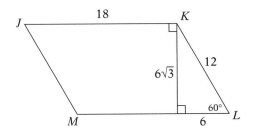

Since the parallelogram's altitude is opposite the 60° angle, the height of the parallelogram is $6\sqrt{3}$. Its area is

$$A = bh = 18\left(6\sqrt{3}\right) = 108\sqrt{3}$$

46. C Start by arranging the test scores in order of lowest to highest:

   60, 67, 74, 78, 81, 83, 83, 86, 88, 90, 92, 95, 100

The median of the data is 83. To find the interquartile range, find the lower quartile by determining the median of the data to the left of the median, 83. Then find the upper quartile by determining the median of the data to the right of the median, 83.

Lower quartile $= \dfrac{74 + 78}{2} = 76$

Upper quartile $= \dfrac{90 + 92}{2} = 91$

The interquartile range is $91 - 76 = 15$.

47. E

$$p \,\square\, 2 = \frac{p^2}{p(2)}$$

$$= \frac{p}{2}$$

48. B The two events are independent. The probability that Alysia *fails* the test is $1 - \dfrac{7}{9} = \dfrac{2}{9}$. The probability that Matt passes and Alysia fails is

$$\frac{9}{10}\left(\frac{2}{9}\right) = \frac{2}{10} = \frac{1}{5}$$

49. D Since the area of the circle is 36π, its radius is 6.

$$A = 36\pi = \pi r^2$$

$$r^2 = 36$$

$$r = 6$$

The area of sector $MNO = \dfrac{1}{4}(36\pi) = 9\pi$.

The area of $\triangle MNO = \dfrac{1}{2}(6)(6) = 18$.

The area of the shaded segment is, therefore, $9\pi - 18$ cm².

50. C

$$f\left(-\frac{1}{4}\right) = 9^{-\left(-\frac{1}{4}\right)} = 9^{\frac{1}{4}}$$

$$= \left(3^2\right)^{\frac{1}{4}} = 3^{\frac{2}{4}} = 3^{\frac{1}{2}}$$

$$= \sqrt{3}$$

Diagnose Your Strengths and Weaknesses

Check the number of each question answered correctly and "X" the number of each question answered incorrectly.

Algebra	1	2	3	4	5	6	9	10	14	17	21	23	24	26	30	Total Number Correct
15 questions																

Plane Geometry	7	8	11	12	22	33	37	45	49	Total Number Correct
9 questions										

Solid Geometry	34	37	41	Total Number Correct
3 questions				

Coordinate Geometry	15	16	19	20	25	44	Total Number Correct
6 questions							

Trigonometry	18	29	36	42	Total Number Correct
4 questions					

Functions	27	28	32	35	38	39	50	Total Number Correct
7 questions								

Data Analysis, Statistics, and Probability	43	46	48	Total Number Correct
3 questions				

Number and Operations	31	40	47	Total Number Correct
3 questions				

Number of correct answers $- \frac{1}{4}$ **(Number of incorrect answers) = Your raw score**

_____ $- \frac{1}{4}$ (_____) = _____

Compare your raw score with the approximate SAT Subject test score below:

	Raw Score	SAT Subject test Approximate Score
Excellent	46–50	750–800
Very Good	41–45	700–750
Good	36–40	640–700
Above Average	29–35	590–640
Average	22–28	510–590
Below Average	< 22	<510